D0863123

THE LION

in the

LIVING ROOM

HOW HOUSE CATS TAMED US
AND TOOK OVER THE WORLD

ABIGAIL TUCKER

SIMON & SCHUSTER PAPERBACKS

New York London Toronto Sydney New Delhi

Simon & Schuster Paperbacks
An Imprint of Simon & Schuster, Inc.
1230 Avenue of the Americas
New York, NY 10020

This Simon & Schuster paperback export edition October 2016

SIMON & SCHUSTER PAPERBACKS and colophon are registered trademarks of Simon & Schuster, Inc.

For information about special discounts for bulk purchases, please contact Simon & Schuster Special Sales at 1-866-506-1949 or business@simonandschuster.com.

The Simon & Schuster Speakers Bureau can bring authors to your live event. For more information or to book an event, contact the Simon & Schuster Speakers Bureau at 1-866-248-3049 or visit our website at www.simonspeakers.com.

Book design by Ellen R. Sasahara

Manufactured in the United States of America

3 5 7 9 10 8 6 4 2

Library of Congress Cataloging-in-Publication Data is available.

ISBN 978-1-5011-5447-8
ISBN 978-1-4767-3825-3 (ebook)

For Mom

"Oh, you can't help that," said the Cat: "we're all mad here."

—*Alice's Adventures in Wonderland* (1865)

CONTENTS

THE LION

in the

LIVING ROOM

Introduction

I N   T H E summer of 2012, Denise Martin and her husband, Bob, were camping in the Essex countryside, about fifty miles east of London and not far from the quaint vacation town of Clacton-on-Sea. Evening was just settling on the campground when Denise glimpsed something unexpected through their bonfire smoke. The 52-year-old factory worker fished out her binoculars for a better look.

"What do you make of that?" she asked her husband. He, too, peered at the tawny creature lolling in a field a few hundred yards away.

"That's a lion," Bob said.

For a time they watched the beast and it seemed to watch them back. Its ears twitched, and it started cleaning itself. Later it ambled down a hedgerow. The couple's reaction was serene, even philosophical. ("You don't often see something like that in the wild," Denise later told the *Daily Mail*.)

Others at the campsite took a less tranquil view.

"Christ, that's a lion," a neighbor said to himself as he peered through Denise's binoculars.

"It's a fucking lion!" another man reportedly screamed, and took off running for his camper.

The cat—rumored to be "as big as two sheep"—soon disappeared into the night, and panic spread. Police sharpshooters converged on the country field. Zookeepers came armed with tranquilizer guns. Helicopters hovered ahead, deploying heat-seeking technology. The campground was evacuated and the press arrived to chronicle the big game hunt. British Twitter exploded with news of "the Lion of Essex."

But nobody could find any trace of it.

The Essex Lion is what is known as a Phantom Cat or, to the cryptozoologically correct, an ABC (Alien Big Cat). Like its many elusive brethren—the Beast of Trowbridge, the Hallingbury Panther—it's a kind of feline UFO, a strange visitation that's particularly common in parts of the former British Empire—England, Australia, New Zealand—where big cats no longer exist in nature, or never did.

A few of the phantoms have been revealed as calculated frauds, or legitimate escapees from exotic menageries. But often these patrolling panthers and leopards on the loose turn out to be something much more familiar: the common house cat, mistaken for the awesome relatives whom he resembles in all but scale.

So it was with the Lion of Essex, who was almost certainly just a burly orange pet named Teddy Bear. Teddy's owners—who were on vacation at the time of the lion hunt—suspected him as soon as they saw the evening news.

"He's the only big gingery thing around there," they told the newspapers.

And so the farcical safari was over.

Yet perhaps the campers were not fools but visionaries. Actual lions, after all, are no longer anything to fear, and many of us have come practically to pity the poor things. (Remember the international outcry for Cecil, the Zimbabwean lion dispatched by a safari-happy Minnesota dentist.) Former lords of the jungle, lions are now relics, ruling nothing: 20,000 holdouts barely hanging on in a few African preserves and a single Indian forest, dependent on our conservation money and our mercy. Their habitat shrinks each year and biologists fear they may vanish by the end of the century.

Meanwhile, the lion's little jester of a cousin, once an evolutionary footnote, has become a force of nature. The global house cat population is 600 million and counting, and more of them are born in the United States every single day than there are lions in the wilderness. New York City's annual spring kitten crop rivals the wild tiger count. Worldwide, house cats already outnumber dogs, their great rival for our affections, by as many as three to one, and their advantage is probably increasing. The tally of pet cats in America rose by 50 percent between 1986 and 2006, and today approaches 100 million.

Similar population jumps are happening across the planet: the pet cat population of Brazil alone is climbing at the rate of a million cats per year. But in many countries the quantities of owned cats are negligible compared to the burgeoning colonies of strays: Australia's 18 million feral cats outnumber the pets by six to one.

Wild and tame, homebound and footloose, these cats increasingly preside over nature and culture, the concrete jungles and the real ones beyond. They have seized control of cities, continents, even cyberspace. In many ways, they rule us.

Through the billowing bonfire smoke, Denise Martin may have glimpsed the truth: the house cat is the new king of beasts.

By now it's obvious that our culture—both online and off—is in the grip of a cat craze. Celebrity house cats ink movie deals, make charitable donations, and count Hollywood starlets among their Twitter followers. Their plush likenesses fill the shelves at Nordstrom; they promote their own fashion lines and iced coffee blends; their images swarm the Internet. Indeed, house cats oversee entire cat cafés, bizarre establishments where people pay to sip tea among random felines, now opening their doors in New York and Los Angeles and in cities around the world.

All this high silliness, however, distracts from something far more interesting. Despite our confessed cat obsession, we know very little about what these animals are, how they came to dwell among us, and why—both in and outside of our homes—they wield such immense power.

The plot thickens when you consider how little we seem to get out of this fraught relationship. People are accustomed to driving a very hard bargain with domesticated animals. We expect our dependents to come to heel, schlep our stuff, or even obediently proceed to the slaughterhouse. Yet cats don't fetch the newspaper or lay tasty eggs or let us ride them. It's not often that human beings are left scratching our heads about why in the world we keep a creature around, let alone hundreds of millions of them. The obvious answer is that we like cats—love them, even. But why do we? What is their secret?

It's especially confusing because this same cherished creature is also classified as one of the world's 100 worst invasive species, accused of damaging a range of ecosystems and even driving some endangered animals to extinction. Australian scientists recently described stray cats as a bigger menace to the continent's mammals than global warming or habitat loss: in a landscape teeming with great white sharks and common death adders, it is the house cat that Australia's Minister of the Environment has singled out as a "savage beast." Bewildered animal lovers sometimes can't decide if we should spoon-feed cats canned salmon with crème fraîche or harden our hearts against them forever.

This same uncertainty permeates American laws: in some states, "pet trusts" enable house cats to legally inherit millions of dollars; in other places, cats who live outdoors are classified as vermin. New York City recently shut down a large swath of its mighty subway system in an effort to rescue two stray kittens, even as our country routinely euthanizes millions of healthy kittens and cats each year. When it comes to house cats, contradictions reign.

The confounding nature of the human-feline affiliation helps explain house cats' persistent associations with black magic. Indeed, the idea of a witch's "familiar"—with its hints of both intimacy and uncanniness—is an excellent definition of the domestic feline. Maybe sorcery is as good an explanation as any for the cats' mysterious and sometimes maddening power over us. Tellingly, an updated version of this medieval paranoia often surfaces in discussions of a common disease that cats spread, which infests human brain tissue and is said to compromise our thinking and behavior.

In other words, we fear ourselves bewitched.

I should confess that I myself have always been among the mesmerized. I haven't just owned cats: for most of my life, I was the sort of person for whom you might purchase a whiskered Brie dish with matching potholders, and I've been known to decorate with cat blankets and coordinating pillows, and fill entire vacation albums with random Mediterranean cat photos. I have purchased pedigreed cats from Fabulous Felines (once rumored to be the world's largest fancy cat emporium) and adopted stray kittens from shelters and the street. I have done these things at my personal and professional peril: I recently learned that a friend's highly allergic mother crosses the road when she sees me coming, and once on a magazine assignment—while I toured a famous research colony of prairie voles—a scientist began wordlessly plucking cat hair off my sweater, lest the scent terrify the study rodents and threaten the integrity of various experiments. In the privacy of my own home, I continue to select carpeting based on a narrow spectrum of colors that best disguise cat barf.

Few people can say they owe their very existence to felines, but I can: my parents vowed not to have children until they "trained" their first cat. (She eventually learned to chase a cork, and that was considered good enough.) Our family has never had anything but cats. My sister once traveled 400 miles to rescue a panicked Russian Blue from a dog lover's bathroom. On long car trips, my mother has been known to wear her tabby draped around her shoulders like a fur stole as she whizzes past astonished toll keepers.

Because cats were so much a part of my own background, I seldom considered the sheer oddness of harboring these tiny archcarnivores—until I had children, that is. Faced with my own offspring's merciless demands, my devotion to another species' appetites and potty habits began to seem silly and even a bit deranged. I studied my cats with fresh suspicion: How exactly had these crafty little creatures gotten their claws into me? Why had I treated them like my own babies for so many years?

But even as these doubts flickered, I had the experience of seeing house cats through the eyes of little children. "Cat" was the first word both of my girls ever said. They begged for cat-themed outfits, toys, books, birthday parties. To toddlers, these pedestrian little house pets were very nearly lion-sized, and living with them seemed to ignite questions about a wilder world: "I want to be like Lucy with Aslan," one sighed, soon after a foray into Narnia, while watching a neighbor's cat from the window.

"Does God love tigers?" they asked at bedtime, clutching plush house cats in their cribs.

So I vowed to learn more about these creatures, and what makes our mystifying relationship tick. As it happens, I've spent much of my professional life writing about animals for newspapers and magazines, and I've gone almost to the ends of the earth in pursuit of the truth about various creatures, from red wolves to jellyfish, trying to understand them as independent organisms in a human-dominated world. But sometimes the best story of all lies directly underfoot.

Which is where you can always find Cheetoh, this book's bright-orange muse.

Cheetoh is my present pet, adopted from an upstate New York trailer park where his father probably fought raccoons, and he weighs in at twenty pounds before breakfast. His unusual size has caused the plumber to pause in wonder upon entering our living room and the Comcast guy to snap cell phone pictures to show his friends. Cat sitters have occasionally refused to return, because Cheetoh—in furious pursuit of food—has chased them, belly waggling. His unusual proportions lend domestic existence an Alice in Wonderland–like quality: you constantly wonder if you've shrunk or he's grown.

It's hard to believe that this oversize croissant curled up at the end of my bed belongs to a species that has the capacity to upend an ecosystem. But, biologically speaking, a cosseted indoor cat is no different from a hardscrabble Australian stray or an urban alley cat. Owned or not, purebred or mongrel, inhabiting a barn or in a multifloor luxury cat condo, house cats are all the same animals. The domestication process has forever altered their genes and behavior, even if they've never seen a person. Kept and stray populations regularly interbreed, sustaining and propelling each other, and an individual house cat may begin life in one category and end up in another. The only differences are circumstances and semantics.

And even if Cheetoh doesn't seem like he would survive far from his food dish, his bludgeoning, feed-me-now persistence points toward an important truth: house cats are quite commanding animals. This is not because they are the smartest of creatures—nor the strongest, especially compared to near relations like jaguars and tigers. In addition to their small size, they are saddled with the same body plan and burdensome, protein-heavy dietary requirements that are driving other members of the cat family toward extinction.

But house cats are supremely adaptable. They can live anywhere and, while they must have plenty of protein, they eat practically anything that moves, from pelicans to crickets, and many things that don't, like hot dogs. (Some of their imperiled feline relatives, by contrast, are adapted to hunt only a rare species of chinchilla.) House cats can tweak their sleeping schedules and social lives. They can breed like crazy.

As I dug into their natural history, it became hard not to admire these creatures in new and ever-wilder ways. And after interviewing dozens of biologists, ecologists, and other researchers, I have the sense that many of them—sometimes despite themselves—admire cats, too. This was a little unexpected, as the divide between cat lovers and the scientific profession has deepened in recent years, and not just because scientists are frequently in league with groups that regard cats as an ecological menace. The clinical side of science also seems to insult the heart of feline subtlety and mystery; for enchanted cat fans, it may be jarring (not to mention dull) to read of "the advantageous amino acid substitutions" that help explain their pets' miraculous-seeming night vision.

Yet some of the most eloquent and original descriptions of cats also come straight from journal papers: cats are "opportunistic, cryptic, solitary hunters," "subsidized predators," and "delightful and flourishing profiteers." And many, if not most, of the scientists that I interviewed while researching this book—whether they study imperiled Hawaiian fauna, brain-dwelling cat parasites, or the gnawed-on bones of our ancient human ancestors—keep house cats of their own.

Which, perhaps, should not be so surprising after all, as the most significant aspect of house cats' adaptability, and the greatest source of their strength, is their ability to navigate a relationship with us. Sometimes this means riding the coattails of global trends, turning what we've done to the world to their absolute advantage. Urbanization, for instance, has been a boon to their prospects. More than half of the earth's human population now lives in cities, and the compact and (allegedly) low-maintenance cat seems better suited than dogs to cramped city life, so we are buying more of them as pets. More pets also means more strays, who share the genes that allow cats to tolerate humans at close quarters, giving them a leg up over other animals lurking in our noisy, stressful metropolises.

But when it comes to managing a relationship with humanity, cats aren't just coasting: they also boldly take the initiative, and this has been true from the first. They're a rare domestic specimen that's said to have "chosen" domestication itself, and today, via a combination of lucky good looks and deliberate behaviors, they hold sway over our homes, our king-size mattresses, our very imaginations. Their recent sweep of the Internet is just the latest victory in an ongoing global conquest, with no end in sight. Indeed, countless little takeovers happen in our own homes every day; while most people must go out looking for a new family dog, pet cats are statistically likely to just show up at the back door one evening, and invite themselves in.

Though the house cats' play for survival in a human-dominated world is striking and unique, their story has universal implications. It's an example of how a single, small, and seemingly innocent human act—taking up with a petite species of wild cat, and giving it the run of our hearths and, ultimately, our hearts—can have cascading global consequences, stretching from the interior forests of Madagascar to schizophrenia wards to online message boards.

In certain ways the house cat's rise is tragic, for the same forces that favor them have destroyed many other creatures. House cats are carpet-baggers, arrivistes, and they're among the most transformative invaders the world has ever seen—except for *Homo sapiens*, of course. It's no coincidence that when they show up in ecosystems, lions and other megafauna are usually on their way out.

But the house cat's story is also about the wonder of life, and nature's continuing capacity to surprise us. It offers a chance for us to set our self-centeredness aside and take a clearer look at a creature that we tend to baby and patronize, but whose horizons stretch far beyond our living rooms and litter boxes. A house cat is not really a fur baby, but it is something rather more remarkable: a tiny conquistador with the whole planet at its feet. House cats would not exist without humans, but we didn't really create them, nor do we control them now. Our relationship is less about ownership than aiding and abetting.

It may seem treasonous to consider our adorable consorts in this cold light. We are used to thinking of cats as companion animals and dependents, not evolutionary free agents. I began fielding reproachful comments from my mother and sister as soon as my reporting for this book began.

Yet real love requires understanding. And despite our mounting feline fascination, we may actually be giving our cats less than their due.

The correct response to a creature like Cheetoh might not be *awwwww*, but awe.

Chapter 1

CATACOMBS

B UBBLING AWAY on Wilshire Boulevard in the middle of downtown Los Angeles, the La Brea Tar Pits look like pools of toxic black taffy. California colonists once harvested tar here to waterproof their roofs, but today these asphalt seeps are far more precious to paleontologists studying Ice Age wildlife. All kinds of fantastic animals mired themselves in the sticky death traps: Columbian mammoths with pretzeled tusks, extinct camels, errant eagles.

But most famous of all are the La Brea cats.

At least seven types of prehistoric feline inhabited Beverly Hills 11,000 years ago and earlier: close relatives of modern bobcats and mountain lions but also several vanished species. More than 2,000 skeletons of *Smilodon populator*—the biggest and scariest of the saber-tooth cats—have been recovered from the 23-acre excavation site, making it the largest such trove on the planet.

It's late morning. The asphalt is softening as the day warms and the air smells like melting pavement. Ugly black bubbles popping on the tar pits' surface make it look as though a monster is breathing just beneath. My eyes water a bit from the fumes and, plunging a stick into the goo, I find that I can't pull it out.

"You only need an inch or two to immobilize a horse," says John Harris, chief curator of the museum here. "A giant sloth would get stuck like a fly on flypaper." There's a touch of pride in his voice.

The only way to get the asphalt off your skin is to massage it with mineral oil or butter, as a few local fraternity pranksters have learned the hard way. Given time enough, the tar even seeps into bone, preserving the remains of the giant animals that died in agony here so well that pit specimens aren't even truly turned-to-stone fossils. Drilling into a preserved saber-tooth rib produces the same smell you get at the dentist's office: burning collagen. It smells alive.

In the murk of the tar pits, I'm searching for clues to the primordial human-feline relationship. Human patronage of cats, which seems so intuitive to us, is in reality a quite recent and radical arrangement. Though we've shared the earth for millions of years, the cat family and mankind have never gotten along before, much less gotten cozy on the couch. Our competing needs for meat and space make us natural enemies. Far from sharing food, humans and felines have spent most of our long mutual history snatching each other's meals and masticating each other's mangled remains—though to be perfectly honest, mostly they ate us.

It was cats like the La Brea saber-tooths, colossal cheetahs, and giant cave lions—and later their modern-day heirs—that dominated the untamed planet. Our prehistoric forebears shared habitats with these sorts of behemoths in parts of the Americas, and in Africa we tangled with various species of saber-tooths for millions of years. So powerful was the ancient feline influence that cats may have helped make us human in the first place.

In a storage room, Harris shows off the milk teeth of a *Smilodon* kitten. They are almost four inches long.

"How did they nurse?" I ask.

"Very carefully," he answers.

The adult upper canine teeth are eight inches; their shape reminds me of a reaper's blade. I run my finger along the serrated inner curve and get the chills. Scientists still don't know much about these animals—researchers once made a steel model of saber-tooth jaws in an effort to figure out how in the world they chewed, and "we only recently learned to tell male from female," Harris admits—but it's safe to say they would have been absolutely terrifying. Weighing about 400 pounds, they likely used their burly fore-limbs to wrestle down mastodons before stabbing their saber teeth through the thick skin of the prey animals' necks.

Then my eyes stray to a nearby skeleton of an American lion, which stood a head taller than the saber-tooths and probably weighed about 800 pounds enfleshed.

So this is what our ancestors were up against.

The sheer awesomeness of such predators, and the grisly legacy of our interactions with them, make it especially remarkable that today people are on the cusp of wiping the cat family off the face of the earth. Most modern cat species, big and small, are now in grave decline, losing ground to humans daily.

With one exception, that is. Harris marches me out to an ongoing pit excavation near one of the oozing seeps not far from the museum's door. As two women in tar-smudged T-shirts chip away at a *Smilodon* femur, there's a sudden brownish blur around my ankles, and up hops Bob, a tailless female house cat with a potbelly and a proprietary air. The giggling excavators tell me how they rescued her from the traffic accident in which she forfeited her tail and then nursed her back to health. "No more surprise mice," one woman says, patting Bob's amputated rump.

Which is stranger, I wonder: the fact that Beverly Hills is a graveyard for giant local lions, or that a tiny, unassuming feline stowaway originally from the Middle East thrives here today?

But in fact, the house cat's rise is the flip side of the lion's ruin. The story of the cat family's ongoing downfall helps explain what organisms like Bob and Cheetoh and all of our beloved house cats really are: fully loaded feline predators, like lynx or jaguars or any other kind of cat, but also extreme biological outliers.

Absent human civilization, the Greater Los Angeles area could still be a prime habitat for the native cats that survived the Ice Age. A few straggling mountain lions continue to haunt the Santa Monica Mountains, though the population is hopelessly isolated and inbred and the rare kittens often end up as highway roadkill. A mountain lion known as P-22 was recently photographed loitering in the hills beneath the Hollywood sign, and gazing out over the glowing city at night.

But it's Bob who rules the tar pits now.

The La Brea saber-tooths and giant lions died out around the end of the last Ice Age for unknown reasons. But we can piece together the narrative of why most of the surviving wild cats—even the smaller species, some of which look very much like our beloved house pets—are in dire trouble today. The story begins where so many of our ancestors ended: inside the mouth of a cat.

The cat family is part of the mammalian order Carnivora, the "flesh devourers." All carnivores, from wolves to hyenas, eat flesh as part of their diet, and why wouldn't they? Meat is a precious resource, full of fat and protein and wonderfully easy to digest. But it's also hard to come by, and so most animals, including almost all of those classified as carnivores, pad their diets with other food groups. In the bear family, for instance, black bears chomp acorns and tubers with plant-crushing molars that wouldn't look out of place in the mouth of a cow; pandas famously subsist on bamboo; and even the big-fanged polar bear occasionally munches on berries.

Not cats. From the two-pound rusty-spotted cat to the 600-pound Siberian tiger, all three dozen or so cat species are what biologists call hypercarnivores. They eat pretty much nothing but meat. The plant-chewing molars of cats have shrunk to a vestigial size, like something a child would leave for the tooth fairy, and the rest of their teeth are extremely tall and sharp, a mix of steak knives and scissors. (The difference between a cat's teeth and a bear's is like the Alps versus the Appalachians.) Though called canines, the killing teeth at the front of the mouth are actually larger in cats than in dogs, which should come as no surprise: cats require three times as much protein in their diets as dogs, and kittens need four times as much. Dogs can even get by on a vegan diet, but cats can't synthesize key fatty acids on their own—they must get them from other animals' bodies.

The singular purpose of a cat's teeth—butchery—explains why all cat maws look alike, even to biologists. The jaws of an insect-sucking sun bear look nothing like a grizzly's, but sometimes even experts can't tell a lion's from a tiger's because they are designed for exactly the same job.

So it goes for the rest of cats' bodies. There are tremendous, almost comic differences in body size—some cats are 14 inches long from tip to tail, and some are 14 feet—but very few differences in form. "The important thing about big cats and small cats is not that they are different but that they are the same," Elizabeth Marshall Thomas writes in *The Tribe of the Tiger*, her history of the feline family. House cats and tigers, she says, are "the alpha and omega of their kind." Sure, tigers have stripes, lions have manes, and pumas have eight nipples while margays have two. But the blueprint endures: long legs, powerful forelimbs, flexible spine, a tail (sometimes up to half the length of the body) for balance, and short guts for digesting meat and meat alone. Cats are armed with retractable claws, sentient whiskers, and ears that rotate for uncanny directional hearing and the broadest possible auditory range. With eyes located at the front of the face, they possess excellent binocular and night vision. Cat skulls are domed and their faces round and short with powerfully anchored jaw muscles, a design that maxes out bite force at the front of the mouth.

Whether the prey is bunny rabbit or water buffalo, almost all cats (with the notable exception of ultraspeedy cheetahs) hunt in the same way: stalk, ambush, tackle, and enjoy. Even lazy Cheetoh hunts like this, plump rear wiggling in anticipation as he pounces on a hapless shoelace. Cats are largely visual predators and depend on surprise, delivering the killing bite by sliding their canines between neck vertebrae like (as the animal behaviorist Paul Leyhausen puts it) "a key in a lock." Cats can get the best of animals up to three times their size, and their ambitions don't always stop there: as a child, I used to watch one of our Siamese stalk deer, crouching on boulders above the oblivious herd.

The modern Felidae have enjoyed worldwide success for ten million years or more, across a remarkable range of habitats. Cats are partial to the tropical forests of Asia, but the feline archetype performs in almost all climates: the snow leopard in the Himalayas, the jaguar in the Amazon, even the sand cat in the heart of the Sahara. Thousands of years ago, lions lived not just in Beverly Hills but also in Devon, England, and Peru—pretty much everywhere on earth except for Australia and Antarctica. Lions are believed to have been the most widely distributed wild land mammal ever, king of a thousand jungles plus deserts and marshes and mountain ranges in between.

What wild cats need to succeed is space. This is why, in nature, they are typically less common than other big carnivores like bears and hyenas. Even the littlest cats need comparatively huge tracts of land to harvest the necessary animal protein. A very rough rule of thumb is that 100 pounds of prey animals living in an environment can support one pound of resident carnivore. But for hypercarnivores, the stakes are even higher. These animals have no evolutionary backup plan. They must kill or die. In fact, cats quite frequently kill each other. Lions eat cheetahs, leopards eat caracals, caracals eat African wild cats. Cats even dispatch members of their own species, and this animosity—in addition to their secretive hunting style, and a given ecosystem's inability to support large numbers of them—explains why most are solitary creatures.

Although humans devour stunning quantities of flesh these days, we are not members of the carnivore family. We are primates. Our great ape relatives don't eat much meat, and neither did our early human-like kin, who started coming down out of the trees in Africa 6 or 7 million years ago, long after cats had settled into their spot at the tippy-top of the food chain.

Not only did we not eat meat, we generously supplied it in the form of our bodies and our babies. A host of creatures dined on us: supersize eagles, crocodiles, bus-length snakes, archaic bears, carnivorous kangaroos, and maybe jumbo otters. But even amid such fearsome company, cats were almost certainly our most formidable predators.

Humanity's early ancestors came of age in Africa during the "heyday of cats," according to anthropologist Robert Sussman, whose book, *Man the Hunted*, details our history as a prey animal. In regions where we "overlapped" with cats, he tells me, "they took advantage of us completely"—

dragging us into caves, devouring us in trees, caching our eviscerated corpses in their lairs. Indeed, we might not know nearly so much about human evolution if not for big cat kills. The world's oldest fully preserved skull representing the *Homo* genus, known as Skull Number 5, was recovered from caves in Dmanisi, Georgia, which likely served as a sort of picnicking ground for extinct giant cheetahs. In caves in South Africa, paleontologists endlessly puzzled over piles of hominid and other primate bones, trying to figure out the source of the carnage. Had our forefathers massacred each other? Then somebody noticed that the holes in some skulls lined up perfectly with leopard fangs.

The contemporary landscape also gives clues about the toll that cats likely took on us. Sussman and his colleague, Donna Hart, surveyed modern primate predation data and found that the cat family is still responsible for more than a third of all primate kills. (Dogs and hyenas account for just 7 percent.) One study at Kenya's Mount Suswa lava caves showed that leopards there eat baboons and practically nothing else. Even our strongest, smartest living kin can fall prey to felines half their size: scientists have picked stubby black lowland gorilla toes out of leopard poop and chimpanzee teeth from lion feces.

Scientists are just starting to formally study our own legacy as prey, finding, for instance, that our color vision and depth perception may have first evolved as a system for detecting snakes. Experiments have shown that even very young children are better at recognizing the shapes of serpents than lizards; they also spot lions faster than antelope. Antipredation strategies persist in a host of modern human behaviors, from our tendency to go into labor in the deepest part of night (many of our predators would have hunted at dawn and dusk) to, perhaps, our appreciation of eighteenth-century landscape paintings, whose sweeping vistas give the pleasing sense that we would have seen danger coming before it ever got close. The goose bumps that I felt at La Brea, while holding a saber-tooth's fangs, date back to a time when my body hair would have stood on end at a predator's approach—making me appear larger and, I hope, intimidating.

Predation pressure likely also helped shape our body size and posture (tall, upright bodies allowed us to scan more distant horizons), our preference for community and social life (a glorified form of safety in numbers), and our sophisticated forms of communication. Even less exalted primate relatives like vervet monkeys have a bark that means "leopard." (Though not to be outdone, small Amazonian cats called margays have been observed mimicking primate baby calls while hunting.)

But the cats' most significant contribution to our species' evolution may not have passed from predator to prey, but rather from predator to scavenger. That gift was our own first fateful taste of meat.

The earliest evidence of our meat-eating dates back about 3.4 million years. Cut marks on hoofed animal bones found near Dikika, Ethiopia, show how hard our largely vegetarian ancestors labored to slice off the meat; at other sites, they hammered into the rich marrow. But where did those first delicious bones come from? Our ancestors would not develop hunting technology for millions of years.

According to Briana Pobiner, an expert in human carnivory at the National Museum of Natural History, it's possible that our unarmed, meat-mad predecessors simply chased some of our first prey animals to death, or threw rocks to kill them. But Pobiner—who works in her office beneath the photographed gaze of two very large lionesses—believes that it's more likely that we were shameless thieves and scavengers, or "kleptoparasites." Our ungracious "hosts" would have been the big cats who felled gazelles and other grazing animals, ate their fill, and then wandered away to come back later. That's when our pesky ancestors sneaked in to snatch what they could. We may have lifted antelopes from the trees where leopards stashed them (perhaps to hide them from even mightier cats, like lions). But the saber-tooths would likely have generated the best leftovers, as the anthropologist Curtis Marean has pointed out, because their big teeth were good for killing but not necessarily for chewing, leaving plenty on the bone. Some scientists have even proposed that saber-tooth table scraps were so bountiful and essential to the diet of early humans that we followed the cats out of Africa and into Europe, in the first great migration of our species.

Once our ancestors tasted meat, rich in nutrients and amino acids, they wanted more. Some paleoanthropologists have argued that meat-eating ultimately made us human. It was certainly a crucial step.

"Meat-eating was so important that we got better and better at making stone tools," Pobiner explains. "It was a feedback loop. Being able to get more meat requires good perception of your environment, communication, advance planning. We would not have gone on the same evolutionary trajectory if it had not been for meat-eating."

Indeed, meat-eating may have literally expanded our minds, according to the "expensive tissue hypothesis" (which concerns brain development, not brand-name Kleenex). Because vegetarian primates must process large quantities of tough plant matter, they have monstrous, energy-sucking intestines. (This is why otherwise-skinny monkeys look like they have beer bellies.) But an animal with steady access to easy-to-digest meat may have the evolutionary leeway to shrink its guts and spend that digestive energy on something niftier: an enormous brain. This crown jewel of *Homo sapiens* is extraordinarily costly, taking up 2 percent of our body weight but 20 percent of our caloric intake. It may be that we can afford it because of meat-eating.

The biggest jump in our ancestors' brain size happened about 800,000 years ago—not long after we mastered fire, which we used to cook our meat, preserving it longer and making it more portable. A few hundred thousand years later, we figured out how to bring down big game on our own. Fast-forward several hundred more millennia and the *Homo sapiens* twig of the family tree finally sprouted, about 200,000 years ago.

At this point the original, and lopsided, power balance between people and big cats gave way to an uneasy equilibrium, in which our beefed-up brains counterbalanced their brawn. With our new hunting weapons, we could probably sometimes push big cats off their carcasses and even kill a few, though mutual avoidance might have been our best strategy. Yet apparently we couldn't help admiring our beautiful foes. Thirty-thousand-year-old cave paintings in Southern France's Chauvet Cave—some of the oldest art in the world—include magnificent ocher leopards and lions drawn with a biologist's eye for detail, down to the whisker spots.

This ancient stalemate between cats and humans, in which both parties were heavily armed and more or less equally matched in their mutual quest for meat, lasted until about 10,000 years ago, when somewhere in the Middle East, humans got enterprising, or lucky, enough to figure out how to forever satisfy our infinite hunger for flesh: raise and kill our own. The domestication of herd animals and plants, the evolutionary coup known as the Neolithic revolution, allowed hunter-gatherers to settle down in permanent communities, which ultimately led to the birth of culture, and history, and the earth as we know it.

For many other creatures, especially cats, the appearance of our first flocks and gardens signaled the beginning of the end.

We tend to think of the conservation plight of wild cats as a relatively recent phenomenon; and Europeans, the British in particular, often shoulder much of the blame for killing them off. It's true that colonists introduced guns to India and Africa and offered handsome bounties for feline pelts. On one 1911 spree, the hunting party of King George V bagged thirty-nine Indian tigers in under two weeks. The Victorians filled London's zoos with African lions, which languished in captivity and usually died within a few years (though a few managed to take a carriage horse or two with them before they went). The imperial campaigns against cats are chronicled in hunting narratives, a singular category of literature that one biologist described to me as "the torrid side of mammalogy." In the classic *The Man-Eaters of Tsavo*, the British officer James Henry Patterson recounts, with icicle poise, his run-ins with a pair of maneless, seemingly depraved African lions.

But for all their chilly efficiency, the British merely accelerated a process that began with the very dawn of agriculture.

"Cats are very fragile," the feline geneticist Steve O'Brien tells me. "If they don't have a lot to eat, they starve, simple as that. It's not shooting them that's the problem. It's planting farms and neighborhoods."

Cats are biologically at odds with the broadest patterns of human civilization. This was true from the first: Egypt, the first great agrarian culture, gradually lost much of its lion population. The Romans—who bagged big cats for processions and Colosseum spectacles—documented regional shortages as early as 325 BC. By the twelfth century lions were gone from Palestine, where they were once common. Before Europeans arrived in India, Mughal emperors fragmented the tiger population by razing forests. And so it went with all kinds of wild cats.

What's most informative about the British hunting narratives are their settings which illustrate precisely the sort of places and situations where human-cat conflict happens—not in the deep jungle but on the freshly plowed margins of civilization: sugarcane and coffee farms abutting Indian jungle, railroad tracks snaking through the Kenyan bush. Along such edges we push deeper into cat territory and cats wander into ours.

The more we push, the more coexistence with wild cats becomes nearly impossible. First, we clear the land, reaching ever deeper into rain forest and savannah, and devouring or shooing off the prey animals. This hurts wild cats, from the lions and tigers that compete with us directly for the big herbivores that we like to eat, to house-cat-sized felines like the African golden cat, whose smaller prey is exterminated or siphoned off as bush-meat.

After we topple forests and polish off the native prey species, we introduce our own food animals like cattle, sheep, chickens, and fish—which wild cats of all sizes, now without a meat source, naturally want to eat. Now it's their turn to be kleptoparasites, and farmers don't tolerate feline thievery.

And then, too, sometimes the biggest cats still want to eat us. Even in the twenty-first century, the most horrific man-eating episodes continue to occur in border zones where spreading human communities press against cat territory. A lone woodsman can hunt his whole life in Russia's vast birch forests without running afoul of a Siberian tiger, but in India's Sundardans Delta, home to 4 million people, rogue tigers are a problem; and in southwestern Tanzania's booming Rufiji farming district, lions can take hundreds of villagers per decade.

Only today, agricultural poisons have replaced firearms as our weapon of choice. Lace a giraffe carcass with pesticides and you'll eliminate not only the man-eating lion but the whole shifty-eyed pride, dispatching the king of beasts like any other pest. Lacking poison, locals will use any available means. Indian tigers emerging from preserves have even been clubbed to death.

It's easy to blame faraway peoples for the demise of the big cats until you imagine what it would be like to send your seven-year-old herd boy to guard a lion-plagued pasture, or to discover a leopard in your own latrine. And when the problem hits home, Americans are no different. Much of America was, after all, big-cat country once, but settlers long ago dispensed with jaguars in the South and mountain lions east of the Mississippi—excepting Florida's panthers, which are inbred and diseased and subsisting on armadillos in one dismal pocket of the Everglades.

The wild cats' tendency to kill the game animals we covet, the farm animals we raise, and, in the case of the largest feline species, us, makes them essentially incompatible with human settlements. As our populations thicken, theirs must thin, and as surviving cats are pushed into undesirable habitat, other forces related to human settlement patterns start to take a major toll: traffic accidents, distemper outbreaks, trophy hunting, fur trapping, droughts, hurricanes, border security barricades, the exotic pet trade.

At present, some humans are even taking their new status as apex predators literally, by eating big cats, as they once relished us. The Asian medicine market carves up tiger carcasses for human consumption: claws and whiskers and bile, but especially bones, for tonic wine. And loin of lion is a trendy dish among a few American gourmands, including a New York based-group called the Gastronauts. It's apparently best when pan-seared, then slow-cooked, and served with coriander and carrots.

Since so many wild cats are now much easier to find dead than alive, I've traveled to the Smithsonian Institution's off-site storage facility, hidden way out in suburban Maryland's strip mall country, to look for them. These giant buildings house all the pickled dolphins and gorillas that won't fit in the downtown museums; one structure is more or less a hangar for the airplane-sized bones of whales.

A security guard inspects my purse and since there's no food allowed in this sterile graveyard, I discreetly eject my chewing gum. Soon I'm following the jingle of the Smithsonian mammals curator's keys as he walks the aisles of metal cabinets. This particular building is all "skins, skulls and skeletons," Kris Helgen says over his shoulder. He pulls open a drawer to reveal the crumpled pelt of a giraffe shot in 1909 by Teddy Roosevelt just a few weeks after he left office: the long eyelashes are still attached, and coquettishly curly. We examine the yellow whiskers of extinct monk seals, and peer into the tusk sockets of one of the biggest bull elephants on record.

This giant collection of dead animals is a de facto time machine, offering a look at a transforming planet and life-forms in flux. It's a bit like La Brea, except that humans killed and carefully preserved most of these animals, doing the eternal work of the tar pits all by ourselves.

"So," Helgen says, "shall we start looking at some cats?"

He unlocks a cabinet to our left and with a careful clunk fits together the jawbone and cranium of a Siberian tiger, only about 500 of which now roam the wild. Helgen remarks on the width of its cheekbones and the length of the bony crest on top of its head, which would have made its living face a near-perfect orange circle, like the sun. To me, the skull looks like it's gritting its teeth. Helgen unfurls the pelt of a rare black African leopard; I stroke a cognac-colored puma from Guyana and explore the plush undercoat of a snow leopard. I hold a piece of muslin stitched with the tiny skin of a cougar kitten, likely one of the last born in New York State, and finger the ear plumage of an Iberian lynx. The fierce black spikes, I discover, consist of the softest silk.

Helgen is a young man, with just a bit of stubble instead of the wizard's beard favored by his senior colleagues. When we met, he was about to depart on a whirlwind three-month wilderness spree, from Kenya to Burma, taking jungle censuses and looking for undiscovered species of mammals. He's not a doom-and-gloom-prone guy: in fact, he strikes me as an environmental optimist.

But not when it comes to the cat family. "The trend has been in one direction—people have supplanted wild cats," he says. "That trend is not slowing down or reversing, but we are getting to the end of the line for some animals"—including many of the big cats, but some little ones, too. Scientists of his generation fear presiding over the first full-scale cat extinctions, particularly of the Iberian lynx and the tiger—not just some subspecies, but all tigers, period. Back over in the tiger drawers, he points out how the nineteenth-century specimens (many with ragged bullet holes) hail from habitats where today there are no more tigers, like Pakistan, while later pelts come from places where tigers never naturally lived in the first place, like Jackson, New Jersey, site of a Six Flags Great Adventure safari park. "In the late twentieth century, almost everything is from zoos," he says.

Locking up his cabinets of exotic skins, Helgen walks across the aisle and pulls out the skull of one last feline, a little species this time, but one that, according to its specimen tags, enjoys a modern range stretching from India to Indiana: roughly the lion's old lands, and then some. This is *Felis catus*, the common house cat.

"And look," Helgen says, parting the tiny jaws so we can peer into its mouth. "A little tiger. And just as fearsome in its way. Just look at those teeth."

Given the history I've just recounted, a complacent human could see these incredibly numerous little felines—which we most often think of as pets—as living trophies. Just as the Romans flaunted lions in the Colosseum, and medieval kings kept them in royal menageries, perhaps we like to keep our own tiny lions around as evidence of our very recent triumph over our feline archenemies. We like to chuckle at cats' savagery in miniature, to coo over their teeth and claws—but only now that we've won.

Maybe a lion purring in our lap or cavorting in our living room evokes our global mastery, our total control of nature. Maybe it's telling that one of the few places in the world where house cats are *not* popular pets is India, which is also the rare region where big cats can still do real damage.

But there's also a strong case that the feline family actually remains unconquered, and that cats are still on top and calling the shots. Yes, man-eating lions have abdicated, but the humble house cat is pressing the same kingly claim in the new millennia.

Indeed, for all their strength and prowess, lions didn't get nearly as far in the world. The house cat has gained ground from the Arctic Circle to the Hawaiian archipelago, taken over Tokyo and New York, and stormed the entire continent of Australia. And somewhere along the way, it seized the most precious and closely guarded piece of territory on the planet: the stronghold of the human heart.

Chapter 2

CAT'S CRADLE

I ACQUIRED CHEETOH—or maybe he acquired me—at Eastertime. It was 2003, and I was a fledgling newspaper reporter in rural upstate New York. My latest assignment had brought me to a battered couch, where I perched beside a tearful young woman and her mother. I was supposed to write about a recent murder in their mobile home community, and I wasn't sure where to begin.

Suddenly there was a soft thud against my ankle. I looked down to discover the burliest, most barrel-chested orange tomcat I'd ever seen getting ready to ram me with his huge red head for a second time. Reflexively, I reached down and scratched the feathery fur beneath his chin.

"He likes you," the mother said, a note of approval in her voice. "He doesn't like anybody."

Our grim interview quickly digressed into an animated discussion of their community's dozens of cats. These were a sort of shared amenity, belonging to no one in particular, wandering from one household to the next, perhaps more welcome on some couches than others.

The women led me into the trailer's back room, where a slender calico vagabond had recently elected to give birth. Now two orange newborns

mewed by her side, and whatever remained of my professional demeanor
dissolved.

One was a soft peachy shade. The other's fur was a vivid tangerine—or
even a bit brighter: the color of artificial cheese dust. The kittens' hue made
me think that the big, pushy tom hanging around had more than a minor
role in their birth. I scooped up the very orange one, and he lolled in the
palm of my hand, his baby ears still bent at the tips. His bleary little eyes
had only just opened: I became one of Cheetoh's first sights.

Sitting in my car afterward, my newspaper assignment unfinished, but
with an open invitation to return in six weeks to collect my new kitten, I
saw Cheetoh's enormous father leap out of the trailer's open window, off
to his next scrounged meal or amorous conquest. I had never seen cats
wandering freely like this, less sequestered pets than independent contrac-
tors, carving out their own living via gifts of cat food and garbage cans, and
boldly coming and going as they chose. At the time, it struck me as a rather
enlightened, almost futuristic arrangement—like a far-out California com-
mune for cats.

But in fact, the human-feline relationship may have first emerged under
similar circumstances, albeit amid clusters of earthen huts instead of mobile homes. The long, strange, and deeply improbable process of cat domestication probably couldn't have found its footing elsewhere.

The 11,600-year-old village of Hallan Çemi stood along the banks of a trib-
utary of the Tigris River, in modern-day Turkey. Just a handful of Stone
Age families inhabited the mud dwellings. But in such tiny settlements, humanity's monumental transition into agriculture likely began. Our switch
from hunting and gathering to the farming life ultimately spelled doom for
many of the world's hypercarnivores, but it was a golden ticket for a handful of domesticates-to-be, including the wild felines that would become
modern house cats.

Uncovered by archaeologists in 1989, Hallan Çemi is considered one
of the very first permanent communities in the eastern Fertile Crescent,
a primitive base camp for nomadic people who, due to recent environ-

mental changes, no longer had to wander far and wide to find food. The local climate had stabilized as the Ice Age waned, and natural resources abounded, giving rise to what archaeologists call "the broad-spectrum diet." Residents fished the river, raided a nearby pistachio forest, and hunted big game in the hills and on the plains below. They ate practically everything in their path: swans, clams, lizards, owls, red deer, boars, tortoises. All told, the Neolithic villagers left behind some two tons of animal bones.

The archaeologist Melinda Zeder has spent years sorting through these barbecued remains, shipped from the dig site to her Smithsonian lab just down the hall from the museum's big-cat skeleton collection. Zeder, whose eyes sometimes seem to catch the light of long-ago cooking fires, is an expert in animal domestication and humanity's fateful shift to the sedentary lifestyle. The prehistoric villagers of Hallan Çemi didn't yet keep farm animals—at that point only dogs had been domesticated, thousands of years earlier, when humans were still a nomadic race—but the residents may have begun to intentionally manipulate local populations of prey animals, like wild pigs. What's more, Zeder also thinks that Hallan Çemi holds clues to how these protofarmers *unintentionally* recruited certain other types of small, furry beasts.

As we talk in Zeder's office, a graduate student plops a little plastic baggie of what look like cinnamon sticks on the desk. The ancient brown leg bones feel as fragile as fired clay. These meager remains belong to the house cat's ancestor, often called simply "the wildcat."

The 58 wildcat bones identified so far from Hallan Çemi's ancient smorgasbord probably do not represent our first pet kitties—alas, we may have eaten these cats along with everything else. (A small yet graphic body of scientific literature describes Neanderthals and hunter-gatherer humans who were cat lovers in an exclusively culinary sense.) But Zeder and her students have some ideas about how this oddball little carnivore—whose Latin name, *Felis silvestris*, means "cat of the woods"—might have forsaken the forest and thrown in its lot with us. Human sedentism, it turns out, was a lifestyle that Cheetoh's forefathers could appreciate from the get-go.

"What does sedentism do to an environment?" Zeder likes to ask. "How does it change the evolutionary trajectory of other animals?"

The new human lifestyle influenced far more species than just felines: in addition to the wildcats, Hallan Çemi attracted unusual numbers of other mini carnivores, like badgers and martens and weasels and, especially, foxes, all in numbers way out of proportion with their natural distribution in the food web. Such gluts of midsize hunters are actually a common feature of present-day urban zones; our towns and cities are full of raccoons, skunks, and other meat-eating pests, and in modern London red foxes are a major nuisance.

A population spike of little carnivores is a called a "mesopredator release," and these surpluses seem to happen when humans kill off the top predators in an ecosystem. Indeed, leopard and lynx bones from Hallan Çemi suggest that the villagers were successfully hunting big cats, making life easier for diminutive meat-eaters that otherwise would have been outcompeted or even consumed. Humans may not have liked these foxes and badgers and small cats either, but they might not have been worth bothering about—like suburban raccoons today.

Along with offering a safe haven, the first permanent human settlements represented a revolutionary new food source. The weasels and badgers and cats invading Hallan Çemi were probably hungry. Many of the huge roasted animals there appear to have been sloppily butchered—there would have been lots of rotting meat around to steal. ("Must have stunk to high heavens," Zeder remarks.) For wee carnivores, this trash would have been a world-altering windfall. Sometimes the prowling, pint-size predators were captured and served up as a course themselves or skinned for their coats, but presumably the risk was worth it.

So humans unwittingly welcomed a whole array of small predators. But why don't we have badgers or foxes in our living rooms today? Of all the little wild creatures that crept across our threshold at Hallan Çemi, why did cats alone stay with us forever, becoming domesticated? And, especially with so much bad blood between the cat family and our own, why on earth did we let them?

~~

Scientists often describe the process of animal domestication as a road or pathway that animals travel—or often, are led down—over centuries, experiencing a series of profound genetic changes along the way. It's typically a one-way street: once a wild species becomes domesticated, there's no going back even if some individuals return to nature. A "feral" animal is not a wild animal but a domesticated stray, and its offspring are biologically similar to beasts that have never left the barnyard. (Think of Cheetoh's long-lost orange littermate: even if he wound up living alone outdoors, his genetic raw material is no different from his spoiled and pampered sibling's, and his kittens—for countless generations to come—are predisposed to be excellent pets.) A wild animal, on the other hand, may be tamed over the course of its lifetime but not domesticated—the comfort it learns to feel with humans can't be passed along to its young. We've gentled lots of types of wild cats, even lions and tigers and cheetahs. But house cats are the only *domesticated* felines.

The rewards of domestication are great. With access to our plentiful food and powerful protection, domesticated animals enjoy unprecedented reproductive success, some even surpassing ours: today there are roughly three times as many chickens (descendants of wild jungle fowl) as people on the planet, and in some countries sheep (former mouflon) outnumber us seven to one.

In exchange, husbanded animals sacrifice their flesh, fur, or labor to us, along with their freedom, and often undergo an extreme physical metamorphosis to tailor themselves to life in the human sphere. Domestic animals usually look quite different from their wild counterparts. Some of this is the result of deliberate human interference, since we breed animals for qualities that we desire, like thicker fur or more meat. But some of it is an accidental result of living alongside man. Often, for reasons we'll soon explore, domestic animals resemble juvenile versions of their wild peers, or have weird traits like spots and floppy ears. We can trace the domestication timeline of most farmyard regulars simply by studying clear differences in their fossils: archaeologists look for telltale domestication signatures like molar reduction in ancient pigs, or horn shrinkage in cows. Dogs—as the first domesticated animals—have been transformed so completely under our care that it's proved very tough for scientists to determine which wolf lineage the modern diversity of Chihuahuas and golden retrievers and pit bulls derive from, and when their ancestry diverged.

With house cats, however, scientists have the opposite problem. Cats have changed so little physically during their time among people that even today experts often can't tell house tabbies from wild cats. This greatly complicates the study of cat domestication. It's all but impossible to pinpoint the cats' transition into human life by examining ancient fossils, which hardly change even into modernity. "You aren't going to find a collar or a bell," Zeder warns.

Because cats, ever contrary, don't follow the patterns that apply to other creatures, most scientists have simply ignored them: Charles Darwin devotes just a few pages of his book on domestication to these exceedingly difficult creatures, while pigeons get two whole chapters. Indeed, whether or not house cats really qualify as domesticated animals remains a subject of debate, even as they reap the same evolutionary benefits as sheep and chickens. Have cats reached the end of the domestication road, or do they remain en route?

For the longest time, scientists couldn't even decide what kind of wild cat the house cats came from. Scholars suspected that our pets contained ancestral sprinklings from several different types of feline: a little Pallas's cat fluff here, some jungle cat spots there, and maybe a drop of Indian desert cat in the distinctive Siamese. It seemed quite likely that *Felis silvestris* was in the genes somewhere, but which one of the five subspecies, or all of them?

In the early 2000s, an Oxford University doctoral student named Carlos Driscoll decided to settle the question. He set out on his motorcycle with the ambitious goal of sampling genetic material from 1,000 cats across the planet, to see if he could pinpoint a common ancestry. He baited his cat traps with live pigeons in Israel, befriended Mongolian ferals, snipped ears off Scottish roadkill, and even coaxed fancy-cat breeders in America to test their favorites' DNA.

The project took nearly ten years but the results were worth the wait: from blue-blooded Persians to mangy strays, from Manhattan's street-smart alley cats to the ferals of the New Zealand forest, it turns out that all house cats come not from a genetic mash-up of many feline species but only from *Felis silvestris*. More astonishingly, they are descended solely from the *lybica* subspecies, the Near Eastern type native to southern Turkey, Iraq, and Israel, where it still lives today.

Driscoll cross-referenced his genetic analysis with the scant archaeological evidence, like a 9,500-year-old kitten grave from the island of Cyprus that suggests that people had by then taken a shine to cats, and Egyptian artwork from 1950 BC that shows cats as common fixtures in human households. He concluded that our domestic relationship with house cats began in the same time and place as our relationship with sheep and cows and most of the rest of our important animal dependents: perhaps 10,000 or 12,000 years ago, somewhere in the Fertile Crescent at a place not unlike Hallan Çemi, though probably occurring in several spots over a prolonged period. Somehow house cats spread from there to take over the entire world.

So at last we know approximately when and where cat domestication began. The remaining mystery is why and how—and ultimately, who, because it is unclear how much say humans had in the matter.

Cats, by any reasonable standard, are terrible candidates for domestication. The most obvious problem is their social lives—or lack thereof. Mankind's basic strategy for controlling other species has typically been to hijack their dominance hierarchies, to play the role of lead steer or alpha dog so that subordinate animals fall in line and we can mate and command and kill them as we choose. But like almost all the cats (with the exception of lions and sometimes cheetahs), *Felis silvestris lybica* has no social hierarchy. It has no leader. In the wild, it does not even tolerate the presence of other adult cats except during copulation. Herding cats really is hard.

Cats' limited social lives aren't the only strike against them, in terms of their suitability for domestication. The wild *Felis silvestris lybica* is—

like most cats—nocturnal, territorial, highly agile, and difficult to contain, all of which makes sharing a schedule and space with humans far from ideal. It is sexually finicky—domestication typically involves mating the best animals to amplify desirable traits, but Driscoll believes that we have influenced feline sex lives for only 100 of the last 10,000-plus years, and even now supervise only a tiny percentage of (mostly purebred) couplings.

And of course, *Felis silvestris lybica* is a terrifically picky eater: many of our domesticated animals (like pigs and goats) will gladly consume any swill, but all cats are exclusive carnivores and eat only high-quality meat. Today, with pet cats, these demands remain inconvenient, as anyone who's run out of turkey and giblets at 11 p.m. knows, but in previous millennia when meat resources were far dearer, there actually would have been a form of carnivorous competition between cat and keeper. (In some parts of the world, this rivalry subtly persists: the average Australian household cat, for instance, ingests more fish each year than the average Australian does.)

Even if our ancestors, still fending off starvation and leopards, could have worked out all of these kinks, it's not clear why we would have made the effort. Our motives for domestication are usually quite obvious: we covet an animal's body parts, by-products, or labor. What exactly house cats furnish (as we will see in the next chapter) is a much fuzzier matter.

But luckily for *Felis silvestris lybica*, at least some individual members of the species turned out to have one vital "domestic" quality going for them: their temperament. A baseline comfort with humans is by far the most important prerequisite for all domestication contenders. Anxious animals won't mate in captivity and may even die of stress. Preferring that our rabbits reproduce like rabbits, humans have always, deliberately or by default, bred calm animals that can handle our chaotic environment. What's so curious about house cats is that they seem to have cultivated this trait on their own.

Almost all wild cats, even those species big enough to eat humans, are, with excellent reason, shy, reclusive, and often deathly afraid of us—and that includes the several other undomesticated yet nearly identical subspecies of *Felis silvestris*. In the 1930s, wildlife photographer Frances Pitt wrote about her attempt to woo the European wild cat, *Felis silvestris silvestris*, a close cousin of the house cat's ancestor. "Beelzebina, Princess of Devils," as she calls the captive kitten, "spat and scratched in fiercest resentment. Her pale green eyes glared savage hatred at human-beings, and all attempts to establish friendly relations with her failed."

But the Near Eastern wildcat is a remarkable exception. Studies of modern radio-collared wild *Felis silvestris lybica* suggest that, while most shun humans, every so often an outlier will pursue us, prowling our pigeon houses and canoodling with our pet cats, with whom they regularly interbreed. That's not to say that a daredevil *lybica* is capable of anything like the sort of affectionate behavior that we recognize in house cats; these wild animals aren't about to snuggle with you on a Sunday morning or sit on your shoulders or request a belly rub. But personality, Driscoll explains, is a trait that can run in families, the same as milk yield or muscle quality, passed on, and sometimes amplified, through DNA. And some quirk in the natural *lybica* gene pool disposes particular individuals toward a certain natural bravado—a feature that would ultimately become the raw material of the cat-human bond. What we call "friendliness" in our pet cats is, in part, a lack of aggression. But it is also a lack of fear, and an inborn boldness.

So it wasn't the meek and mild cats that first entered our fire circles at Hallan Çemi and elsewhere: it was the lion-hearted. Once the most fearless felines infiltrated, they fortified themselves with our tasty leftovers and mated with other daring cats dining nearby, producing even more audacious babies. These were not domestic recruits, but invaders. And while other little predators like foxes and badgers were content to linger at civilization's edges, where they remain today, bold cats blazed a trail all the way to our beds. In doing so, they hijacked what is normally a human-driven selection process.

In effect, Driscoll tells me, "House cats domesticated themselves." And to get a sense of how the key feline personality traits could have flowed down along bloodlines to our modern pets, he suggests that I visit a certain basement.

The first time I meet Melody Roelke-Parker, she is hammering apart a frozen mountain lion heart in a laboratory of the National Institutes of Health. A globally known big-cat veterinarian, she's diagnosed distemper outbreaks in Serengeti lions and helped discover evidence of genetic bottlenecking in cheetahs, and her personal collection of frozen feline tissue samples from wild cats across the planet is world-class.

But I am interested in another collection: the one living in her house.

For years Roelke oversaw an NIH colony of wild Asian leopard cats, small spotted felines native to South Asian jungles, which scientists crossbred with regular house cats to study topics from fertility issues to the evolution of certain coat colors. When the funding for those experiments stopped, Roelke-Parker—whose heart is far more tender than the ones in her freezers—ended up adopting dozens of the hybrid lab animals, even though they were given to exorcism-worthy behaviors like running upside down on the wire roofs of their cages. Due to lack of handling and their leopard cat genes, most were more or less wild—"absolute hellions," in her fond remembrance. She bred them with each other and with ordinary house cats.

A decade and many litters of kittens later, Roelke-Parker's Maryland basement looks like a miniature zoo, with story-high cages festively decked out with dangling tree branches and hammocks. Visitors find themselves under the surveillance of many, many pairs of slanting yellow eyes. Meows mingle with the determined hum of the washing machine.

The leopard cat/house cat crosses today look mostly like ordinary pets, smoke-colored and tuxedo and swirled tabby. But what now interests Roelke-Parker and her former lab mate Driscoll lies below the surface: it's the animals' behavior, which seems to follow definite genetic pathways.

"What I wanted to show you was the families," Roelke-Parker says. "Let's start with Kiwi." She leads me to a large cage full of cats with flattened ears and furious faces. Water bowls clatter as Kiwi, a blotched tabby, and her adult kittens scramble to get as far away from us as possible. "This is the bad family," she says. "Kiwi doesn't like me, she doesn't want to look at me. Most of Kiwi's offspring are really obnoxious. There's this 'I'm pissed off and I could kill you' thing that they do."

Some of Kiwi's kittens are a beautiful silver color, which might make them especially adoptable, but their temperament forbids it. "That one is called Snow Witch," she says, pointing to the worst offender. Snow Witch was such a pretty kitten that a member of the NIH lab foolishly agreed to take her in. On her first night in her new home, she tore the bathroom fan from the ceiling. Snow Witch went back to Roelke-Parker's basement.

On the other end of the spectrum, there's Poppy. Poppy has mated with some of the same males as Kiwi, but for whatever reason her kittens tend to be friendly, growing snugglier with successive generations. We meet some of them—Pistachio and Pecan and Pyro. "Sometimes you get a really sticky-sweet one that wants to sit on my shoulder," Roelke-Parker says.

Almost on cue, there's a plaintive meow, and to my shock a rusty-brown cat named Cyprus, part of Poppy's lineage, hops out of his cage through a door that Roelke-Parker has opened, the only cat that I see enjoy such a privilege. He gets to munch his own private can of food by the washing machine, and he receives plenty of extra caresses and even kissy-faces from Roelke-Parker, whom he appears to adore, soliciting her eye contact. Indeed, it wouldn't surprise me if this cat eventually sweet-talked his way out of the basement and into Roelke-Parker's living room upstairs: though he bunks with the rest of the colony, Cyprus is practically a pet. But what makes him so different?

As it turns out, I'm not the first interested visitor to Roelke-Parker's basement. She recently hosted a scientist from the most celebrated domestication study ever conducted: the ongoing Russian fox farm experiment. More than 50 years ago, Siberian scientists decided to breed silver foxes, but instead of selecting for fur quality or body size or another standard physical trait that might be prized in farmed foxes, they focused on temperament alone. Their results were mind-blowing: within just a few generations of crossing the friendliest animals, the once-snarling silver foxes—a species that had never been domesticated—licked the scientists like dogs. Today the silver foxes are sold as pets.

The Russian visitors were curious to learn more about agreeable Poppy and mean Kiwi and their respective clans. Scientists hope to one day identify the genes that shape such differences in temperament and that may underlie the mysterious process of domestication.

And yet Roelke-Parker's basement is a highly artificial scenario, with humans in a supervisory role. The true history of cat domestication—in which wild cats underwent key personality changes, above all else—is a tantalizing real-world parallel to the famous fox experiment. In nature and our shared history, feline personality changes happened largely among cats who were left to their own devices, raiding and mating in our settlements with increasing moxie. Humanity wasn't holding the reins.

Because it was a natural process, the house cat's real-world metamorphosis from wild animal to cuddly companion happened very, very slowly. The silver fox's personality transformation took only a few decades, and—even though novice herdsmen 10,000 years ago knew a lot less than the modern Russian scientists—the long-ago domestication of most common barnyard species spanned just centuries. By contrast, house cats are probably a work in progress even today. When researchers from Washington University in St. Louis recently compared the genome of house cats and their wild relative, *Felis silvestris lybica*, they found just a handful of genetic differences, especially unimpressive considering the changes that domestic dogs have undergone. "The number of genomic regions with strong signals of selection since cat domestication," the authors write, "appears modest."

The modern house cat's physique suggests as much. Most domesticated animals share a common set of peculiar physical features, including splotchy coat pigmentation, small teeth, juvenile-looking faces, floppy ears, and curly tails. Scientists call this little-understood suite of traits the "domestication syndrome." Darwin, who first described it, was particularly baffled by the floppy ears, so common in domestic dogs and pigs and goats and rabbits but completely absent in wild animals, with the exception of elephants. As they became friendlier, the Russian foxes suddenly developed these trademark droopy ears, along with white fur splotches that made them look very much like collie dogs. (Even farmed carp can exhibit mottled white spots in their scales.) The cause of the distinctive and slightly goofy domesticated "look" has been one of the great puzzles of evolutionary biology.

The funny thing is that house cats don't really look like this. They lack droopy ears. They don't have curly tails. They don't have tiny teeth compared to their wild counterparts, and their faces—and indeed most of their bodies—are not immature looking. Indeed, they appear almost identical to a full-grown wild *lybica*.

House cats do have pigmentation anomalies, in the form of white bellies, facial blazes, and other unusual markings. But these embellishments apparently are quite new. Evidence suggests, for instance, that house cats' coats began to vary only in the last millennia or so. Before then, it seems, cats came in just one color. Ancient Egyptian funerary reliefs, for instance, don't feature tuxedo cats—the pet felines are all brown mackerel tabbies, à la the wild *lybica*, though cats had already been in human company for thousands of years. The first evidence of changing coats, Driscoll says, comes from a medical writer who mentions it about AD 600.

In addition to sporting these new coat colors, modern house cats fit the domestication mold in a few other ways. Some may, for instance, undergo more frequent reproductive cycles than their wild counterparts, meaning that kittens can be born year-round, contributing to the breeding bonanza that domestication allows. And they exhibit the single most vital and distinctive sign of the domesticated body type: house cats have shrunken brains, smaller than *lybica*'s by about a third.

This statistic initially reminded me of certain of my dimmer-seeming pet cats, but brain reduction is a standard feature of domestication in animals ranging from turkeys to llamas. It does not mean the animals are stupid; rather, it allows them to survive in our settlements. Typically, the reduction involves the forebrain, which includes the amygdala and other components of the limbic system, controlling perception and fear. A whittled-down fight-or-flight response means that an animal is better suited to stress—the crux of domestic existence. In large part because of their reduced fear responses, house cats are brazen, and—if exposed to enough human contact early in the first two months of life—can display the docile and even downright friendly behaviors (rubbing ankles, licking faces) that their owners appreciate today.

But here again, because human beings weren't actually steering the process, it took ages for the cat brain to shrink. Analysis of Egyptian cat mummies from just a few thousand years ago shows that those animals still had brains as big as their wild relatives'.

Scientists now suspect that domestication syndrome may be caused by a deficit in embryonic stem cells called neural crest cells, which help determine an animal's forebrain size. Interestingly, the neural crest cells also influence a remarkable array of factors like skull shape, cartilage formation, and coat colors when they migrate to different parts of the body during fetal development. Favoring tamer animals with smaller forebrains and reduced startle responses in species ranging from cows to carp, humans may have inadvertently selected for these impaired neural crest cells and all their myriad consequences—weird colors and droopy ears and twisted tails included.

Maybe the fact that house cats display some, but not all, of the critical features of domestication syndrome means that their neural crest cells are still in the process of being impaired, and their domestication journey is still very much under way. When the Washington University geneticists recently analyzed the house cat's genome and compared it to *lybica*'s, they indeed found that genes related to neural crest cells were among the few areas that had undergone change. One day we may well see cats with lop ears and corkscrew tails, but sadly not quite yet.

Just a few other measurable differences distinguish house cats from their wild kin. Our pets' legs are a bit shorter. Their meow sounds a little sweeter. They've recalibrated their social lives ever so slightly; many house cats still very much like to live alone, yet unlike the wild *lybica*, they can also form family-based colonies similar to lion prides. House cats can tolerate living with unrelated cats (though often not nearly as well as we owners might imagine), and sometimes seem to enjoy it: my parents' Burmese and Siamese loved to curl up together, forming a furry yin and yang.

And perhaps it should come as no surprise that house cats have also lengthened their intestines—a hypercarnivore's concession to the more varied, difficult-to-digest protein sources available in human settlements.

So after the first intrepid felines breached our communities very, very gradually—much slower than they would have had humans been running the show—the offspring of certain wild cats became ever more frequent and emboldened guests. Over the centuries they shrank their brains so they could stand to live among us and grew their guts so they could help themselves to more of our meaty garbage. Along the way they acquired some pretty white spots.

It was an extraordinary move on the cats' part: with just a few nips and tucks, a feline species ill suited in so many other ways to domestication could reap the benefits of an alliance with humanity. And today these built-in advantages apply not only to the privileged pet cats that share our down pillows and well-stocked pantries but also to stray cats, living in alleyways, wildernesses, and worse, who may never have touched a human but who thrive because of their distant ancestors' decision to sidle up to us.

Apart from those few stingy changes, however, house cats barely twitched a whisker to accommodate humanity—not then, and certainly not today.

Which again begs the question: Why did we let them stay?

Chapter 3

WHAT'S THE CATCH?

O NE OF the deepest mysteries of house cats is what they do with their time. Even the most indulged dog usually pursues some version of his ancestral duties: yapping at strangers, fetching and carrying, loping alongside his owner, looking vainly for opportunities to hunt or herd or otherwise serve us. But Cheetoh's life seems like one unbroken sunbath, disturbed only by frantic sprints to the dry food dish in the moments before the automatic timer is due to deliver a crunchy payout. Food and rest—plus a few pets (grudgingly received) and the occasional promenade around the back patio—account for all the labor of his days. To say that this animal hasn't done much for me lately is a ludicrous understatement.

Perhaps Cheetoh is just a particularly shiftless example of his kind. Or maybe cats were never anything more than a sort of furry ornament or living luxury good. But cats are so cryptic: I must be missing something here. After all, these creatures have been among us for millennia now. Once they insinuated themselves into the human sphere, they must have found a higher purpose, or at least some kind of a discernible function, that explains why we tolerated them.

One September morning I find myself at *Meet the Breeds* at the Jacob Javits Center in New York City. This annual pet festival bills itself as an introduction to various kinds of purebred pets: Is the Dandie Dinmont terrier right for you? How is a Turkish Angora cat different from a Turkish Van? But it's also a primer on the basic differences between cats and dogs, and its daily schedule perfectly distills the gifts and uses of each companion animal.

The dog show ring is a constant flurry of activity. Police dogs execute neat phalanxlike maneuvers; US Customs and Border Patrol dogs search suitcases for narcotics; dogs with Educated Canines Assisting with Disabilities pilot wheelchairs. Atka the Amazing Eskie frisks through her tricks and Shetland sheepdogs perform a conga line.

Meanwhile, over in the cat ring, the cats do pretty much nothing. They purr, they primp, they stare into space. Poker-faced, they allow the MC to lift them overhead to display their cuteness and ask game-show-style cat trivia questions as well as pose a few more controversial inquiries, like "What color is my cat?" (This intense public debate is slated to fill at least a half hour on the show schedule.) As their throngs of human admirers sing "I'm a Mean Ol' Lion" from *The Wiz*, the cats keep mum.

When you get down to it, it's hard to showcase cats' contributions to society. Cats don't detect IEDs, retrieve the drowning, or guide the blind. So why are there so many more cats than dogs padding around the planet today? Why do American households include some 12 million more cats than dogs?

It's obvious why we cultivated canine companionship. The dog's story is unlike any other, since we appear to have begun consorting with them thousands of years—maybe even ten or fifteen thousand—before we domesticated any other animal. We were still hunter-gatherers then, and the "First Friends," as Rudyard Kipling calls dogs, soon transformed our lives as much as we transformed theirs. Almost from the outset they barked warnings, lugged supplies, pitched into the hunt. When we transitioned into farming settlements, dogs came to heel, evolving along with our lifestyle. And while cats made meager, nearly invisible alterations to the stubborn feline body plan over many millennia, dogs—under our direction—went whole hog, producing an endless array of convenient body styles and temperaments to assist in myriad human endeavors. Hunting breeds similar to the greyhound date back to the Egyptians. Romans likely employed guide dogs, sheep dogs, mastiff-like war dogs, and tiny lapdogs that fine ladies kept stored up their sleeves (in later eras, these were apparently used like hot water bottles). A list of antique Tudor dog breed names illustrates their myriad purposes: Stealer, Setter, Fynder, Comforter, Turnspit, Dancer.

More recently, we've fitted dogs with Kevlar vests and parachuted them into war zones. Dogs comfort the victims of mass shootings, help capture Osama bin Laden, locate the scat of rare animals for scientific surveys, discover the graves of lost Civil War soldiers, and support kids with learning disabilities. "Dogs can detect incipient tumors and distinguish the types and grades of numerous cancers, sometimes simply by smelling their owner's breath," writes David Grimm in his book about the animal rights movement, *Citizen Canine*. "Dogs can also sniff out dangerous bacteria like *E. coli* in public water supplies and 'superbugs' in hospital wards."

And cats? "Cat purring," Grimm suggests, "may boost bone density and prevent muscle wasting—a serious problem for astronauts, though as yet no one has advocated for cats in space." For this potential application he cites "anecdotal evidence."

Charmed by the notion of astronaut purr therapy, I started a file called "Uses for Cats," listing our best attempts over the centuries to find a practical purpose for these animals. To encourage rain, Indonesians paraded cats around their fields. Seventeenth-century Japanese musicians settled on cat skin as the perfect sheath for the samisen, a square-bodied lute (and apparently even modern plastics can't compare). The Chinese used the cats' dilating pupils to estimate the time of day—an awed French missionary named Père Évariste Huc described this "Chinese discovery" to his European readers with "some hesitation . . . as it may, doubtless, injure the interests of the clock-making trade."

Cats were also an essential part of several kinds of European tortures. Medieval murderers were sometimes burned in a sack with twelve cats to maximize suffering. During a punishment called "cat hauling," a cat was dragged by its tail down the length of an offender's body.

In the high-tech era, the cat hair that covers so many of us has been at least once submitted as damning DNA evidence in a murder trial; on the other side of the law, prisoners have employed cats as drug mules. In addition to their rather grisly roles as medical test subjects in human bladder and hearing aid studies, cats have served as key indicators for a rare tropical disease known as ciguatera: reef fish can turn toxic after feasting on certain algae, so people let an ultrasensitive cat sample the day's catch first. Cat meat itself is still eaten in some corners of the globe, though it apparently does not taste very good, and cat skins are only seldom worn, although there's a growing hipster craze for harvesting shed cat fur for felting crafts.

Imaginative military leaders sometimes have yearned to let slip the "cats of war" (a sixteenth-century German-language artillery manual presents particularly vivid illustrations of flaming feline siege machines), but few have realized the vision. In the 1960s, the CIA did attempt Operation Acoustic Kitty, in which feline spies implanted with microphones, radio transmitters, and antennae were dispatched as eavesdroppers. But the program was scrapped midway through the maiden mission, since apparently the first reconnaissance cat was so stealthy that a taxi driver didn't see it in time to swerve.

In our litany of cat tasks, only one is obvious and even lionized: cats are supposed to kill mice and rats for us. This, some would argue, is even better than bagging a terrorist. "In silence, in secret, and often at night, the ancient battle between the cat and the rodent, mankind's greatest natural enemy, has continued through the ages," writes historian Donald Engels in *Classical Cats: The Rise and Fall of the Sacred Cat.* "Domesticated cats were the bulwark of Western societies' defense. . . . the presence of a barn cat often meant the difference between starvation and survival for many farm families through the millennia."

Such vermin-slaying does seem the one plausible reciprocal service that cats might provide in exchange for their privileged global status. Rodents, and especially the diseases that they carry, remain a worldwide problem. There's a certain pleasing symmetry to the idea that cats, rocketed to the top by the same agricultural revolution that doomed most of their wild cousins, would become stalwart guardians of barn and silo, not to mention the human immune system.

But is this true? Do cats really keep vermin at bay? Did they ever? For the truth, I decide to ask a rat scientist.

I first learned about the field of "cat-rat interactions" while tramping in a fetid Baltimore back alley, reporting on the Rodent Ecology project at Johns Hopkins University School of Public Health. The subjects of this on-going fifty-year study, Norway rats—aka brown rats, sewer rats, and wharf rats, the major invasive rat species of America and much of the world—are nasty creatures, vectors for plague and hanta virus and leptospirosis and many other grave and unpronounceable ills. In the early 1980s, an ambitious young Hopkins graduate student addressed a question few had considered: How did Baltimore's large alley cat population impact the resident rats?

One winter day I meet that graduate student in his apartment in New Haven, Connecticut, where he is now a senior research scientist at the Yale University School of Public Health. Jamie Childs sits on a leopard-print daybed as the snow falls on skylights above. Since his days in Baltimore, Childs's epidemiology studies have taken him across the world, and his apartment is lined with mammal skulls, some of them human.

When the conversation turns to his old cat-rat work, Childs disappears from the daybed for a moment and returns with what looks like a black-bound telephone book: the original copy of his PhD thesis. He cracks it open to a section of photographs.

They are in black and white. Perhaps because the scenes were shot at night, they have the illicit look of a forbidden tryst—and in a sense, that's precisely what they are. These pictures show cats and rats in the shadows, hanging out *together*. In one image, "the bulwark of Western society's defense" pointedly ignores "mankind's greatest natural enemy" scurrying just a few inches away. Kittens and adult rats stand close enough to touch.

Such shocking scenes, Childs says, were no means uncommon. The two species rarely even tussled. "I never saw a cat kill a rat. They are just not natural enemies in that environment. They are sharing a common resource," which is so bountiful that they need not even compete for it. That resource is trash.

Childs discovered that, in Baltimore, cats do haunt the rat hot spots—precisely what you'd expect of an animal devoted to safeguarding our civilization. But in reality felines lurk near rats because that's where the most garbage is. "What's food for rats is food for cats," Childs says. And even with modern sanitation in effect, there is plenty of refuse to go around. In three years of work, Childs found—via rat remains—just a few cases of cats eating rats, and these were exclusively small juveniles.

Perhaps the feline garbage scarfing shouldn't come as a shock. Cats were most likely lured by trash at Hallan Çemi and other early settlements. Foxes, their prehistoric doppelgängers, still eat so much trash today that in one experiment, fox populations plummeted in areas where garbage was swiftly collected but thrived wherever it was left to fester. Why would any animal waste energy and risk injury to catch a rodent with much easier pickings available?

To be clear, house cats are superb hunters and obviously do kill rodents, sometimes for food, sometimes for fun, just as they kill small animals of all kinds. The average cat owner can attest to the occasional beheaded mouse on the carpet, and the smell of a cat alone may sometimes be enough to keep pests away. I once had a tuxedo cat named Sylvester who seemed to take an almost obscene pleasure in mouse torture: late at night I would awake to the sound of his purring and a terrible squeaking in the kitchen, and cower under the covers, unable to decide whether to rescue the poor maimed victim being batted around on the linoleum or to let my sadistic mouser finish the job, which could take ten agonizing minutes or more.

Cats almost certainly ate some rodents at Hallan Çemi and similar early sites; isotopic analysis of 4,000-year-old cat remains from central China showed evidence of millet, which suggests cats were eating the mice that ate the grain (though it's possible that cats, with their elongated guts, may also have sampled millet directly). Today's Norway rats are quite intimidating animals, much bigger than, say, the reigning black rats of medieval Europe, which might have been more manageable prey. As late as the twentieth century, exterminators rented out cats as means of pest control.

But the question is not whether cats sometimes eat rodents—it's whether they eat enough to make a difference to human civilization.

Beyond the ongoing Baltimore project, only a few other studies tackle the question of how well cats guard our larders. One dates to 1916, when the Massachusetts State Board of Agriculture concluded after a series of farm surveys that many cat-patrolled farms had plenty of rats and that just a third of the cats were active ratters. In 1940, a British scientist charged with protecting food stores for the war effort observed some farms in Oxfordshire and found that cats can indeed deter rats from settling in a building—but only if the existing population is wiped out by poison first. Also, to keep the cats from pursuing happier hunting grounds, each had to be fed half a pint of milk per day. (So much for preserving war rations.) And one recent California study suggested that cats in urban parks prefer to hunt native species like voles rather than invasive pests like house mice.

In fact, the same study found that urban cat populations are actually associated with higher numbers of house mice, which, the authors point out, may have coevolved with cats and learned how to outsmart them. This important point helps distinguish thriving invasive species, like street rats and house mice, from the far more delicate wild rodents that (like many other endemic creatures, as we'll see in the next chapter) house cats routinely threaten. Though these ubiquitous rodent invaders are not themselves domesticated, they are another variety of humanity's furry hangers-on that have tailored their biology to our lifestyle. Scientists call such tenacious creatures "commensals." (One commensal adaptation to city living is, for instance, an amped-up, year-round breeding cycle that yields staggering numbers of rodents.)

When it comes to their pest-control shortcomings, then, it's not that house cats are weak, but that rats and mice are so strikingly robust. Yet even if cats can't suppress rat populations entirely, might they still protect us from some rodent-born diseases by picking off a few in our houses here and there? Sadly, Childs's finding that cats kill only juvenile Norway rats has major epidemiologic implications, for these puny youngsters aren't the key disease spreaders. It's mostly the big old rats—survivors with robust immune systems—that carry the diseases.

But what about places in medieval Europe, where the offending street rats were of the more palatable black variety? In particular, I'd learned from popular books (and from various animal rights activists) that cats had been an instrumental defense against the medieval bubonic plague, carried by the black rats and their fleas. There's even a theory that the Catholic Church ignited the devastation of the Black Death by killing off Europe's cats.

The story goes like this: in 1233, Pope Gregory IX penned *Vox in Rama*, a papal bull that describes orgies of witches fraternizing with Lucifer in the guise of a black cat. Though the document also implicated frogs and ducks, anti-feline prejudice swept across Europe and untold numbers of cats were subsequently targeted and executed on suspicion of devilry. Then, in the very next century, the rat-borne plague spiraled out of control and killed tens of millions of people.

But claiming that an ecclesiastically created cat deficit caused this tragedy is a little silly. First, nobody knows how many cats the witch hunters killed, but house cats (as opposed to their imperiled wild feline relatives, large and small) are incredibly adaptable and hardy creatures, tough to catch and—thanks in large part to their alliance with mankind—shockingly numerous and almost as quick to multiply as rats. No amount of hurling cats from bell towers and burning them in bonfires—the inquisitors' colorful but not particularly efficient methods—would have made more than a tiny dent in cat populations across the vast area of mainland Europe.

Second, due in part to new archaeological evidence, scientists now suspect that rat fleas may not have driven the Black Death after all. The disease also raged in places like Scandinavia where black rat populations were small, and scientists are beginning to think that it was, at least in some spots, actually spread by coughing or by human fleas that jumped from person to person, cutting rats and cats entirely out of the equation.

Finally, house cats themselves can be major plague hosts. If cats indeed managed to dispose of any number of diseased black rats, they likely contracted plague themselves and carried it into our villages and homes. This is a surprisingly common modern scenario, according to Kenneth Gage, a plague expert at the Centers for Disease Control and Prevention. His studies of the plague outbreaks that still occur in pockets of the American West show that nearly 10 percent of human plague victims contract the disease directly from house cats. This is not to say that house cats caused the Black Death, but only that they probably didn't hinder its spread, and might have occasionally helped. After all, it's cats, not rats, that we like to cuddle with.

Just one last note on this matter. The medieval witch hunters suspected a whole menagerie of animals—including crabs, hedgehogs, and butterflies—of demonic mischief. But cats were indeed the most commonly accused "imps," according to one analysis of more than 200 English witch trials, with many villagers testifying that witches' cats "tormented" them and sickened their children. Several theories explain this prejudice, including the fact that cats are nocturnal, and so more readily available for midnight Sabbaths. But the University of Pennsylvania zoologist James Serpell also suggests a convincing medical explanation: cat allergies. Respiratory reactions to cat dander are exceedingly common, impacting up to a quarter of modern people, and can be quite crippling. Perhaps it didn't seem like a stretch to say that sorcery triggered the scary "Hecticks and consumptions" that many people experienced in the company of cats. Maybe cats earned their reputation as a malevolent force.

Funding for cat-rodent science no doubt became scarcer in the 1960s with the advent of effective rat poisons, which, everyone agrees, work far better than cats. For now, "the impact of cats on commensal rodent populations," as the authors of a recent book on urban carnivores conclude, "is probably not substantial, given the reproductive capacity of these species and that they occupy habitats such as sewers or building cavities where they are not readily accessible."

In his own life, Jamie Childs has moved on from the cat-rat field. He has been on hand for outbreaks of Ebola and hemorrhagic fever and other devastating human diseases. And when confronted with rats gone wild in his travels—and it happens to him more than most people—Childs recommends the services of a rat terrier, who will shake scores of rats to death in succession, not stopping to dine or sunbathe.

But despite bearing witness to alleyway events that more or less amounted to interspecies treason, Childs still ended up adopting one of the stray cats from his study area.

"A white and gray one—I called him Boots," he says with a fond smile. "Just a great animal."

Cats, it seems, transcend the practical. Domesticating them made so little sense that we likely never tried; once cats domesticated themselves, they provided few tangible services. They did not save us from starvation, nor did a Continental cat deficit catalyze the Black Death. Yet—tolerated by Stone Age villagers, venerated by the Egyptians, and digitized by modern millennials—cats have stood the test of time, and many of us today confess to enjoying their company immensely. It does seem that, in a way, they bewitched us.

Human whims and affinities are at the heart of the house cat's success. "People tend to think that people are always very goal-directed, and do everything intentionally," the animal domestication scholar Greger Larson tells me. "Well, that's bullshit. There's not always an economic purpose or something logical. Myth and suspicion and just keeping up with the Joneses and all these other things can drive us. It's about culture and aesthetics—and accidents."

One very important accident is the fact that, though cats and humans last shared an ancestor about 92 million years ago, cats look uncannily like us. Even better, they look like our infants. Their oft-cited "cuteness" is not an arbitrary or benign quality, but a set of highly particular and powerful physical features that scientists have taken the trouble to tease apart and study. House cats are blessed with a killer set of what Austrian ethnologist Konrad Lorenz calls "baby releasers": physical traits that remind us of human young and set off a hormonal cascade. These features include a round face, chubby cheeks, big forehead, big eyes, and a little nose.

Mentally inventorying my own pets, I seem to have a particular weakness for this look. "Wow," said my sister-in-law the first time she saw Cheetoh. "He has such a human face!" And indeed he does.

As with our own helpless neonates, the "baby releasers" of other animals cue a pleasurable, drug-like "oxytocin glow" in human adults and trigger a set of nurturing behaviors, including enhanced fine-motor coordination that prepares us to cradle a baby. Pet-keeping has thus been called a "misfiring of our parental instincts." Or as the evolutionary biologist Stephen Jay Gould suggests, we are "fooled by an evolved response to our own babies and we transfer our reaction to the same set of features in other animals."

Of course, lots of animals are adorable, especially baby ones, and domesticated animals in particular tend to retain infantile features into adulthood. Some of this juvenile look is a consequence of selecting for docile temperament, but also reflects our tastes. With their long faces and sharp snouts, wolves are not cute, but many dog breeds are, and our weakness for baby releasers must have influenced the development of animals like the pug. Indeed, some fancy dogs, like Pomeranians, look an awful lot like cats.

But house cats, including adult ones, and even the original wild *lybica*, just naturally happen to resemble human progeny, without any engineering at all. Part of it is their size, which—at an average of about eight pounds—is of precisely newborn proportion. (I've been known to carry my more tractable cats cradled in my arms, baby style.) Part of it is sound—the cat's meow is reminiscent of a baby's cry, and studies show that cats may have modulated their vocalizations over time to mimic the cry more precisely. Part of it is those key facial features, which actually reflect the cats' deadly anatomy—their short, powerful jaws give rise to sweetly rounded faces, and they have little snub noses because smell isn't the keystone of their hunting strategy the way it is for dogs.

But the real secret may be their eyes.

With their slitted pupils and hypersensitive retinas, which glow at night like moons, cats' eyes are not much like ours. But in important ways they look similar. For one thing, feline eyes are gigantic: an adult cat's eyes are almost as big as a human's, and a kitten's jumbo eyes look larger still in a small face. Likely because of the subconscious association with our own saucer-eyed offspring, an animal's eye size predicts its commercial appeal:

with its black eye patches that make its relatively beady eyes look a hundred times bigger, the World Wildlife Fund's panda is conservation's ultimate poster child. Yet house cats—though hardly endangered—could probably give pandas a run for their donor money.

As big as cats' eyes are, their placement may be even more fortuitous. Many other cuddly animals, like rabbits, have eyes on the sides of their heads, which allows for a wider field of vision, and even dogs' eyes are slightly more off-center. But cats are ambush predators. To pounce upon fast-moving prey, especially at night, they need to be able to judge distances, so they evolved the best binocular vision of any carnivore. This ocular strategy requires overlapping fields of view, so cat eyes face forward, planted front and center in their heads.

That's how our eyes face, too. Primates are not ambush predators but largely vegetarian browsers, and we've used our centrally located eyes for very different purposes: scanning bushes for ripe fruit at close range, and much more recently, for reading the facial expressions of others. Cats' eye placement is a major part of what makes their faces appear so person-like to us. (Owls, another visual nocturnal predator, have similar facial composition, which perhaps explains why we prefer them to, say, vultures.)

So a cat's features are a perfect cocktail of cuteness, yet they still look a whole lot like the animals that once slaughtered our ancestors. A cat's face is the face of a supreme predator, but it is also the face of a child, and there's a mesmerizing tension in that combination.

Particularly, it seems, to women: in fact, the "baby release" effect of oxytocin seems to be particularly potent in women of reproductive age. And while it's conventional wisdom that the hardcore cat world of Persian fanciers and rescue groups is female-centric, I wasn't prepared for how explicitly maternal it is. In even the upper echelons of cat shows, champions with page-long names and pedigrees are referred to simply as "little boy" and "little girl," as in: "Can you believe that Russian judge dumped my little girl?" From organic meat purees to high-end strollers, many baby products have feline equivalents, and the founder of Hauspanther, the wildly successful cat swag website, got her start in infant gear.

This is not to say that the Stone Age ladies of the Near East were dandling cats on their knees—these mommying impulses are the strange fruit of a long, slow, complex, and frequently inscrutable history. But raw cuteness, combined with inborn boldness, helps explains how the cat got a paw in the door when so many other species stayed out in the cold.

For humans, the effect of having fake babies—"fictive kin," in the jargon of evolutionary psychologists—is unclear. Some scholars suggest that humans may reap benefits from faux parenting a fur baby, since it's practice for rearing our own children, and a display to potential mates of our human parenting skills. Others claim that a cat is more akin to a "social parasite" that pirates our nurturing instincts and robs our actual young of time, attention, and other resources.

For now, it's enough to say that, through a combination of evolved behavior and natural good looks, house cats exerted a kind of subtle control over us. We became their creatures as much as they became ours. They ate our food without much to offer in return. And yet they had far grander conquests in store.

For while cats cozy up to humans, sitting pretty in our settlements, gobbling trash, and eschewing sewer rats, they don't *need* to remain among us. They are still cats, after all. They can always step back into what's left of the wild. Midlevel hunters no longer, they are now the apex predators of a man-made world.

Chapter 4

THE CATS THAT ATE
THE CANARIES

O BSERVING SOME neighborhood cat stalking a front lawn or slinking around a corner, I've often marveled at its striking resemblance to Cheetoh . . . only to realize—with dawning horror—that it *is* Cheetoh, who has somehow squeezed his vast bulk through the slats of the back porch, and is now out on the lam. I've spent far too much free time trying to secure the perimeters of various apartment patios and condominium decks in an effort to protect my precious charges from the mean streets beyond.

And yet in a growing number of places on this planet, fences are seen not as a way to keep beloved cats *in* but rather as a last-ditch way to barricade them *out*. In these locations cats are not considered pets but nightmarish invaders, capable of ransacking whole ecosystems and annihilating feebler life-forms in their path.

I arrive at the Crocodile Lake National Wildlife Refuge in the pulverizing rain, after buying the last umbrella at the first gas station in Key Largo. It's not a great day to comb the Florida woods for a highly endangered subspecies of rodent, but the three guys in the refuge trailer don't acknowledge the cats-and-dogs downpour. In fact, refuge manager Jeremy Dixon carries wraparound sunglasses. PhD student Mike Cove lets fat raindrops plop into his mug of morning coffee. Ralph DeGayner, a septuagenarian Michigan snowbird, has been out since 4 a.m. in the monsoon, checking his cat traps, and his day is just beginning.

This trio of determined optimists may be all that stands between the Key Largo wood rat and oblivion. Walt Disney and Jane Goodall couldn't stop the house cats that are wolfing down the last of the rare wood rats, but these three men refuse to yield. And currently they are in the market for the best anti-cat fences that money can buy.

Wincing a little as I unfurl my new umbrella, which turns out to be patterned with tiger stripes, I follow them into the rain.

The KLWR, as this type of Eastern wood rat is briskly referred to in official documents, is a cute little cinnamon-colored creature with big, worried eyes. Unlike Norway rats and other superfit, more or less cat-proof pest species that can live practically anywhere, the wood rat is an indigenous animal that insists upon a very particular type of dry Floridian forest called hardwood hammock. Here, the KLWR pursues a singular passion: building huge, byzantine stick nests, which it beautifies with snail shells and Sharpie caps and other treasures.

Once common throughout Key Largo, the wood rat is now found only in a handful of public preserves, which together amount to a few thousand acres of forest. The wood rat's woes likely started in the 1800s, when Key Largo farmers razed hardwood hammocks to plant pineapple trees, and worsened in the twentieth century when large-scale construction projects transformed this former coral reef.

Then the vacationers came with their cats, and the rest was very nearly history.

Dixon, the refuge manger, is a no-nonsense North Floridian who used to work at the Wichita Mountains Wildlife Refuge, where federal scientists brought back the near-extinct bison. At Crocodile Lake he's the guardian of several obscure, imperiled local creatures—the Schaus swallowtail butterfly, the Stock Island tree snail—but he came here specifically to take a stand for the wood rats. One of his first moves was to install a flashing KEEP CATS INDOORS sign on County Road 905, a rather startling directive amid the refuge's still, green trees.

DeGayner, the volunteer, is scrawny and white-haired, with a keen eye for an injured waterbird glimpsed in the distance. (He sometimes rehabilitates them in his spare time.) He lacks academic bona fides, but the retired pool company magnate has been aiding the wood rats longer than almost anybody. He is the refuge's wiliest trapper, bagging dozens of cats and then delivering them alive to a local animal shelter.

The house cats are still winning, however. Even though much of the wood rat's fragile range is now off-limits to people, the population has dropped precipitously since the species was rushed to federally protected status in the 1980s, and Dixon and his team say it's because the local cats don't abide by refuge boundaries or the Endangered Species Act. Current wood rat estimates hover around a thousand individuals, and at one point it was feared that there might be only a few hundred left. The besieged wood rats even gave up on building their trademark nests, perhaps because slowly dragging large sticks seemed suicidal with so many house cats afoot.

"The wood rats were living in a landscape of fear," says Cove, the graduate student who has previously studied South American jaguars and ocelots, and knows a superpredator when he sees one.

But, though close kin to lions and tigers, house cats are also like flatworms and jellyfish and other simple organisms that are just good at taking over ecosystems. The International Union for Conservation of Nature ranks house cats as one of the world's 100 worst invasive species, an unusually glamorous addition to the icky litany of advancing fungi, mollusks, shrubs, and other brainless, aimless beings. The dreaded list includes few carnivores, let alone hypercarnivores. But the house cat's extreme adaptability and reproductive prowess, its tweaked domesticated physique, and its special relationship with man make it a very formidable alien. And while it's tempting to pretend that only stray cats cause problems, in truth our cuddly pets are as suspect as the mangiest ferals.

Ten thousand years after their ancestors invaded our Fertile Crescent settlements, house cats have spread like dandelion fluff. There are now some 600 million of these formerly obscure felines worldwide, and some scientists put the number at closer to a billion. America alone has nearly 100 million pet cats, a number that has apparently tripled in the last 40 years, and perhaps just about as many strays. (These are remarkably good at keeping out of sight—living in Washington, DC, I discovered my neighborhood cat colony only when I started taking my kids on back-alley safaris.)

House cats have populated every imaginable habitat, from Scottish heaths to African tropical forests to Australian deserts. They colonize urban nativity scenes and Navy missile test sites and Louisiana State University's Tiger Stadium, thriving in bogs and Brooklyn bodegas alike. In addition to the hearts of our major cities, they've staked claims on helicopter-accessible-only wilderness tracts where even people don't dare live.

In all of these niches, they eat pretty much everything alive: star-nosed moles, magnificent frigatebirds, tarantulas, kakapos, katydids, freshwater crayfish, sawfly larva, Brewer's blackbirds, bridled nailtail wallabies and bats and boodies (aka burrowing bettongs) and fantails and scarab beetles and small fish and ruby-throated hummingbirds and chickens and eastern barred bandicoots and brown pelican nestlings. They even stalk (small) animals in zoos.

"Beefsteak and cockroaches," reads one nineteenth-century description of an orange house cat's diet. "Moths and poached eggs, oysters and earthworms . . . its belly became a realization of Noah's ark." And since the feline family has always had a hankering for our kind, it should come as no surprise that house cats have even been known to prey on a species of primate, the white sifaka, and maybe other Madagascar lemurs as well.

Cats can drive extinctions, particularly on islands. One Spanish study found that cats contributed to 14 percent of all vertebrate vanishings on islands worldwide—an extremely conservative estimate, the authors say. Scientists in Australia recently released a mammoth *Action Plan for Australian Mammals* report that fingered house cats as a factor in the fate of 89 out of Australia's 138 extinct, threatened, and near-threatened mammals, many of which are only found Down Under. The continent has far and away the highest rate of mammal extinctions in the world, and the scientists declare house cats to be the single biggest threat to mammalian survival there, far more dire than habitat loss and global warming. (Domestic dogs, on the other hand, have been sent to safeguard some endangered Australian species, like little penguins.)

"If we had to choose one wish for advancing the conservation of Australia's biodiversity," the authors write, "it would be the effective control, indeed eradication, of cats." Australia's environmental minister promptly declared war on the world's favorite pet, which he described as "a tsunami of violence and death."

Bird lovers, in particular, have long squawked about the house cat's appetite. In 2013, federal scientists released a report suggesting that America's cats—both pets and strays—kill some 1.4 to 3.7 billion birds per year, making them the leading human-related cause of avian deaths. (And that's not to mention the 6.9 to 20.7 billion mammals and untold millions of reptiles and amphibians they also do away with.) A Canadian governmental study reported similarly grim findings a few months later.

Of course, house cats are small and stealthy hunters in a big world and it's hard to prove what precisely they are snacking on. But records from wildlife rehabilitation centers give some idea: one California facility reported cat injuries in nearly a quarter of its thousands of avian patients, a huge sweep of species from chickadees to waxwings to whip-poor-wills. Prey animals are found "maimed, mauled, dismembered, ripped apart, and gutted while still alive," the veterinarian David Jessup writes, "and if they survive the encounter, they often die of sepsis."

Now new technology is giving an especially clear and gory picture, via a recent spate of studies that equipped house cats with remote cameras and other digital tools. Jiggling footage from the University of Georgia's 2012 "Kittycam" study of more than 50 well-fed suburban house pets ("subsi-

dized predators" is the formal term) showed that almost half are active
hunters, though they seldom bring home their catch, often leaving it un-
eaten at the kill site where their owners don't see it. Australian scientists
snagged an infrared reel of a cat rousing itself from a nap to snatch a native
dragon: the camera is tucked beneath the cat's fuzzy chin, which chews
thoughtfully as the lizard's skinny tail disappears by degrees like a strand of
spaghetti. And one Hawaiian researcher recorded a cat dragging a downy
Hawaiian petrel chick from its nest, powerful proof of house cat predation
on an endangered species.

The Key Largo wood rat's defenders are gunning for a similar money shot.
So far they have nighttime stills of iridescent-eyed cats pawing at the endangered wood rat's nests, and a blurry photograph of what they think is
a neighborhood pet carrying a dead wood rat in its mouth. But they don't
have frames of a cat killing a wood rat outright. Such an image would be
not just a form of witness but a potential legal weapon. The refuge workers
hope that the owner of a wood-rat-wolfing cat could be prosecuted under
the Endangered Species Act.

As we walk beneath the sodden canopy of Key Largo's remaining hardwood hammocks, we come across a long, low mound of brown leaves and
twigs. It looks like a shallow grave, but is actually the opposite—a lifeboat.
After the persecuted wood rats swore off nest building, DeGayner and his
elderly brother, Clay, vowed to build nests for them. The first bunker-like
models were fashioned from old Jet Skis, easy to come by in the Keys. The
DeGayners carefully camouflaged these "starter chambers" and placed
them upside down close to food sources. This particular fake nest even has
a hatch so the Disney scientists could peek in.

Yes, Disney scientists. In 2005, fearing that wood rat numbers would
pass the point of no return, the US Fish and Wildlife Service teamed up
with biologists and other "cast members" from Disney's Animal Kingdom in Orlando to raise and then release captive wood rats into the
wild. (At first this struck me as an unusual alliance, but if you think
about it, the Disney franchise is staunchly pro-rodent, and its best-

known pet pussies, from Cinderella's Lucifer to Alice's Cheshire Cat, are all at least mildly villainous.)

For years at Rafiki's Planet Watch, a *Lion King*–themed conservation facility inside the park, the Disney scientists lavished care upon captive wood rats, which were warmed with portable heaters and cooled with fans to mimic a balmy Key Largo–like climate. The wood rats were given romaine lettuce to eat and pinecones to play with. They pooped in wax-paper-lined trays. The subject of diligent medical exams, the wood rats, which don't live long in the wild even under cat-free conditions, reached the Methuselah-like age of four.

Before long, Disney visitors could watch wood rat highlight reels and listen to the raspy vocalizations of a wood rat in heat. When the film *Ratatouille* came out, children were invited to don chef's toques and prepare a meal for the wood rats. Jane Goodall even paid a visit and featured the wood rat on her Hope for Animals and Their World website.

Finally it was time to take the Key Largo wood rats back to Key Largo. They were fitted with tiny radio telemetry collars, fortified with native foods, and allowed to acclimate in a caged artificial nest for a week.

"It went real well—until we let them out," Dixon says. DeGayner trapped cats around the clock, but he "couldn't get them out of there fast enough," he says. "I could see it coming. We'd let the wood rats out, and the next night it would be over." When researchers tracked down the bodies, they often found them half-eaten and buried under leaves, exactly the way a tiger caches its kill.

"How do you train a Key Largo wood rat to be afraid of a cat?" Disney biologist Anne Savage asks me. The wood rat's natural predators are birds and snakes: murderous felines are "not something they are supposed to be encountering. If the Key Largo wood rats can't even set foot out of their nests it wouldn't matter how you train them."

Disney's breeding program was scrapped in 2012. The refuge is redoubling its efforts to build hundreds of artificial fortress nests and to capture invading cats. Some of the invaders are thought to be local pets; others may inhabit feral cat colonies near the refuge. But, of course, to scientists, this is just a technical distinction. Conservation-minded biologists do not necessarily categorize house cats as "pets" or "strays" or "ferals," because all house cats with access to the outdoors are, in their eyes, identically dangerous.

It has stopped raining in Key Largo, though the hardwoods still drip, and Dixon hasn't donned his wraparounds just yet. "I'll tell you what we want," he says with narrowed eyes. "We want the wood rats to build their own damn nests. And we want these cats off our refuge. We are trying to save an endangered species here."

cᴖ─

To understand how cats got their claws into so many ecosystems, it's help-ful to know how they reached them in the first place.

Water, in the forms of rivers and seas, is the major barrier to mamma-lian dispersal. Birds can waft across oceans, but mammals must swim or surf on vegetation rafts, preferably in pairs, or arrive via even more pecu-liar circumstances. Domestic dogs had to enter the New World the hard way, trekking with their masters across the frozen land bridge. Mammals never reached some faraway isles: New Zealand does not have any native mammals save three species of bats, which borrowed a page from the avian playbook. Much rarer than herbivores even on the mainland, on islands carnivorous predators are often completely absent.

But house cats have become a major exception to this waterproof rule: though cats are said to hate water, it has always been their way around. This is largely because they have sold themselves as the perfect shipboard companions. For starters, there's their reputed rat-catching ability—and perhaps a closed system like a ship is the rare circumstance where resident felines could be relied on to make a difference. Certainly there are records of ships' cats killing rats, which hungry sailors sometimes confiscated for their own dinners. After the sudden loss of several cats, one eighteenth-century voyager lamented that cats can "be but ill Spared from Ships so overrun with rats as ours." (Of course, if the ship was persistently infested, perhaps the missing cats weren't indispensable after all.) Some cats also enjoyed choice galley rations in addition to their rat kills; there's even a nineteenth-century account of one plucking a morsel of mutton from the gunroom steward's mouth.

Hunting prowess aside, these creatures from the often-arid Middle East were peculiarly suited for life on the high seas—not as strange a coincidence as it may sound, since the open ocean has often been compared to the desert. Cats don't need much drinking water and can get by for long stretches without any at all; nor do they require vitamin C, so scurvy is not a concern.

Yet the ancient mariners' motivations may not always have always been so practical. Perhaps the sailors of old, from merchants to pirates and deckhands to captains, wanted cats aboard for the same reasons that you and I might: because their cute antics offered a pleasant respite from the doldrums. Sailors invented cat toys out of musket balls and twine and some even rigged up miniature hammocks. Over the centuries, cats became such a quintessential part of ship culture that many superstitious old salts wouldn't come aboard unless cats were also conscripted. Catless ships were sometimes considered derelict under maritime law, and even today nautical lingo is rife with cats: cat-o'-nine-tails, cat's paw knot, catwalk.

By 9,500 years ago, we know—from the ancient kitten grave—that cats had sailed to Cyprus, perhaps their first port of call. Millennia later, they made it to Egypt, though the Egyptians probably stalled their dispersal pattern somewhat (in addition to being landlubbers, they had strict laws regarding the export of house cats). It was more likely the seafaring Phoenicians who salted much of the Mediterranean basin with felines, introducing them to Italy and Spain. The ancient Greeks also furnished their far-flung colonies with cats, depositing them around the Balkans and the Black Sea. In the Greek seaport of Massilia (modern Marseille), the coins of the realm sometimes featured prowling lions, but it was house cats that used the city as a staging area for continental conquest. Cats mainlined up the Rhône River, and later hitchhiked the Seine, likely jumping ship at their leisure.

The Greeks' successors, the Romans, were die-hard dog people. Still, cats managed to ride the coattails of the imperial legions as they trampled Europe, and cat skeletons dot the Danube frontier. House cats beat the conquering Romans on the long march to Britain: they were already holed up in Iron Age hill forts held by barbarian chieftains, perhaps delivered there centuries earlier by tin-trading Phoenician ships. Cats were probably distributed through central Europe by the time of Christ.

And just as cats did not need Caesar's caresses to succeed, neither did they require the blessing of the pope. Medieval Catholic suspicion was a mere hiccup—or, perhaps more accurately, a hairball—where cats were concerned. Whatever the extent of the cat Inquisition, many monks and nuns held on to their pets, papal bulls be damned; Exeter Cathedral listed cat food among its expenses from the years 1305 to 1467 and had its own cat door.

And of course, cats had plenty of friends among the so-called infidels. Because the Prophet Muhammad was a feline admirer, Muslim armies sweeping into North Africa and Spain despised "unclean" dogs and adored cats. Just decades after Pope Gregory's Vox in Rama hit the stands, a wealthy Cairo sultan established what may have been the world's first cat sanctuary. Cats were also beloved by the Vikings. Feline genetics suggest that, around AD 1000, the flame-haired raiders took a shine to the orange cats they found near the Black Sea and spirited them off to outposts in Iceland, Scotland, and the Faroe Islands, home to unusual numbers of Cheetoh's fellow gingers today.

But of all the empires ancient and modern, Christian and otherwise, it's Britain, perhaps the greatest sea power the world has ever known, that gave cats their biggest boost. The explorer Ernest Shackleton even dragged a cat to Antarctica in 1914. (Perhaps sensing the epic suffering to come, Mrs. Chippy was prudently swept overboard.) Her Majesty's Navy outlawed ships' cats only in 1975.

British ships ferried house cats to the Americas. Starving Jamestown settlers ate theirs, but that didn't prevent cats from gaining a claw hold, and then spreading westward, where they were installed in frontier garrisons and Wild West outposts. Miners chauffeured them to California and Alaska, where they were sold for gold dust. The hope, as usual, was that cats would quell the boomtowns' riotous invasive rodents. Yet there are subtle hints that cats were not quite equal to the task. The cats at one Kansas fort "were perfect wrecks," an army sergeant complains in the 1850s. "They could not digest mice enough to counteract the ravages of fleas, and moped about utterly discouraged." Some cats apparently forsook the flea-ridden human settlements to take their chances on the prairies, where tasty native critters abounded.

Perhaps most critically, though, from a conservation perspective, the British colonists stashed cats on all sorts of Pacific islands and opened Australia to feline conquest. As early as 1770, James Cook's HMS *Endeavour* docked in North Queensland, and "it would be illogical to assume that the cats were supervised in any way," one observer notes. In Sydney today stands a bronze statue of Trim, the cat aboard the first ship to sail around Australia. Trim's British master, the intrepid Matthew Flinders, kept a logbook that was a tad cat mad, cheekily detailing Trim's onshore escapades: "Many and curious are the observations he made in various branches of science, particularly natural history of small mammals, birds and flying fish, for which he had much taste."

Confident in the cats' rodent-routing skills, the British thoughtfully marooned cats on far-flung islands with colonial potential, including twenty on Tahiti. A few colonial introductions were less deliberate: cats paddled ashore after shipwrecks.

Perhaps the most arresting ships' logs describe the cats' reception on inhabited islands. Here, native people who had never seen a cat of any sort, nor guessed such creatures existed, encounter them for the first time.

Nowhere is their species' power over ours more apparent.

"Our cats . . . struck them with particular astonishment," the colonial official John Uniacke wrote, after several Aborigines came aboard the HMS *Mermaid*, docked off Queensland in 1823. "They were . . . continually caressing the cats, and holding them up for the admiration of their companions on shore."

Among the Samoans, "a passion arose for cats," noted Titian Peale, an American explorer, "and they were obtained by all possible means from the whale ships visiting the islands." On Ha'apai, natives stole two of Captain Cook's "Catts." On Eromanga, natives exchanged cords of fragrant Polynesian sandalwood for the explorers' felines.

Cats instilled fear in a few prescient natives, but the prevailing emotion seems to have been wonder. When Christian missionaries arrived, their charming pets no doubt enticed many converts. By the 1840s, some Australian natives were observed toting cats and kittens in bags, à la Taylor Swift, and by the end of the next century the Aborigines viewed the magnificent invader as an indigenous animal.

Of course, cats didn't really need a welcome wagon. Wherever they disembarked, they landed on their feet.

This self-reliance further distinguishes them from dogs. Roving dogs remain a problem in many cities in the developing world and sometimes behave as invasive predators—in 2006, twelve wild dogs were thought to be wiping out a population of rare Fijian ground frog, for instance. But it turns out that dogs, biologically reborn in human company and so intimately suited to our use, have a terrible time without us. It's as though they've left the wild too far behind them, while cats keep a paw in both worlds, making them far more flexible and formidable invaders.

Feral dogs, for one thing, are incompetent mothers. Puppies born on the street tend to die. Packs of street dogs are sustained through recruitment of new strays rather than through births.

House cats, on the other hand, are doting mothers and unsurpassed breeders both in and outside of the human sphere. Females reach sexual maturity at six months of age and thereafter reproduce more like rabbits than tigers—a key ecological advantage that's in part a function of their small size and their hyped-up reproductive cycles. Indeed, they can outbreed some species of wild rodent. (KLWR, we're looking at you.) By one calculation, a pair of cats could produce 354,294 descendants in five years, if all survived. In real life, five cats introduced to forbidding Marion Island (permanently snowcapped and actively volcanic, it's hardly a feline paradise) bore more than 2,000 surviving descendants within 25 years.

And even these kittens know how to kill. Feral dogs don't seem to pick up pack-hunting and other ancient lupine habits and depend almost entirely on garbage, which cats, while certainly enjoying a nice, easy meal of trash, can also do without, going off the grid and subsisting on their own kills. (Cats are said to prefer warm, moist, still-twitching entrées anyway.) Diligent feline mothers teach their kittens to hunt starting at just a few weeks of age by bringing live prey, if it's available. Even if no mother is around, kittens figure out how to stalk and pounce. "The behavior of kittens at play," Elizabeth Marshall Thomas writes in *The Tribe of Tiger*, "is hunting behavior and nothing else."

As predators, house cats have almost supernatural powers: they can see in the ultraviolet, they can hear in the ultrasound, and they have an uncanny understanding of three-dimensional space that allows them, among other things, to judge the height of sounds. They combine these distinctly feline gifts with a gastronomical flexibility that few of their relatives share. Rather than specializing, like some wild cats, in a particular chinchilla or hare, house cats hunt more than 1,000 species—and that's not including all the exotic odds and ends in the garbage.

Their lifestyles are similarly elastic. They can live alone, as in nature, or in groups. They can rule a thousand acres of territory or a studio apartment, roam over boulders or pick a path across traffic. They are largely nocturnal, but tailor daytime hunting excursions to prey types, temperatures, and seasons. They can even rejigger their anatomy. Behavioral ecologist Michael Hutchins, former head of the Wildlife Society, told me about his travels on the Galápagos Islands, which—for all their rare and celebrated wildlife—have a shortage of fresh water and so are inhospitable to many land animals. But not to house cats: the archipelago's thriving imported population survives by drinking "blood and dew," Hutchins says, and develops noticeably enlarged kidneys as a result. Today these very fit survivors are preying upon a type of endangered petrel and even one of Darwin's species of iconic finches.

By far the supplest aspect of the domestic cat is its relationship with us. House cats enjoy a range of options unavailable to other mammals, especially carnivores, because of their species' special standing with ours. It's not often that we knowingly promote the invasive plants and animals that we transport around the world in ballast water or on the bottoms of our shoes. With cats, though, we load the dice in obvious ways: not only by introducing them to landscapes where they have no business being, but by feeding them generously, and taking some of them to the vet for shots, and allowing them to live in our houses and under our porches for decades when, left to their own devices, they might die young.

These advantages enable cats, as hunters, to defy basic laws of nature. An ecosystem generally supports as many predators as the prey base can bear—any more, and predators starve. But, especially in urban areas, house cat populations reflect human populations, not prey populations, both because of household pet-keeping and the large numbers of strays that frequent our dumps. In Bristol, England, there are some 348 house cats per square kilometer. In cities like Rome and Jerusalem, and in parts of Japan, densities of 2,000 cats per square kilometer have been recorded. All these extra apex predators put stress on the local prey species. In some places cats actually outnumber adult birds. This is a little like lions outnumbering wildebeests.

Rather bafflingly, these ridiculous densities of cats also exist in places where humans and our can openers are scarce. That's because in many remote regions where we've introduced cats, we've deliberately loosed other prey animals, particularly domestic rabbits, or accidentally ditched ship mice and rats. These cunning human affiliates—which are, in their way, just as impressive and capable as house cats—invade the new ecosystem and breed at staggering levels. Their populations can sustain huge numbers of cats, which—eating bunnies and mice to their hearts' content, without ever diminishing the overall population—need not depend on delicate, rare native animals for survival. Instead, they hunt these opportunistically, picking off endangered specimens one by one when they encounter them, for a snack or amusement, to the point of extinction.

This phenomenon is called hyperpredation.

~

By now, cats inhabit thousands of once-feline-free islands, and further introductions keep happening, thanks to pleasure cruises and tribal relocations and even (to ecologists' lasting shame) scientific expeditions. Long-isolated islands are biodiversity havens. The lack of native predators makes it easy for cats to parachute in at the top of the food chain, and there's nowhere for the prey to go. Not that they would necessarily flee. Naive island animals often lack antipredatory strategies, even fear itself, a condition called "island tameness." They are more or less sitting ducks—or, often literally, flightless birds.

On South Africa's Dassen Island, where cats were introduced in the late 1800s, they've hunted African black oystercatchers, crowned lapwings, and helmeted guinea fowl.

A dove species disappeared off Mexico's Socorro Island soon after a military garrison imported cats in the 1950s.

On Réunion Island, in the western Indian Ocean, cats down the endangered Barau's petrel. In the Grenadines, they binge on the critically endangered Grenadines clawed gecko. On Samoa, where cats roused passionate local affection at first, they attack the tooth-billed pigeon. In the Canary Islands, they pursue three types of threatened giant lizard and one threatened bird, the Canary Islands stonechat. On Guam, they've targeted the Guam rail, a "secretive, flightless" and extremely endangered bird. "Due to predatory cats," the US Fish and Wildlife Service writes, "it is believed that no Guam rails exist on Guam at this time."

Fiji, the Cayman Islands, the British Virgin Islands, French Polynesia, Japan. The list goes on, though each ecosystem has a unique story. The sub-Antarctic island of Kerguelen is so windy that insects can't survive there—Captain Cook nicknamed it Desolation Island—but it grows the Kerguelen cabbage, long a sailor's staple, because it's rich in vitamin C and useful in staving off scurvy. (The plant also has a "peculiar flavor," the assistant ship's surgeon Joseph Hooker wrote in 1840, delicately noting that it produced no heartburn "or any of the unpleasant symptoms" usually associated with cabbage—a very happy discovery in the close quarters of the ship.) But soon the cabbage-sated sailors got a hankering for some rabbit, so they introduced bunnies to the island. The population exploded, and in 1951, scientists at a French research station tried loosing a few cats as a countermeasure. By the 1970s, the few had become a few thousand, and they were eating an estimated 1.2 million native birds per year, surfeiting themselves on the white-headed petrel and Antarctic prion.

Hawaii is another cat disaster in progress. In 1866, cat lover Mark Twain observed the archipelago's "platoons of cats, companies of cats, regiments of cats, armies of cats, multitudes of cats," but 150 years later he could for once be accused of understatement. Cats even live 10,000 feet up on the lava flows of Mauna Loa. Unfortunately, our forty-ninth state is also home—sometimes, the only home—to several less enterprising bird species. Wedge-tailed shearwaters, for instance, don't lay eggs until they are seven years old, and then it's only one per year. Endangered Hawaiian petrels can't fly from their ground burrows for fifteen weeks. On the island of Kauai, the Newell's shearwater has a mothlike relationship with city lights and, enthralled yet confused, then suddenly exhausted, it plummets from the sky. Good Samaritans are encouraged to collect birds and deliver them to aid stations, but cats have learned to wait beneath the lights.

In New Zealand, cats eat bats, the island nation's only native mammals. A lone cat called Tibbles was said to have erased the Stephens Island wren in the late 1800s—scientists now blame several cats, but to the exterminated bird these details are of little consequence. Cats have also been implicated in the declines of sooty shearwaters and kiwis. In the 1970s, they cornered the last population of kakapo, and today there are just over 100 of the huge flightless parrots left. Some of these birds might otherwise have enjoyed a life expectancy of ninety-five years.

In addition to quieting the "dawn chorus" of island birds, the cats have zeroed in on the silent tuatara, a rare New Zealand reptile whose roots on the main island date back to the dawn of the dinosaurs. But now, thanks to house cats, its tenure there is over.

Then there is the case of Australia, an island that also happens to be a whole continent. Australia contends with many rough-and-tumble animal invaders: cane toads, starlings, smooth newts, red fox, camels, blackberry bushes, water buffalo. But house cats are, in the minds of many, the most egregious offenders, a prime component in what the head of the Australian Wildlife Conservancy has dubbed "the ecological axis of evil."

There are about 3 million pet cats and some 18 million free-roaming cats Down Under, making the continent's human and feline populations roughly equal. Australian ecologist Ian Abbott has pieced together how the feline invasion might have played out between 1788, when cats made landfall after several coastal introductions, and 1890, by which time the whole continent was taken. In a rather heroic work of scholarship, he pored over colonial journals for mentions of cats, searching for key words that previous historians had seldom indexed. In the early 1800s, most cat mentions are rather incidental—cats are listed in a catalogue of livestock, a cat drags a fat-tailed dunnart into a house, a cat is "eaten for a wager," and so on. But by the 1880s, accounts from the outback grow somewhat more alarming: unknown cats start stepping out of the shadows in the darnedest places to join bushwhackers by their campfires. In 1888, one observer claims that cats had "spread throughout the whole country and many were seen as far as Mount Aloysius." In 1908, another explorer notes that "numerous cat tracks were seen in every direction."

The cats seem to have tailed miners and pastoralists into the interior, and after the humans and their livestock reached the limits of their endurance, the cats soldiered on. However, a few decades passed before the house cats penetrated the deepest wilderness, and given their tremendous invasive capacity Abbott wondered what took them so long. He now thinks that it was because Australia, unlike most islands, did have a few formidable native predators—the tiger quoll, the wedge-tailed eagle—capable of preying on cats. It wasn't until we shot or starved or otherwise eliminated these carnivorous competitors that cats multiplied off the charts.

Also, blame their British blood, but the Australians kept loosing more cats on purpose. They dispatched cats to protect fruit trees from birds, and to prevent seabirds from roosting on pearling luggers, but most often to duel with invasive rabbits, which as usual had hopped far beyond the dinner pot to wreak havoc on the local vegetation, not to mention the settlers' crops. In the Rabbit Suppression Act of 1884, the Australian government formally allied itself with cats, which it suddenly became a crime to kill. The government launched 400 cats on the Tongo station near the Paroo River and "liberated" 200 cats from Adelaide to the wilderness around Mount Ragged. It transported cats to western New South Wales and purchased cats in Perth for release at Eucla.

In some places, tiny houses were erected for these feline civil servants, a legacy evident in the names of places like Victoria's Cat House Mountain. But, ever adaptable, the cats secured their own accommodations. Just like in Wonderland, cats could now be found at the bottom of rabbit holes, as cats learned to occupy the burrows of the very bunnies they were supposed to be eliminating. "Rabbits have aided [the cats'] spread by providing food and . . . shelters," states the betrayed, and possibly overburdened, Department of Sustainability, Environment, Water, Population and Communities in a memo. Ultimately, not only did cats fail to rout the rabbits, but they stuffed themselves on native animals as well. As early as the 1920s, naturalists battling the rabbit "plague" also began to speak of a cat "scourge." Turncoat cats are even said to conspire with another environmental threat—wildfires—lurking in fire scars to mop up the exhausted survivors.

The carnage is still being accounted for today. Many of the cats' prey animals are small, retiring, nocturnal, and obscure: creatures like numbats and pygmy rock-wallabies and swamp antechinuses and long-nosed potoroos. The greater stick-nest rat, a rodent that sounds not unlike the Key Largo wood rat, once had a million-kilometer natural range, but was later confined, in part because of house cats, to a single five-kilometer island. Still, that's far better than the fate of its compatriot, the lesser stick-nest rat, which has entirely vanished from the earth.

The Australians have tried hoarding endangered species on offshore islands to protect them from cats, and they've erected high-tech anti-cat fences that supposedly anticipate the cats' sobering ability "to tolerate electric shock, dig, climb vertical surfaces, and jump at least 1.8 meters." In places like the Wongalara Wildlife Sanctuary, home to a few remaining pale field rat refugees, conservationists patrol the perimeters of these anti-cat corrals with spotlights and dogs.

But you know what they say about the best-laid plans of long-tailed hopping mice (which are now extinct) and men.

One at-risk Australian mammal is the greater bilby, a shy gray marsupial that resembles the love child of a mouse and rabbit: a little awkward and quite long of nose, it's also very cute. Its close relative, the lesser bilby, is the mascot of the Australian Wildlife Conservancy, much like the World Wildlife Fund's panda. Sadly, the lesser bilby went extinct in the 1960s, in part due to house cat predation. The greater bilby hangs on, but its range— which once covered 70 percent of the continent—has imploded.

Unusually for cat food, the bilby has its own appreciation society, and there has been a recent national movement to celebrate Easter with foil-wrapped chocolate bilbies instead of candy replicas of those hateful invaders, the bunnies. In Queensland a few years ago, the Save the Bilby Fund shielded a few acres of bilby habitat with a $500,000 predator-proof fence and herded dozens of precious survivors inside. To everyone's delight, the rare marsupials began to breed and by 2012 had produced more than 100 newborns—a regular embarrassment of bilbies, at least compared to wild populations.

But, unbeknownst to the bilby boosters, heavy rains and flooding rusted a hole in the fancy fence. When scientists entered the breached sanctuary afterward, they found 20 cats and no baby bilbies.

Ecologists in Australia and beyond note that focusing on house cat predation alone actually downplays the cascading ways in which these invaders can transform an ecosystem. Several studies suggest that the mere presence of cats can scare birds out of breeding and make them too jittery to feed their young properly. Bristle-thighed curlews in the Phoenix Islands have learned to avoid cat territory entirely so they may molt in safety. Just a whiff of cat pee makes tammar wallabies breathe more heavily.

Rival predators, too, find themselves oppressed. In one Maryland study, cats took out so many chipmunks that local hawks switched to hunting songbirds, which were much harder to catch, resulting in lower hawk nestling survival. Cats likely spread feline leukemia to the last remaining Florida panthers, and they're also carriers of rabies. And to a staggering array of animals, from beluga whales to barnyard pigs to Hawaiian crows (which no longer exist in the wild) to human beings, cats introduce a vicious and sometimes fatal disease called toxoplasmosis.

Adding an alien feline superpredator can even jeopardize plants. In the Balearic Islands, cat predation hastened the disappearance of one seed-eating endemic lizard that was the only distribution mechanism for an equally rarefied kind of indigenous plant. In Hawaii, the droppings from imperiled seabird colonies are a key fertilizer.

House cat predation is less well studied on mainlands, in part because the sheer numbers of cats and potential prey animals make for a rather unwieldy study subject. The 2013 American predation meta-analysis, conducted by Smithsonian and other government scientists, led to a petition signed by scores of conservation groups to remove all unowned cats from federal lands. The scientists extrapolate their (instantly controversial) findings from small study zones to the huge mainland area, so the results include "wide ranges and uncertainties," according to the *New York Times*. The biologist Stanley Gehrt of Ohio State University told me, hopefully, that another important mainland predator—the coyote, a large carnivore that is actually expanding its historic range—may be helping to suppress the cats more than the Smithsonian numbers suggest. But many conservation biologists accept the data.

At the same time, the lessons of island ecology may increasingly apply to the American mainland, which some scientists say is in the process of becoming "islandized." With warmer temperatures, brighter lights, more noise, and plentiful food and water, our cities and towns are unique, if highly irregular, ecosystems that are radically different from surrounding areas.

Likewise, thanks to habitat fragmentation, the remaining wilderness areas are becoming islands as well: they're cut off by roads and subdivisions instead of rivers and oceans, but to resident animals the effect is similar.

In many cases, the wild animals adapting to twenty-first-century mainland life might as well be castaways in the Pacific.

Unable to safeguard the last stragglers of various endangered species, the worldwide ecological community is, in some areas, attempting full-on felinicide. People bomb cats' lairs with targeted viruses and deadly poisons. They rain hell on cats with shotguns and hounds. Australia is leading the fight. Even though it's illegal to declaw a pet cat in Australia, the government has bankrolled pioneering research in cat poisons, including the development of a toxic kangaroo sausage called Eradicat. The Australians have also tested the Cat Assassin, a metal tunnel into which cats are lured under false pretenses and misted with poison. Scientists have considered dispatching Tasmanian devils to the mainland to dismember cats.

The trouble is that once cats are entrenched in an ecosystem, they are almost impossible to dislodge. Bait poison rarely works, as cats prefer to eat live animals. And because of their breathtaking reproductive capacity, just a couple of overlooked cats can rebound from bio warfare and restock the population.

Cat banishment is possible on much smaller islands, though it can cost up to $100,000 per square mile. Here's an idea of the process: to get rid of several thousand resident cats on uninhabited Marion Island, in 1977, South African scientists introduced a deadly feline virus called panleukopenia. That dropped the population to roughly 615, nowhere near low enough. So the anti-cat crusaders tried traps of various kinds, hunting with and without dogs, poisoning, and shooting by day and night. Between 1986 and 1990, eight teams of hunters embarked on four eight-month deployments, crisscrossing the tundra. It took a combined 14,728 hours to shoot 872 cats and trap 80 more. The last one was killed in July of 1991, but just to be sure, sixteen hunters continued to rove the island for two more years. This might be considered overkill for some invasive species, but not cats.

Likewise, the hard-won victory over the house cats of tiny San Nicolas Island, off the coast of California, was a "monumental achievement " for the United States Navy, according to the commanding officer overseeing the missile-testing base there. It took years of planning, 18 months of trapping, and $3 million to expel the cats, which were hunting an endemic deer mouse and a federally protected species of night lizard. The cat stalkers had to be careful not to disturb Native American archaeological sites and to use special radio channels so they didn't accidentally trigger naval munitions. Meanwhile, the battle-tested cats employed guerrilla tactics, eluding dogs and custom-built computerized traps and spurning "felid-attracting phonics," aka digitally recorded meows. Finally, a professional bobcat hunter finished the job.

Nearly 100 islands have been cleared so far, giving a new lease on life to the Turks and Caicos rock iguana on Long Cay in the West Indies and to the false canyon mouse on Coronado Island in the Gulf of California. Cat eradication is now under way in the Galápagos. Many more critically endangered creatures await salvation, including the Margarita Island kangaroo rat, the Amsterdam albatross, and the San Lorenzo mouse. At the same time, about 20 percent of these large-scale eviction efforts have failed outright. On New Zealand's Little Barrier Island, the cats shrugged off the panleukopenia released in 1968 and by 1974, their numbers, which had dropped by 80 percent, were back to normal. And sometimes, cat-ridden ecosystems are so thoroughly broken that removing the cats does more harm than good: following a successful feline purge on Macquarie Island in 2000, the subsequently soaring bunny population gobbled 40 percent of the island's vegetation, causing landslides that swamped penguin colonies. (The devastation is visible from space.)

But even more than the cats' own remarkable resilience, the biggest obstacle to cat eradication is the people who love them.

Sometimes our objections to these efforts are quite rational and self-interested: on inhabited islands and the mainland alike, locals don't want their venison tainted with aerially broadcast cat poisons, and they're not wild about cat-hunting marksmen roaming with guns.

But mostly it's a more delicate matter of what scientists call "social acceptability." The first time I heard cats—so very familiar to me, and a fixture in my own personal landscape since birth—characterized as an invasive species, I was quite offended. Apparently, I'm not alone. While visiting Crocodile Lake, I picked up a government-issued brochure that described dangerous Floridian alien species like "exotic purple swamphens" and "nonnative Gambian pouched rats" but never even mentioned the wood-rat-routing house cats, perhaps because the subject is too controversial.

People simply don't want cats killed, and imagining whole islands full of massacred Cheetohs is enough to make the average cat owner queasy— or furious. Indeed, the trend in opinion and activism runs in the opposite direction: toward treating the swarming cats themselves as imperiled creatures, in need of protection from ecologists. Thus the renegade cats rounded up from the California naval base were neither gassed, shot, nor fed doctored kangaroo sausage but rather delivered to a mainland cat sanctuary.

Even such bloodless methods may meet with resistance. "It really feels like I've taken on the gun lobby," says Gareth Morgan, a philanthropist who launched a "Cats to Go" campaign to rid his native New Zealand of free-roaming house cats through sterilization and natural attrition. "Every animal has its place in this world, but this one is so protected that it's proliferated to an extreme extent."

"Why do we show such affection and care for some animals but disregard the welfare of others?" the Australian ecologist John Woinarski writes to me. Most Australians have "no affinity" for the majority of indigenous Australian animals, "and hence regard their loss as relatively inconsequential."

"We are not into treating all organisms equally," the conservation biologist Christopher Lepczyk tells me from Hawaii. "We pick and choose what we like."

And what we like are cats.

Chapter 5

THE CAT LOBBY

WHEN I met Annie, she was cowering in a French fry container, alone in the very back of an animal shelter cage. My mother's pride of condominium cats had thinned in recent years, and I had vowed to help replenish the population with a new kitten. This eight-week-old tabby had Cleopatra-like markings at the edges of her luminous green eyes and a pointed little chin.

"I'll take that one," I declared.

The shelter workers exchanged glances. "But she's feral," one finally said. The other brought out an armload of kittens from a tame litter to show how much cuddlier they were. The tabby kitten, meanwhile, dodged my hands and resolutely avoided eye contact. This cat probably wasn't a good candidate for adoption, the workers explained, since her optimal socialization period had almost passed. Annie's mother, caught in nearby woods in the same Havahart trap, had already been put to sleep.

Far from dissuading me, the mention of euthanasia was all the motivation I needed, and it was Annie that I carried home in a cardboard box with punched-out airholes. Nearly fifteen years later, she remains a treasured—

if exceedingly reclusive—family companion, and I'm glad I had the chance to choose her. At the time I considered it a good deed.

Yet some in the animal welfare community might shake their heads over this story. They believe that unsocialized house cats belong in the wild, that they have no business being imprisoned in an animal shelter in the first place, and that the question of euthanasia should not even come into play. In a perfect world, Annie and her mother would have been left together in the woods.

To understand this somewhat counterintuitive cat-loving perspective means entering a domain where a house cat's fabled "staff" includes not only feeders and veterinarians but lawyers and lobbyists, and where a feline's worth is not determined by whether it makes a nice pet.

Cats, these advocates argue, have a higher claim on our affections. As the saying goes: if you really love something, set it free.

The Hilton Crystal City has seen much of this before: the name tags and microphones; the workshops, moderated panels, and networking sessions; the banquets and exhibit halls, and all the other trappings of a high-end professional conference. Only the line for the women's bathroom is perhaps a little longer than usual. Come to think, there is hardly a man in sight. One of the few to be found is huddled in a corner of the jam-packed ballroom, desperately trying to launch a video for the opening plenary lecture under the scrutiny of many female eyes, not to mention the slanted green feline gazes, clear and hypnotic, staring up from programs and down from posters everywhere.

Suddenly a lone woman's voice rises to fill the awkward silence: "Soft kitty, warm kitty!"

By the time she reaches the final "purr, purr, purr!" of the cat song from *The Big Bang Theory*, hundreds of women have joined in.

And so begins the first-ever Alley Cat Allies National Conference. Entitled "Architects of Change for Cats," the event has drawn hundreds of house cat advocates from all over the country, plus Canada and Israel, for a long autumn weekend in Arlington, Virginia, just across the river from

Washington, DC. The choice of location is, perhaps, both a show of political might and a nod of approval: in recent years, our nation's capital has become well known for its hundreds of cat colonies and general policies of feline largesse.

Alley Cat Allies and its affiliates are known as the "cat lobby," or sometimes among themselves, the "cat mafia." Cat advocates come from all walks of life, from nuns to sorority sisters and retired admirals to prison guards. Some are casual volunteers; others find full-time careers in the work. Not all are affiliated with Alley Cat Allies, but the group boasts thousands of supporters and a nationwide influence. Celebrity allies have included Portia de Rossi, Angela Kinsey (the famed cat lady of NBC's *The Office*) and Tippi Hedren, the actress who came under avian assault in Alfred Hitchcock's *The Birds* (and went on to found a big-cat wildlife sanctuary).

Alley Cat Allies agitates for the rights of all house cats, but particularly for free-living strays. Images of these ownerless animals hang throughout the hotel, most shown with the tops of their left ears clipped, a flaw that somehow only underscores their "fearful symmetry."

There are many million—perhaps up to 100 million—free-roaming cats in America today, a near-perfect shadow of the owned population, and they live everywhere from parking lots to nature preserves. Wandering dogs have been mostly eliminated from the modern American landscape, and from much of the developed world, but how to deal with roving cats— ignored for much of our mutual history—is today a mounting controversy. Should these cats be treated as the wild animals that they act like, or the domesticated creatures that they are?

I hunt for cream for my coffee and find only soy milk—at this archcarnivore's convention, the human fare is strictly vegan. In the hallway, women wearing "Ask Me About My Colony" T-shirts make hushed phone calls to check on their many cats back home. Somewhere roams an official cat hunk—John Fulton, host of Animal Planet's *Must Love Cats*—who poses in the conference program alongside a kitten whose eyes are the exact same shade of hazel as his own. He seems to be making himself scarce, perhaps wisely, while the women talk of Tomahawk traps and tuna bait versus mackerel.

The conference covers many such practical matters, like kitten season survival tips and updates on the National Cat Help Desk and the Purrfect Pals prison program. But the how-to tidbits, chitchat, laughter, and occasional tears accompany hard-core political strategizing. People speak of "the revolution," "the work," and "the movement"; of "paradigm shift," "mission drift," "burnout," and "vision." Attendees bone up on the Bill of Rights and learn how to turn veterinarians into activists, win over city councils, and sway mayors.

The cat advocates' central goal is to reform the US animal shelter system and stop feline euthanasia. Cats are by now proving such resourceful survivors that we routinely execute them. Our country kills millions of healthy but homeless cats every year—nearly half of all house cats that enter shelters, and almost 100 percent of the unsocialized cats, which are especially hard to place with owners.

The better solution, according to the cat lobby? Just leave the cats outside—but stop them from reproducing in such staggering numbers. Though conference speakers counsel against the public use of acronyms, among themselves they call the strategy TNR: Trap, Neuter and Release, or—as many prefer—Return. Roaming cats, which the advocates sometimes call "community cats" or "wild cats," are captured in traps, sexually defused (and ear-tipped to prove it), and then set free to live out their lives where they "belong"—"as part of the natural landscape."

The neuter-and-release method is sweeping the country and has been embraced in recent years by many major municipalities: joining Washington are New York City, Chicago, Philadelphia, Dallas, Pittsburgh, Baltimore, San Francisco, Milwaukee, Salt Lake City, and more. There are now some 250 pro-TNR ordinances nationwide, a number that, according to Alley Cat Allies, rose tenfold from 2003 to 2013, and some 600 registered nonprofits have emerged to do the work officially, though there are far more groups trapping, neutering, and returning under the radar. Abroad, entire countries—like Italy—have adopted the strategy.

The cofounder of Alley Cat Allies is Becky Robinson, a slight middle-aged woman with a pixie cut and a pacing gait that prompts inevitable cross-species comparisons. At the conference Robinson is an even bigger draw than the cat hunk: I glimpse her only from distance, always mobbed, but several times over the course of the weekend I get the chance to hear her speak—about Sugar Bear and Gremlin, the feral kittens that she discovered in her very first alley more than 25 years ago, but also about truth and justice.

"What matters most," she says in the opening plenary session, "is that we're humans. We have strong emotions. We have a moral compass." Where cats are concerned, people "want to do what's right, but they don't know what's right.

"And that's what we have to show them."

The modern animal welfare movement began in Victorian England, at a time of migration from agrarian communities to cities. Increasingly removed from both the perils of the wilderness and the realities of the farm, with its barnyard menageries and daily calculus of life and death, people began to think of animals in a new light.

Even as the British slaughtered tigers overseas and seeded the Pacific with feisty feline aliens, back at home they cultivated a sentimental domestic ethos—"the Eden of home," as the historian Katherine Grier calls it. In addition to extremely well-behaved wives, this idealized ecosphere included household animals, which had to be treated with kindness, lest the gentility of the gentleman of the house be called into question. These ideas soon crossed the Atlantic to America, where mothering manuals began to stress the importance of teaching children to be nice to animals: one dire maternal primer warned that little Benedict Arnold had loved to "torture quiet, domestic animals."

In America, Grier explains, the first animal rights organizations formed shortly after the Civil War. Yet these pioneers were not primarily concerned with cats, or even dogs; the American Society for the Prevention of Cruelty to Animals, for instance, was founded in 1866 to protect carriage horses.

Where exactly felines figured in this brave new world of animal welfare is difficult to say, in part because cats—though they'd been humanity's associates for millennia—were still not considered proper companions in the way that other animals increasingly were. Grier describes one eighteenth-century Philadelphia family that fled with a pet cat during a yellow fever outbreak, but most house cats would have been left to fend for themselves. Cats had our blessing, but they were also a part of the background, and we did not micromanage them—a cat was more a presence than a pet. Cats were often excluded from early American pet-owning guides, but perhaps this is because they didn't need much care, living most or all of their lives outdoors. They were underrepresented, too, in nineteenth-century pet-purchasing catalogues, one of which boasted thirty-four dog breeds, seven types of squirrels, four monkey varieties but only two kinds of cats. This may be because cats were already so numerous that the idea of paying money for more seemed insane.

People tended to use generic names for cats, like "tomcat" and "pussy," while dogs had distinct and rather florid names, such as "Pompey." Pet owners also took many more pictures of their dogs. Besides, the most popular American pet through the early 1900s seems to have been neither dogs nor cats but caged birds, which amused lonely housewives with their singing.

Since pampered pet felines were an exception and most cats were more or less unattached, in the early twentieth century many municipalities simply ignored the stray cat population, which grew with the new megacities and, later, suburbs. Even as cities hired dog catchers and drafted nuisance laws to curtail feral dogs, there were no cat catchers, because footloose cats were so much less visible and dangerous than dogs, not to mention much harder to apprehend. Their reputation as pro bono exterminators probably didn't hurt either.

People called the stray cats "tramps." As their numbers swelled, pandemic-prone metropolises did occasionally panic. The cats were falsely accused of carrying diseases like polio, and during one 1911 scare, the New York SPCA gassed 300,000 in New York City.

At the time, though, many cat lovers supported such killings. The anti-slavery activist and early-animal-rights booster Harriet Beecher Stowe was also a prolific kitten drowner; dispatching unwanted cats was, she once said, an example of "real brave humanity." Throughout the modern animal rights era, people have massacred alley cats for the animals' own supposed benefit, perhaps convinced that a life outside the newly glorified domestic sphere was no life at all. In the 1930s, bands of well-meaning women roamed New York City's streets, rounding up cats for the gas chambers out of the goodness of their hearts. It was simply the animal welfare fad of the day.

A few early cat lovers looked beyond asphyxiation for ways of helping strays. In 1948, Robert Kendell, president of the American Feline Society, unveiled a scheme to deliver planeloads of excess American cats to fight postwar Europe's rat problem. (Kendell believed that the war had leveled the Continental cat population, though this seems presumptuous—some of London's first cat colonies are said to date from the days of the blitz, because cats don't evacuate.) When the State Department declined to fund this Cats for Europe initiative, foreign powers did not protest.

The problem of cat overpopulation compounded in the second half of the twentieth century, when cats' popularity as house pets really took off. Technology may have hastened this change: in 1947, the invention of kitty litter allowed cats to more elegantly undertake an indoor existence and become constant companions instead of occasional visitors. (As far as Alley Cat Allies is concerned, the advent of kitty litter forever partitions time, like the invention of bronze, or the wheel.) Around this period, too, effective rat poisons permanently relieved cats of their supposed mousing duties, and perhaps our firesides were as good a place to retire to as any.

But more sweeping social changes also drove the trend. Ongoing urbanization, with the new skyscrapers soaring a hundred stories above the nearest dog park, made cats an increasingly appealing pet. The entry of women into the workforce, which left no one at home to feed Lassie, has been another feline blessing, as is the rapidly aging population of the Western world. (Even the frail can crack open a can of Friskies.) Since the 1970s, the number of pet cats has been skyrocketing.

These lucky creatures have today amassed considerable legal rights: house cats can inherit property in many states, and veterinarians and neighbors may sometimes be sued for harming our feline family members. At the same time, though, more pets in general means still more surplus cats and more unwanted kittens. Rigorous pet sterilization campaigns and shelter adoption programs have helped to take the edge off the population spike: something like 85 percent of owned cats are today spayed or neutered. Alas, only about 2 percent of free-roaming cats are. Euthanasia has long been America's solution to the problem of cat overpopulation: California alone kills about 250,000 cats annually, and in some jurisdictions the numbers are reportedly rising.

Another modern "humane" alternative involves warehousing unwanted cats in no-kill animal shelters. But it's understandable that cat lovers see this as a poor option for their cherished consorts. High-capacity shelters, which can be crowded and loud and smell powerfully of kibbles and disinfectant, are for the most part twentieth-century relics designed for dogs, cats' temperamental opposites in many respects.

Developed in postwar England, Trap-Neuter-Return is the most plausible-seeming third way to come along. Marrying humanity's sense of global stewardship to our desire not to kill cute cats, its logic sounds sensible enough: neuter cats to nip the problem in the bud, and then live and let live. The method is often spun as a "return" for us as well—to an older, better, more natural way of doing business with cats, in which they move in and out of human civilization, hanging around our margins without any obligation to be pets.

"Allowing a cat or any living being to exist in an environment to which it is adapted," says the veterinarian Kate Hurley in an online webinar on the policy, "is not abandonment, any more than we are abandoning the jackrabbits."

In 1993, San Francisco was the first big city to endorse public cat-colony management, but the real sea change has happened just in the last few years. The laws vary—some local governments merely tolerate the managed cat colonies, while others help fund the work. But today even in cities that haven't formally adopted the legislation, the colonies are everywhere— behind supermarkets, beside railway tracks, in boatyards and in backyards. In Washington, DC, there are hundreds of managed colonies; in Oakland, California, one woman supervises twenty-four herself.

The official purpose of the colony management is mass sterilization, but in reality the colony keepers may enjoy a variety of relationships with the cats. Some may neuter the animals and release them the next day, never to see them again. But others name the cats and maintain daily contact.

The cat advocates say the outdoor cats should have the right to live and die as Mother Nature dictates. But just as stray house cats are not really wild animals, since the effects of domestication are always stamped in their bodies, brains, and DNA, Mother Nature is never truly given full rein in the TNR model. Along with food, colony managers may provide the cats with emergency veterinary care, insulated shelters, coyote escape posts, and other amenities seldom available to those jackrabbits that Kate Hurley mentions. In harsh climates, cat caregivers may supply pond aerators so that water sources don't freeze over and even indoor cat beds.

Not that cats in warmer climates get less attention: at my Miami Beach hotel recently, the stray cats sunning on the boardwalk—which was elaborately posted with NO ANIMALS ALLOWED signs—were served an al fresco breakfast on large, frilly tropical leaves, a presentation more festive than brunch at the resort restaurant.

And in the event of less pleasant weather, like hurricanes and tornadoes, Alley Cat Allies helps lead national feline relief efforts and even coaches the caregivers of coastal colonies on how to shield their cats from a storm surge. So much for nature's wrath.

As the new cat-colony laws gain traction, the animal welfare community is deeply divided on the strategy. People for the Ethical Treatment of Animals opposes managed colonies because of concerns about lack of access to steady veterinary care and other welfare issues. (Other cat-colony critics, however, argue that the feral cats' quality of life is actually quite good—indeed, too good.) The Humane Society of the United States is in favor of the colonies, with some ecologically sensitive restrictions. The American Veterinary Association remains agnostic.

"The profession is grappling with it," says veterinarian Bruce Kornreich, associate director of the Cornell Feline Health Center. "The TNR folks are very passionate. In terms of intentions, people who do TNR come from a very humane and loving place."

The fiercest opponents within the animal-loving world are, unsurprisingly, "the bird people." When it comes to outdoor cats, the two constituencies have been at each other's throats since at least the 1870s, when the so-called Army of Bird-Defenders asked American schoolchildren to sign their names to a "muster" demanding "perfect peace for birds," and suggested that wandering house cats be fed into a stupor or shot. And while certain plush, imperious creatures may have since booted birds from their perch as America's favorite pet, outdoor bird-watching is an increasingly popular pastime, with nearly 50 million hobbyists in the United States alone. Peering through their binoculars, the birders can't help but notice that today's neutered cats have one conspicuous disadvantage over yesterday's euthanized felines: they keep on hunting.

To battle the rising tide of cats, the American Bird Conservancy runs a Cats Indoors program, whose lone staffer is a young man named Grant Sizemore. "I have trouble explaining my job to people," says Sizemore when we meet in his cramped office in Washington, DC. In a show of diplomacy, Sizemore has been pictured on the Conservancy's website with his own indoor cat, Amelia Bedelia. ("She's technically my girlfriend's cat. She's a handful, I'll put it that way, but she adores me.") He tells me a bit about what Cats Indoors is up against. "There are a lot of folks who really, really, really love cats and when it is suggested that anybody is doing anything that might take their cat away from them—it's like guns, sort of."

Sizemore's duties involve making the rounds on Invasive Species Awareness Day, filming public service announcements, and distributing anti-outdoor-cat literature. He hands me two Cats Indoors brochures, which seem to be aimed at rather different audiences. In one, a comely cartoon woman in red high heels and her three cartoon cats look out a window at a bird feeder. "The world outside your front door can be a brutal place for your beloved pet," the text says. "There are cruel people who want to hurt animals. Each year, animal shelters and vets treat cats that have been shot, stabbed or even set on fire . . ."

The other pamphlet makes a less gentle case for Cats Indoors. With no snazzy red footwear in sight, nor a single cartoon, it presents photographs of downed birds and mutilated rabbits and feasting feline predators.

Sizemore himself comes across as a little overworked and not at all militant, but the birders have sometimes gone to rather egregious extremes. In recent years, the head of the Galveston Ornithological Society was accused of shooting an outdoor cat, and a researcher at the Smithsonian Migratory Bird Center was sentenced for trying to slaughter a whole cat colony. A writer for *Audubon* magazine raised a firestorm when he wrote an op-ed suggesting the use of a common household painkiller as a handy cat poison.

Another group of wildlife scientists published in a scientific journal those words that some ecologists will whisper only behind closed doors: that managing cat colonies is "cat hoarding without walls."

Kornreich, the Cornell veterinarian, phrases the objection rather more delicately. "Mathematical models and papers," he says, "suggest that this is not always the best way."

The problem, of course, is that cats are just too good at surviving. For neutering to effectively reduce stray cat numbers, it's estimated that 71 percent to 94 percent of a given population, including virtually all of the females, need to be trapped and operated upon. Anything less and the colonies don't shrink: intact cats can simply ramp up their reproduction until the environment again contains as many cats as it can bear.

"Cats are reproductive machines," says the Tufts University veterinarian Robert McCarthy. "All you need is males and females around. I pulled every paper. There is zero—zero—data that TNR works. It just doesn't work at the level that it needs to work. If you have 100 cats and you neuter 30 of them, it's not like the problem is 30 percent better. It's nothing. You didn't make any progress. It's zero percent better."

Success is possible with one or two stray cats in your yard, or even, with extreme diligence, in larger areas with defined boundaries, like a university campus. The veterinarian Julie Levy has tirelessly practiced TNR at a 2,000-acre University of Florida tract in Gainesville, Florida, for nearly twenty years. Through managerial vigor, a steady supply of volunteers, free surgeries, and bold adoption tactics, she has reduced the campus population, and published some of the few TNR studies to show favorable results.

"If you make an effort to do a conscientious job, a couple of thousand acres is not a problem," she says. "Our problem is more whole communities." Her campus-focused clinic performs about 3,000 surgeries per year—but she estimates that there are about 40,000 feral cats in Gainesville and the surrounding county. Which means that as impressive as her achievement is, on a regional basis it's likely meaningless, far below the targets that ecologists cite.

For even a small city like Gainesville, such goals are almost certainly beyond reach. It is just too difficult, expensive, and time-consuming to catch and castrate so many cats, and neutered cats die off while new intact cats enter the system all the time. (The Florida city also has 70,000 pet cats, and even if the national average of 85 percent of the pets are neutered, that's still more than 10,000 potential breeders in the mix.) Now imagine this scenario in a much larger metropolis. Levy calculates free-roaming cat numbers by dividing a human population by six—other groups divide by fifteen—which suggests that there are roughly 1.4 million such cats in New York City alone. More than a million cats would need to be trapped and neutered in greater Gotham for an effect to be felt.

Skeptics also contend that neutering and releasing cats may actually make overpopulation worse. The neutered cats are hormonally compromised, which changes their behavior. Back home on the streets, the males are calmer and the females are no longer subject to the constant stress of mating. When kittens are inevitably born into colonies that include these less aggressive neutered cats, their chances for survival increase. Plus, colony feeders provide a nutritious windfall for all nearby kittens and cats, neutered and not. (It's been speculated, too, that the availability of free food gives malcontent cat owners an excuse to dump their pets, expanding the outdoor population by nonreproductive means.)

Just as a colony's kitten survival rate may rise, the neutered cats themselves tend to live longer: now that they don't care about sex, they don't get into nearly as many fights. In his paper on the issue, McCarthy of Tufts expresses the environmental impact of TNR via the increased total number of "cat days" lived. To the cat advocates, the prospect of more "cat days" is quite delightful—Alley Cat Allies often touts the longevity of its original alley colony of 54 tuxedo cats, the last three of which lived to be 14, 15, and 17 years old, far above the average stray's life-span of a few years.

But of course, though certain other desires may have forever slipped their minds, the neutered cats still hunt for the duration of their lives.

To get a feel for the reality of the situation, I tag along with Alley Cat Allies on several neutering expeditions. The first, on a wintry afternoon, is a major triumph, in part because the target is perfectly contained: one family in suburban Maryland had been feeding a fluffy bunch of half-grown feral kittens around their backyard pool, which the cats use a bit like a Serengeti watering hole. A few months earlier, the kittens might have been socialized and adopted out, but by now they are fierce and almost ready to start having kittens of their own. The Alley Cat Allies staffers set out half a dozen Tomahawk traps and then we retreat to the warmth of the sun porch to watch alongside the couple and their Siamese. "I hope they'll come back to eat here!" the wife frets as we wait. Dusk falls, and the faux flowers planted around the pool begin to glow with artificial lights, and one by one the traps snap shut. "Come on, little fuzzy butt!" one of the trappers whispers in exultation as the last cat creeps in.

The second cat-trapping trip is in inner-city Baltimore—a multiday, multirescue group attempt aimed at an entire city zip code. I enlist with a group of workers who have just come from a cat hoarder's house, where they cut apart a couch to extract two kittens. Together we drive into one of the city's bleaker neighborhoods, turning heads as our caravan of a Volvo, a Prius, and a bright-yellow, brine-and-mackerel-scented cat paddy wagon rolls into a trash-strewn alley.

We are here to collect the stray cats overseen by an older man named Mohawk. He does not know how many cats he's been frying up hamburger chuck for lately—perhaps a dozen? He has named them all Fi-Fi, except for one tremendous gray tomcat that he calls Fatty. Once a sickly kitten, Fatty owes a lot to Mohawk, who nursed him on Enfamil baby formula. (In Baltimore I learn of many creative sources of cat nourishment, including Chinese food, Thanksgiving leftovers, and Cinnamon Toast Crunch.)

Mohawk's alley backs into a chain-linked lumberyard that looks a little like a forest; snakes and hawks live back there, he tells us. It is frigidly cold out, but I can see several cats surveying the landscape from atop an over-flowing garbage bin that I at first mistake for a dirty snowbank. Mohawk loudly shakes a Doritos bag, and many more cats come running—Fatty, Fatty's brother, Fatty's other brother, and lots and lots of Fi-Fis.

"I think you may have more cats than you realize," one rescuer says.

"You got your day's work cut out for you," Mohawk agrees.

The rescuers load cats into the van. "You gonna bring them back?" Mo-hawk asks. "They're like family." The rescuers promise they will, and also to return with vegetarian pizza and more traps. After several hours, and a heated dispute with a neighbor over a pet cat named Snowball that the trappers attempt to shanghai and neuter anyway, a number of the cats are in custody, though there is no way to tell how many more of Mohawk's affiliates lurk beyond the fence.

The population of Baltimore City is over 600,000—that's roughly 100,000 stray cats, according to Levy's math. Despite this single-alley bo-nanza, in which the cats were handily trained to come at the crinkle of a Doritos bag, the entire multiday, multiagency round-up—which adds up to many dozens of "human days" of hard work—yields just over 100 neu-tered cats.

If neutering cat colonies does not always work as advertised, why are major American municipalities and even whole nations embracing the practice left and right? Part of it may have to do with public opinion. According to a 2011 Associated Press poll, seven out of ten American pet owners want only "sick" and "aggressive" animals euthanized. This preference has practical implications: TNR and euthanasia are both costly options, but volunteer labor is vital for both, and animal lovers are much more apt to sign up for population-control scenarios where cats make it out alive. Also, politicians do not want to introduce anti-cat legislation or otherwise rub cat lovers the wrong way. More than 40 million American households include cats, and with their fund-raising power and grassroots following, the cat people do not pussyfoot around. Deep-pocketed TNR sponsors include PetSmart

Charities and Maddie's Fund, a no-kill animal rescue group founded in honor of a billionaire's schnauzer. The annual Alley Cat Allies budget is about $9 million, which pays for—among other services—a multiperson legal team, an in-house graphics department, a public relations officer, and a social media director.

After attending the conference, I signed up for Alley Cat Allies email alerts. These soon ranked among my favorite correspondence. Many of the emails came from Becky Robinson herself and were signed off, simply, "For the cats." Some messages were tender, others tragic, and all were highly determined. I read "urgent kitten safety advisories," and many, many requests for money: "This is the only way we can be there for kittens everywhere. Click here to donate $35 or more." When more than two dozen dead cats were found hanging in a tree in Yonkers, NY, Alley Cat Allies distributed white flowers at a memorial vigil "as a symbol of the cats' innocence," and I received an electronic white rose that I could email around.

Though often criticized for being too softhearted, Alley Cat Allies and other cat advocacy groups don't shy away from confrontations. They demanded the dismissal of Ted Williams, the *Audubon* journalist who wrote the cat poison op-ed (he was suspended, but later reinstated). After the Smithsonian bird group published their meta-analysis of cat predation in mainland America, Robinson personally protested "the junk science" on the National Mall and presented a petition of more than 55,000 angry signatures.

The advocates also use their clout against private businesses and citizens whose attempts to handle out-of-control cat populations fall short of Alley Cat Allies' ideal. In 2008, after five years of practicing the TNR method, a Chantilly, Virginia, mobile home community attempted to jettison its still-thriving colony of 200 cats; the *Washington Post* was summoned, and after three days of negative "local and national attention," the management caved, and the "wild" cats (as the headlines called them) returned to pooping in the trailer park's snapdragon beds. "We got hate mail from as far away as Europe," the man behind the property management desk tells me when I visit.

Other entities that have attracted the cat lobby's ire include senior citizen complexes, concrete plants, and the Loews Hotels chain in Orlando, not far from where Disney scientists sheltered their doomed wood rats.

If private groups refuse to yield, cat advocates often contact elected officials. Politicians take such outreach very seriously, and the Alley Cat Allies conference placed major emphasis on working the right political channels; the website provides a political toolkit. These aren't necessarily small-town matters: recently, the wife of Stephen Harper—then the prime minister of Canada—spoke at a cat charity dinner. "Mrs. Harper, raising awareness about cat welfare is a good look for your husband's upcoming campaign strategy," a protestor—pro-human, this time—shouted in the middle of her speech. "Don't you think supporting an inquiry into missing and murdered indigenous women in this country would be a better look?"

"That's a great cause," replied Mrs. Harper, who was apparently wearing cat ears at the time, "but tonight we're here for homeless cats."

Yet because American cat laws are typically determined at a city and county level, national groups like Alley Cat Allies often wade into very local politics, where running afoul of the cat lobby can be quite an experience for a hometown politician.

I speak with Michael Taylor, then the mayor pro tem of Sterling Heights, Michigan. In his early thirties, and only lately fledged from his alma mater's branch of the Young Republicans, Taylor is accustomed to handling such hot-button issues as library book purchases and pothole repairs. He is also a cat owner himself. But when the Macomb County Animal Shelter announced that it would be switching to a TNR model, Taylor and the rest of the town council didn't think too hard about their decision to hire another shelter that would cart away offending cats for good. In fact, Taylor's first impulse was reflexively political: he envisioned voter backlash if "a cat terrorizing the neighborhood" was collected, neutered, and then promptly returned to said neighborhood for perpetuity. Then he and the town council examined the science behind mass neutering and were unimpressed. "There wasn't any evidence," he says. "It was really all raw emotion, was what I found."

After considering the matter, and hearing the arguments of local cat lovers, the council "said no, we are not going to be putting any feral cats back," he remembers. It wasn't long before—at my home hundreds of miles away—an alert popped into my in-box about an ongoing "rampage against feral cats." "You know us at Alley Cat Allies," another email said. "We won't back down when cats are in danger, in Macomb County and anywhere else in the nation. We will be there fighting for their lives and their safety."

A Twitter skirmish ensued between Taylor and some cat advocates, in which Taylor unwisely referred to them as "troll(s) . . . Kidding!" A local television station was notified that "an elected official was harassing cat advocates," Taylor says. "Of course, the reporter jumped on it." The story spread, and the young mayor pro tem was soon receiving enraged emails from across the country and beyond, some signed by cats themselves. "I sincerely HOPE KARMA gives right BACK to you what you sow!! DEATH & DESTRUCTION!!" one woman wrote.

Online, people wished that Taylor would contract AIDS. One constituent informed him personally that she herself would rather die than have her cat impounded in a cat-killing town. Taylor faced threats of a recall and was told that a political action committee was being formed to prevent his reelection and that a Sterling Heights tourism boycott would soon be under way.

"Sometimes life is stranger than fiction," Taylor says. "I never would have believed it if they hadn't come at me with everything they had. I think they figured 'they all crack,' that I'd throw my hands up."

Sterling Heights did not surrender, though several neighboring municipalities did—much to Taylor's disappointment. "I told them, 'Stick to your guns!' but the pressure was just too much. If you have enough people, like the Alley Cat Allies does, you can exert a lot of influence over elected officials. If you chip away at community after community, you've gotten across the legislation you want one city at a time. I give them a lot of credit."

The Sterling Heights cat scandal happened in early 2014. On February 14, another email appeared in Taylor's lengthy queue: "Someone has sent you an eCard from Alley Cat Allies!" the subject line said.

It was a Valentine. Beneath a picture of a fluffy white cat lolling in a red rosebush, the caption read: "Please Don't Kill Me! I just want to live :) Meow?"

⌒⌒

The headquarters of Alley Cat Allies in posh downtown Bethesda, Maryland, occupies a floor and a half of an office building, a striking contrast to Grant Sizemore's lonely cubicle at the American Bird Conservancy. The entranceway is adorned with brass memorial plaques for Tuffy Beige, Darth Vader, Bashful, and other presumably deceased cats. ("To Zane Gray, Goodnight, Sweet Prince," "Blackjack Hartwell, My King.") Inside, the office bursts with avant-garde cat furniture that is conspicuously unoccupied by the Royals, as three office cats are collectively known: today they are nesting in file boxes. Around the office at regular intervals hang pillowcase-like bags. In the event of a fire, every staff member has been trained to capture the Royals in these duffels and transport them to safety. This is difficult even absent an inferno. The Royals were socialized shortly after the optimal window and remain disobedient and resourceful.

I am here to meet Becky Robinson.

More than an hour late, she arrives in a flowing tangerine jacket. She looks cautious, tired, elegant. She offers me water and then, distressingly, breath mints. It quickly becomes apparent that she is one of the most charismatic people I've ever met. She has a big, goofy laugh, shimmering brown eyes, and excellent elocution.

At her insistence, I have sent her a list of questions in advance, but we do not discuss them. Not at first, anyway. Robinson wants to talk about her childhood. She grew up in the farm country of rural Kansas; her mother left when she was young and her father remarried. She remained more or less in place, tended at times by a grandmother and an aunt. It was the original free-range childhood, with long hours staking out prairie dog burrows and watching hawks hunt.

The Robinsons were community pillars: church elders, hospital volunteers. They were also the sort of people who wanted to save everything, even the town's old opera house. They would catch rattlesnakes in advance of the annual rattlesnake hunt and harbor them until the danger passed.

Her aunt was particularly kindhearted. When she took the Robinson children to shop in town, the first stop was always Duckwall's, the five-and-dime. "It was a little store on Main Street," Robinson says, "and what do you think they sold in the back?" She gives me a little smile. "Animals. They sold pets. They had birds and rats and mice. And of course that was where we stopped first every day. We might have had a shopping list, but the list was in your back pocket until you went to the back of Duckwall's, and you could smell it before you could see it." On each occasion Robinson's aunt would ask to see the manager. She insisted that the cages be cleaned and that the animals be fed. "And after the animals we'd also water all the plants," Robinson recalls, "because they are living things, too."

Robinson eventually got a degree in social work and joined the welfare system, but the horrors of child abuse overwhelmed her.

"It was just too much," she explains. "I could not have continued on as a social worker. I left, I resigned." She sought out animal rights groups, moved to Washington, and formed Alley Cat Allies in 1990, launching the national movement to make TNR mainstream. She calls it her "life's work."

Asked to defend the method against its many critics, Robinson notes that it's a little absurd to crack down on house cats for global environmental woes, considering what humans have done to the world. At the same time, she makes a powerful case for human decency. She directs me to an online presentation where I later see a picture that lingers in my mind for days: a fluffy, multicolor mound of stiffened cat and kitten corpses that represent one morning's work at a single California shelter. The biggest threat to our favorite companion animal is not disease but our poisons and crematoriums. Many modern animal pounds, in Robinson's view, are no better than slaughterhouses. Americans are a compassionate people, she says, and should not have to finance institutionalized violence that most aren't even fully aware of. "That's why we exist," she says of her organization. "We had to break that wide open. We had to say: let cats stay, let them live outside. These are families! There isn't just one way for cats." At the very least, she says, local agencies should be required to publicize the numbers of animals they are killing.

But her most powerful argument is that even if neutering cat colonies doesn't always deliver on its promises, euthanasia doesn't work either. Critics sometimes acknowledge this as well: as impossible as it may be to catch and neuter enough cats to change populations, it is equally hard to catch and kill them. One model showed that lethal control is the best management tool only if a whopping 97 percent of cats are destroyed. The overwhelming majority of America's stray cats don't come into contact with animal control at all. "They're *never* going to catch all the animals," Robinson says, her voice rising. "There are millions and millions of cats!"

"Whether you like it or not," she goes on, "whether you accept it or not, whether you have cats or like cats, they are part of the environment. There is no way around that. And they've been part of the environment. And this idea that we are going to change this, we humans have this idea, this arrogance, that we are somehow going to change this overnight, and do away with all cats, is quite frankly quite preposterous. It's a bit hysterical."

A backlash against TNR is under way, with environmental lawsuits ongoing in Los Angeles and Albuquerque. Even Washington, DC—Alley Cat Allies' core turf—recently reconsidered its pro-colony policies, in a newly proposed city Wildlife Action Plan that equates stray house cats with dreaded invasive species like northern snakeheads.

Animal welfare activists, veterinarians, and scientists continue to pursue other population-control solutions. One proposed alternative is to give ownerless cats vasectomies and hysterectomies instead of neutering them: though vasectomies are more expensive and complex, these procedures would leave cats' hormones intact, and perhaps neutralize the neutered cats' survival advantage. This method, the veterinarian Robert McCarthy told me, has been discussed for possible use in Japan's Fukushima zone, where, in the wake of the killer tsunami and nuclear meltdown, colonies of house cats have apparently prospered.

The Holy Grail is a contraceptive vaccine, perhaps like the kind sometimes used for deer, but house cat loins are quite well-armored. Knocking out a single hormonal pathway doesn't seem to be enough to curtail feline lusts, says the pro-TNR veterinarian Julie Levy, who has worked on developing the technology. "All of biology is based on reproduction," she says. "We're really trying to overcome what drives life."

As various contraceptive scenarios are considered, some animal welfare groups have tried partnering with wildlife ecologists to study population impacts. But such relationships may often be fraught, in part because many ecologists continue to question whether cat activists really want to shrink cat populations.

And understandably so. According to TNR's governing logic, new kittens should be a dispiriting sight, furry proof of the movement's failure. But, of course, to many people, and especially to cat advocates, kittens are also the cutest things in the entire world. I'm not surprised to learn that advocates do everything that they can to save even the sickest kittens, incubating them in their bras, and cooling their fevered ears with rubbing alcohol.

At the Alley Cat Allies conference, I sit through a very technical presentation on Tomahawk trap trip plates, postoperative temperature control, and other TNR mechanics. As the sober PowerPoint concludes, the presenter suddenly flashes a slide of an adorable feline neonate: "And this is my kitten Rex!" she says. The room explodes in squeals.

It was a bit like ending a lecture on the war on drugs with a picture of a lit crack pipe—especially since there is actually some evidence that cats, like street drugs, have clinically compromised our minds.

Chapter 6

CAT SCAN

I ALMOST BECAME cat food once.

This was Tanzania, 2009. I'd just spent a happy week on a magazine assignment rattling around in a Land Rover with researchers from the famous Serengeti Lion Project. Though I tried to be all business and stifle my squeals at the sight of their sublime study animals, a few sighs slipped out. But mostly I managed to stay still and quiet while we counted whisker spots and staked out water holes from the safety of the truck.

On my last night, we left the Land Rover behind to climb a big pile of rocks in the middle of the grasslands. We wanted to admire the sweeping view of the savannah before sunset, and to inspect a grizzled old tree that the lions had used as a scratching post for centuries.

But once on top of the kopje, we discovered something far more spectacular: in a crook between the boulders huddled two tiny, unattended lion cubs. We'd accidentally stumbled into a lion's den—and the mother was nowhere to be seen.

Now, it doesn't take a PhD in biology, or even a background in wildlife writing, to grasp that this was probably not the safest situation: while the local lions mostly regarded the scientists with jaded disdain, getting between a lioness and her vulnerable young is a potentially grave mistake. It would have been wise to tiptoe back to the Land Rover, and fast, before an enraged mother came barreling out of the shadows. We had no weapons, not even the umbrella the scientists sometimes brandished at emboldened lions.

And yet I felt in no hurry to leave. A strange kind of euphoria overtook me, and suddenly the prospect of a slavering lioness didn't seem distressing in the least. I posed for elaborate pictures among the boulders, the cubs peeking over my shoulder from a few yards away. I begged the scientists to linger just a little longer. It was almost like I wanted to be eaten.

The feline family has long been linked with hypnotic powers: just as uncanny house cats are staples of Western witchcraft lore and superstition, lions are shamans in various African traditions, jaguars are disguised Amazonian prophets, and so on. Cats somehow seem to tamper with our logic. Perhaps cats have picked off so many people over the millennia, and otherwise taken advantage of mankind, because they have a wizardly way of enchanting us.

Or maybe science can explain it. The memory of my rather singular flirtation with death-by-lion came flooding back the first time I read about *Toxoplasma gondii*, also known as the cat parasite. This mysterious microorganism is spread by felines and is by now believed to inhabit the brains of one in three people worldwide, including some 60 million Americans. In rodents, the parasite seems to catalyze bizarre behaviors, making infected animals lose their inborn fear of cats and even become "attracted" to them, thus upping their chances of becoming prey. Some scientists think it has similarly strange effects on people—predisposing us to risk taking, raising our odds of violent death, even driving us insane.

Reflecting on my Serengeti recklessness, I began to wonder: Had a cat sickness transmitted to me via Cheetoh in my own den lured me into the den of a far larger feline, as dinner? And furthermore, could a bug in my brain help explain otherwise inexplicable aspects of my long-standing cat "attraction"—for instance, my penchant for commissioning formal portraits of Cheetoh, or my eccentric habit of lying awake at night, wondering how much ransom I would pay if he was ever kidnapped?

As it turns out, I'm far from alone in nursing such suspicions. Many cat lovers, pondering their blind devotion to a savage little archcarnivore, privately wonder if they might be a little touched in the head. Then they hear a snippet on the nightly news or NPR about a ubiquitous yet invisible cat-borne organism that currently dwells inside many of our skulls. The headlines can read like horror movies, suggesting that house cats even practice "mind control."

There is no question that the global explosion of *Toxoplasma*—now perhaps the most successful parasite the world has ever seen—is the strangest fruit of humanity's relationship with the house cat. But are theories about the parasite's impact on human behavior based on legitimate science? Or are they just our latest flawed attempt to rationalize the enigmatic house cat's power?

Such questions occupy the thoughts of quite a few researchers across the country—not least because the parasite itself often lives inside their brains.

Just beyond the gridlocked limits of Washington, DC, is a little slice of the American heartland: acres of cornfields, silos, cows. This quaint vista belongs to the United States Department of Agriculture's Maryland research center, where I find the lab of J. P. Dubey, the world's foremost expert on the cat parasite.

Dubey is a sprightly older man who speaks with a faint Indian accent. He has been studying *Toxoplasma* since the 1960s. Back then, researchers were well aware of the parasite, which was already notorious for causing human birth defects, but they had no clue how it spread. Dubey was part of the international scientific team that first identified cats as the carrier.

Though *Toxoplasma* can infect any kind of warm-blooded animal, it reproduces itself in cat guts and in cat guts alone. All of the parasite's "secondary hosts," from camels to skunks to humpback whales to human beings, are just pit stops between cats. Only the intestines of infected felines are the site of epic parasitic orgies, reproductive frenzies that produce a billion new copies of *Toxoplasma*, which are then spewed out into ecosystems via cat poop.

Any kind of cat will do: all feline species, from the tiger to the ocelot, are the single-celled organism's "definitive hosts." But the domestication and global spread of the house cat has likely been the key to *Toxoplasma*'s dizzying expansion. Today it's perhaps the most cosmopolitan parasite on the planet, infecting birds and mammals everywhere from the Amazon to Antarctica. Far more people have toxoplasmosis—as the associated disease is known—than own cats.

Nearly five decades later, Dubey is still probing the parasite's role in our food web. *Toxoplasma* follows two main avenues of transmission: in addition to being broadcast by the billion in cat feces, which people and animals accidentally ingest, it's also spread when we eat the infected flesh of a secondary host. The first method is far more efficient: a billion parasites could theoretically infect a billion new animals, while meat-eating merely transfers the sickness from a single prey animal to its predator. (It's a bit like the difference between a machine gun and a bayonet.) But working together, the multiple modes of transmission make *Toxoplasma* very difficult to study, let alone stop.

"This is a very clever parasite," says Dubey with a faraway smile. He himself has been infected since 1969.

Brain-burrowing parasites are almost always devastating, like the rare brain-eating amoeba that haunts swimming holes in the American South and kills people every summer. *Toxoplasma* sounds similarly scary: it forms untreatable cysts in animals' brains and muscle tissue and, in addition to harming livestock, can indeed be fatal to many species of wild animal, from crows to wallabies.

There is no cure for toxoplasmosis and, after the initial infection subsides on its own, the cysts in our brains and bodies never go away. Yet in healthy adult humans, this ultracommon illness has long been considered harmless. The acute phase of infection usually causes only mild, mononucleosis-like discomfort, or often no symptoms at all, before it settles down into its dormant state. The greatest known danger has always been to the developing human fetus, which lacks a strong immune system:

this is why pregnant women are warned to steer clear of litter boxes. A simple blood test—and I'll be taking one shortly—can tell if you've had the disease, but most healthy people don't even bother checking.

Lately, though, scientists have grown suspicious of the supposedly benign parasite, and are investigating whether long-term brain infections alter human neurology and behavior.

Dubey is not waiting for the result of these studies. His goal is to stop the parasite in its tracks. He walks me through his own crowded lab, where I meet visiting scientists from Spain, India, and Brazil. Worldwide infection rates vary by climate and regional culture: for instance, certain dietary habits, especially an acquired taste for raw and rare meat—pork and lamb, in particular—almost certainly increase the parasite's spread. Rates are highest in South America, southern Europe, and parts of Africa, with 80 percent of the population infected in some countries. The American infection rate is somewhere between 10 percent and 40 percent, and South Korea is perhaps the toxo-freest nation, at less than 7 percent.

On a countertop nearby are blenders full of what appear to be delicious strawberry-banana smoothies. These are chicken hearts flown in from Grenada, ground into a pink soup that the lab will check for signs of the parasite. I also spy the splayed form of a skinned mouse. The brain of this toxoplasmosis-positive rodent has already been removed, Dubey explains, and will soon be fed to a research cat. Within a few days, the newly infected but otherwise healthy cat will begin defecating millions upon millions of invisible egg-like *Toxoplasma* forms called oocysts, which Dubey and his team will harvest and study.

"Can I see your cats?" I ask Dubey.

"I would rather you not do that," Dubey says. "We have very strict security for them. You have to change clothes. These organisms, the oocysts, are highly infectious and very hardy. You cannot kill them. You can put them in Clorox and nothing will happen. They will survive without a problem."

Even in the lab itself, protocols are extreme. "Everything here will be incinerated," Dubey gestures at the mouse corpse, the crumpled paper towels. "Everything that comes out of here. This must all be burned."

In 1938, pathologists at Babies Hospital in New York City examined a newborn who developed convulsive seizures when she was three days old; peering with an ophthalmoscope, they saw lesions in the baby's eyes. She died a month later, and the autopsy revealed similar lesions covering her brain.

This was perhaps the medical community's earliest diagnosis of human toxoplasmosis. It was the dreaded congenital form, still the best-known and most devastating iteration of the disease, which is passed from cat to pregnant human to unborn baby, causing spontaneous abortions, still-births, and severe complications like blindness and mental retardation. But it would be decades before we figured out how the condition was acquired—and from what.

By the 1950s, scientists suspected a carnivorous connection: they noticed that pigs that ate undercooked meat from the garbage had higher rates of infection. In 1965, researchers decided to test this idea in a Paris sanatorium. Hundreds of young tuberculosis patients were fed barely cooked lamb chops. (Because a raw meat diet was also thought to be a tuberculosis remedy, the experiment was—at the time, at least—considered ethical.) Some of the meat must have contained tissue cysts, because the sick children's toxoplasmosis rates surged. But the keystone species in the transmission pattern remained a mystery.

The breakthrough finally came when a Scottish parasitologist switched, on a whim, from studying dogs to cats and just happened to spot *Toxoplasma* in his feline subjects' droppings. Dubey and other researchers picked up on this providential lead, and by 1969, several groups converged on the conclusion that cats were the parasite's definitive host, their bellies its command center.

The medieval inquisitors had nothing nearly so damning on cats: they may have once been rumored to steal baby's breath, but now there was hard evidence that they could blind the unborn and destroy their brains. After the journal *Science* published the finding, "many cats were killed, because people didn't understand it," Dubey remembers.

The fact that cats were able to overcome this public relations disaster, and even accelerate their rise during the 1970s, is yet more proof of their unusual hold on our affections. But now we also know that certain types of cat ownership, particularly keeping an indoor cat, aren't all that risky. In fact, average cat owners don't even have unusually high rates of infection. Indoor cats eat mostly commercially prepared food—which has been frozen, cooked at high temperatures, or otherwise industrially treated to kill the parasite—and don't have much contact with outdoor animals. They acquire the infection only rarely.

It is outdoor cats, which catch and eat infected prey, that typically transmit *Toxoplasma* to human beings. As cats deposit invisible oocysts, their owners may accidentally acquire the organisms while changing a litter box, or a neighbor may ingest some by working in contaminated garden soil. Or another animal in our food chain—a lamb, say—might ingest the organisms instead, and we get it by eating lamb burgers, one secondary host consuming another. (Barn cats, in addition to not catching enough mice, can also spread toxoplasmosis to livestock, and Dubey advises keeping cats far away from pigs, which are particularly susceptible to the disease.)

Cats usually get infected just once in their lives, and the oocyst-shedding phase lasts just weeks before the parasite goes dormant. But at any given moment, scientists estimate that 1 percent of the earth's cats and kittens are spreading the parasite, and that's more than enough to saturate ecosystems. In the United States, roughly 80 percent of Pennsylvania's black bears (which eat all kinds of garbage, and are not known for thoroughly cooking their meat) have been infected. Another study found that nearly half of Ohio's deer have toxoplasmosis; they likely get it from munching cat-poop-tainted grass.

Humans are more sanitary than stags or bears, but it's still harder than you might expect to protect ourselves from toxoplasmosis. For instance, a major perk of modern pregnancy is being medically excused, for nine blissful months, from kitty-litter scooping. But if you have an indoor cat, like I do, this measure is mostly pointless, as the real risks lurk elsewhere.

Abstaining from rare meat may be more effective. Yet vegetarians are by no means exempt from the sickness. When John Boothroyd, a Stanford

University microbiologist, gives toxoplasmosis talks to the general public, "the vegetarians start looking very smug. Then I show them a picture of carrots." Soil-dusted veggies can be packed with cat-deposited oocysts. One Indian study showed that vegetarians and meat-eaters actually had similar rates of infection.

In fact, people may get sick just from drinking water. A well-known outbreak happened when more than a hundred people drank from a contaminated Canadian reservoir, and water supplies tainted by cat excreta may be an important transmission mechanism, particularly in the developing world. Breathing the air isn't necessarily safe either. Another well-studied toxoplasmosis epidemic occurred when people simply inhaled dust at an Atlanta, Georgia, horse stable that housed cats.

No one is sure when and why cats and *Toxoplasma* first joined forces, but the relationship is likely quite ancient. Because lions, leopards, and other wild cats once ruled so much of the earth, the parasite was likely well distributed eons before *Felis silvestris lybica* invaded the first human settlements. In fact, signatures in our DNA suggest that *Toxoplasma* influenced primate evolution: to help us better ride out the infection, one of our genes seems to have shut down, becoming an unexpressed "dead gene" still present in our cells today.

But it is the very modern and evolutionarily radical relationship between humans and house cats that's made the parasite omnipresent. In pristine nature, cats—even more than other creatures at the top of the food chain—were quite rare, limiting just how common a cat-dependent parasite could become. Then along came human civilization, packing in thousands of pet felines per city mile. And whenever we and our cats toured a new ecosystem, *Toxoplasma* tagged along. The parasite is now found even above the Arctic Circle, in beluga whales and other creatures, and it is particularly devastating in regions without native feline species, like Australia. Kangaroos and other animals that didn't coevolve with cats often die of toxoplasmosis, because their immune systems can't cope with the alien sickness.

As we hauled house cats hither and yon, we likely also reshaped the parasite's biology. European colonists sailing to Brazil, for instance, brought ships' cats ashore, where they no doubt contracted exotic strains from jaguars and pumas. If some of the cats already carried European strains when they acquired the Brazilian ones, the two varieties would have the unprecedented opportunity to scramble together in the cat's intestines, giving rise to new, potentially superfit mutations.

Why are cat intestines so hospitable to this parasite? "It's probably a whole bunch of things, from body temperature to what they eat to what other microbes are in there," says Boothroyd. And the mutations that have likely taken place during the parasite's long residency, he notes, may have helped it become even more "exquisitely fine-tuned" to the feline host.

Toxoplasma-like organisms dwell in many other animals' guts—chickens poop out a similar parasite perfectly suited to chicken innards. But this parasite inhabits only chickens; it can't be carried by other barnyard animals, let alone humans. For a single parasite to infect such a vast network of secondary animals in addition to its definitive host is quite extraordinary.

The key to this network effect may be the cat family's hard-core carnivory.

Imagine that a mouse accidently ingests the chicken poop parasite, and the chicken parasite figures out how to survive inside the mouse. That's a huge leap—"not something you see often, thank God," Boothroyd remarks—but in this case a totally pointless one. Because once inside the mouse, the chicken parasite is trapped: another chicken is not going to eat the mouse, and so the chicken parasite has no way to get back to its heaven, the chicken stomach, and make a billion copies of itself and its nifty new mouse-friendly mutation.

A cat-poop parasite with a similar mutation in the same mouse, on the other hand, has many more options. "Because cats are carnivorous, there is a chance that mouse is going to end up eaten by a cat and get back where it needs to be," replicating ad infinitum, Boothroyd says. Instead of a dead end, the mouse becomes an opportunity.

Some of *Toxoplasma*'s secondary hosts are true parasitic culs-de-sac—humpback whales can carry the parasite, and even lions don't stalk humpbacks. But because cats consume so many kinds of meat, it behooves the parasite to cast a wide net. Just a few hits amid billions of misses mean success.

Like the house cat itself, then, *Toxoplasma* is fine-tuned yet flexible, picky but promiscuous. While other single-celled parasites focus on trashing one type of human cell—like *Toxoplasma*'s cousin, malaria, which hunts down red blood cells—*Toxoplasma* commandeers practically every kind in our body: stomach and liver cells, neurons, the cells of the heart. When I watch a high-magnification movie of *Toxoplasma* in action, it even looks a bit like my Cheetoh. The plump little paisley-shaped parasite sidles up to a much larger human cell with a gliding gait that recalls the way a cat coasts about your ankles when it wants to be fed. Then suddenly, the parasite rams the cell and squeezes itself inside, like a water balloon squishing through a peephole.

It can even invade immune cells, which it appears to use to sneak into our brains, a place that most parasites can't penetrate. This is an excellent thing, since the brain is perhaps our most vital and vulnerable organ: immune responses are muted there because they cause swelling, which can be deadly in the close confines of the skull. The best strategy is to keep invaders out in the first place. The brain-body barrier is closely guarded by specially lined blood vessels and almost impossible to breach.

But *Toxoplasma* may use the body's own trusted immune cells as a Trojan horse to smuggle itself through the barrier. And once it's in, the brain can't do much about it. The parasite is there to stay. Hibernating in armored tissue cysts, it waits patiently to be devoured by a cat.

But maybe the parasite doesn't just bide its time inside. Perhaps it pulls strings behind the scenes and stacks the deck in its favor, increasing the odds that it will become feline fare. That was the gist of a sensational series of 1990s experiments, in which scientists at Oxford University exposed *Toxoplasma*-positive rats to cat urine.

Though largely mediocre rat catchers, cats do have one thing going for them in the pest control department: the smell of their urine is, to a rodent, the most horrifying odor in the world. Even a lab rat whose forefathers have been bred for dozens of generations in captivity, far from a house cat's clutches, will flee from the scent of cat pee.

From the perspective of a parasite transmitted via cat poop, this inbred terror of cat pee would be "a huge obstacle in transmission," says Joanne Webster, who led the Oxford study. "We wanted to see if the parasite could dampen down that effect."

What they observed was more than a dampening—the parasite seemed to completely mute the rats' fear instinct. The infected rodents no longer avoided cat urine. "It actually made them attracted," Webster says. The rats that cozied up to the cat urine didn't seem to change their social behavior, nor did they lose their wariness of other classic rat deterrents. They just lost all fear of cat pee. The researchers coined the phrase feline "Fatal Attraction," to newspapers' delight.

The finding, which has since been replicated in many other labs, jibed with scientists' growing interest in the so-called manipulation hypothesis. Certain parasites have been shown to puppeteer the behavior of their hosts for their own selective benefit; sometimes, the unlucky host animal is even induced to offer itself up as a sacrifice. In one famous example, a parasitic fluke infects an ant, then prods the ant to scale a blade of grass where it is more likely to be eaten by a sheep or a cow, the fluke's preferred hosts.

Scientists now hypothesize that the reckless behavior of *Toxoplasma*-infected rats—their newfound courage around cat urine, combined with increased activity levels that researchers have also noted—may be engineered to increase cat predation.

If correct, then the finding is even wilder than it sounds. Most classic cases of the manipulation hypothesis occur in simpler organisms, like those luckless ants. In mammals, there are no other examples of a parasite manipulating its host so dramatically.

Which brings us back to my very personal inquiry: If this cat parasite uses mice like marionettes, might people become its pawns as well? Had I been neurologically induced to "sacrifice" myself in the lion's den? With morbid fascination, I read a study of our closest primate relatives, which found that toxo-infected chimpanzees are drawn to the urine of their major predators, leopards.

Alas, scientists have not yet undertaken an analysis of how many un-lucky human victims of lion mauling are toxo-positive. But there has been some intriguing work on the parasite and risk-taking behavior in infected people, who do seem more likely to die violently in a variety of ways.

For instance, individuals with toxoplasmosis have an elevated risk of suicide, and countries with higher infection rates likewise tend to have higher suicide and homicide rates. The same spike shows up in car crash statistics, where people with toxoplasmosis are more than twice as likely to be involved in a motor vehicle accident.

Is crashing your Jaguar the modern version of getting eaten by a jaguar? It's possible. "Maybe you take a toxo-infected human," says Stanford neu-robiologist Robert Sapolsky in an online interview, "and they start having a proclivity towards doing dumb-ass things that we should be innately averse to, like having your body hurtle through space at high G-forces."

But some scientists think it's more likely that these sloppy drivers (and other infected people and animals) suffer from something far less extraor-dinary than parasitic manipulation, like a suppressed but ongoing immune response that lasts much longer than the brief bout of illness that most people experience. These hard-hit individuals may have had weaker or more sensitive immune systems to begin with, and their toxoplasmosis in-fection leaves them feeling persistently under the weather. In the case of the accident-prone motorists, perhaps their reaction time slows, making them less likely to avoid perils on the road.

This second hypothesis finds support in another gory data point: the toxo-positive sea otters of Monterey Bay are three times more likely to be slaughtered by a super predator, but not of the feline variety. Rather, the infected otters fall prey to great white sharks. It seems odd that the cat par-asite would engineer its victims to be somehow "attracted" to giant fish; more probably, the sick otters are just a little dazed and confused, making them easier marks.

Speaking of easy marks, whenever I mention my homegrown hypoth-esis about the lion's den, scientists chuckle heartily. They suspect that the parasite does tailor itself to life inside certain secondary host species, but probably not humans. That kind of adaptation would make sense only for a species that's much more available and easy to hunt, like mice or pigeons. The fact is that not too many people get eaten by cats big or small these days, and a *Toxoplasma* strain designed to lure foolish journalists into lion's lairs would probably have perished long ago. To a parasite that's born by the billion, the human population is small potatoes.

But that still doesn't mean that it's irrelevant to *us*. The consensus that only pregnant women need fear toxoplasmosis took a major hit in the 1980s during the HIV epidemic. The overwhelmed immune systems of AIDS patients let the parasite run roughshod, creating tennis-ball-sized brain lesions. As many as 30 percent of AIDS patients in some European countries (and 10 percent in the United States) died from the infection. Indeed, the microorganism became a hot topic in the 2016 American presidential debates, after a toxoplasmosis drug manufacturer suddenly jacked up the price of certain lifesaving treatments for the immunocompromised.

Even in people with healthy immune systems, researchers are now picking up correlations between the parasite and a laundry list of ailments: Alzheimer's disease, Parkinson's disease, rheumatoid arthritis, obesity, brain cancer (an especially contested association), migraines, depression, bipolar disorder, infertility, heightened aggression, and obsessive-compulsive disorder. A University of Chicago study recently noted a connection to road rage incidents.

Then there is even more eye-opening research. A Czech scientist named Jaroslav Flegr thinks the parasite helps sculpt our individual personalities. According to his work, infected people are more guilt-prone than others, infected men tend to be suspicious and dogmatic, while women are more social and snazzier dressers. Perhaps inevitably, Flegr exposed his human subjects to cat urine, and found that infected men rather liked the smell while women did not.

That's not, by a long shot, as peculiar as this branch of science gets. Another toxo researcher speculates that the infection may explain our fondness for sauvignon blanc, the fragrance of which resembles cat urine. (True to form, one of my go-to vintages is indeed called Cat's Pee on a Gooseberry Bush.) New Zealand specializes in this style of wine, and New Zealand just happens to have the highest levels of cat ownership in the world—and national toxoplasmosis rates hovering around 40 percent.

Even if these curious findings withstand further scrutiny, how would our shopping habits and wine cellar contents possibly boost cat predation rates? They probably don't. The parasite could catalyze a range of behavioral changes in its many secondary carriers, only a few of which need to benefit the invader.

But because the human brain is an organ without parallel in the animal kingdom, human beings may suffer subtle effects that don't concern other host species like sea otters and wallabies. The best studied of these possible toxo-complications is worrisome indeed: there's a persistent link between the parasite and schizophrenia.

E. Fuller Torrey is the associate director of the Stanley Medical Research Institute, America's largest private funding source for the study of schizophrenia and bipolar disorder. African tapestries decorate his airy office in Chevy Chase, Maryland, a nod to his days as a Peace Corps physician. There's a painting of an elephant herd, but I don't see any lions. There is, however, a small picture of a house cat with an X through it.

Torrey doesn't own cats, and family members that aspire to may be out of luck. "The reason that my grandchild does not have a cat is that I strongly urged my daughter not to buy one for her," the research psychiatrist says. "And I would not advise anybody to own a cat that is an outdoor cat if they have small children. And I would not advise anybody to ever play in a sandbox that had not been covered twenty-four hours a day."

On the other hand, Robert Yolken of Johns Hopkins University, a pediatric virologist and Torrey's frequent collaborator, is the owner of indoor cats Cinnamon and Tibby. As a prank, Yolken once used Tibby as a bookend for a shelf full of the many books that Torrey has written.

Despite their different personal relationships with felines, the men are mutually alarmed by the house cat's world conquest, and by extension, *Toxoplasma*'s. "There is no historical precedent for such numbers of cats," they write in a recent *Trends in Parasitology* paper, citing a 50 percent jump in cat ownership between 1986 and 2006. We may be just beginning to understand the consequences.

Torrey believes that schizophrenia is a disease of recent origin, almost nonexistent before the early 1800s, when mentions first appear in historical documents, and potentially caused or exacerbated by various elements of modernity. But he's become particularly interested in one specific nineteenth-century lifestyle trend: increased cat ownership. As we've seen, the 1800s were the period when cats started inching along the path to becoming catered-to members of our households. Many of the first wave of cat enthusiasts, he notes, were artists, a population not typically known for its mental health.

"The rise of cats as pets, in fact," writes Torrey in his book *The Invisible Plague*, "closely parallels the rise of insanity."

Yolken and Torrey introduced the notion of a "typhoid tabby" to the medical community in a 1995 issue of *The Schizophrenia Bulletin*, describing such far-flung and provocative phenomena as a schizophrenic spike in people born during the 1944–1945 Dutch "hunger winter," when starving pregnant women supposedly ate cats.

Perhaps more persuasively, they presented a study they'd conducted that showed that 51 percent of surveyed mentally ill adults had a house cat in childhood, versus only 38 percent of healthy people. (The only other major childhood difference detected was breast-feeding rates.) "House cats," the paper concludes, "may be an important environmental factor in the development of schizophrenia."

Later, the scientists repeated the study, this time controlling for dog ownership to be sure that schizophrenic kids weren't more likely to have companion animals in general. They again found that schizophrenics were more likely to have owned a childhood cat, while dog ownership rates remained similar to healthy people's.

When the two scientists first floated the connection between cats and clinical-grade craziness, "everybody thought it was an absolutely nutty idea," Torrey recalls. Initially, he and Yolken wondered if feline retroviruses might be the schizophrenic agents. But the blossoming *Toxoplasma* field has revealed stronger links to the disease.

Schizophrenia is a devastating and medically inscrutable sickness that afflicts roughly 1 percent of the American population with symptoms like hallucinations and paranoia. Obviously, the vast majority of people with toxoplasmosis—that is to say, a third of the global population—do not have schizophrenia, and studies increasingly indicate a major genetic component to the disorder. But Yolken and Torrey believe that toxoplasmosis, paired with other environmental and genetic factors, may be a risk factor that tips predisposed people into full-blown mental illness.

One compelling fact is that people infected with toxoplasmosis are nearly three times more likely than uninfected people to receive a schizophrenia diagnosis. Yet even that finding is not as cut and dried as it seems. There is typically no way to determine which a person developed first, toxoplasmosis or schizophrenia. Critics suggest that perhaps schizophrenics are more likely to acquire the parasite due to lapses in hygiene associated with their psychiatric condition.

But Yolken and Torrey, while they obligingly acknowledge tensions in their theory, cite a rich array of supporting correlations. In addition to the seemingly abrupt appearance of schizophrenia in the 1800s, there's a perplexing seasonal component to the disease that's unusual among mental illnesses. Schizophrenics tend to be born in the winter and early spring. Torrey speculates that indoor-outdoor cats, though still actively hunting, spend more time in homes during the cold months and are perhaps more likely to infect a winter or early spring baby in its last trimester of gestation, when *Toxoplasma*'s effects are particularly profound. Several studies suggest that pregnant women more frequently acquire *Toxoplasma* in the winter.

There are other scattered shards of evidence. Like women with acute toxoplasmosis, schizophrenic women tend to have more stillbirths, and no one knows why. In some places where cats (and by extension *Toxoplasma*) have been historically absent, such as the highlands of Papua New Guinea, schizophrenia is apparently quite rare. Like schizophrenia, toxoplasmosis tends to run in families—not because of genetics, but because families share exposure to food, water sources, and cats—and maybe some of what has been taken for schizophrenia's heritability is *Toxoplasma*'s transmission pattern in disguise. Schizophrenia is, for unclear reasons, more common in crowded, poor households. So is toxoplasmosis. Finally, some toxoplasmosis patients develop psychotic symptoms, and—even when psychotic symptoms are absent—antipsychotic drugs designed to treat mental illness have proved curiously effective in fighting the spreading parasite before it goes into its dormant mode.

Many toxoplasmosis researchers find the schizophrenia theories at least intriguing. However, there are counterarguments. While schizophrenia is thought to be more common among those who grew up in cities, toxoplasmosis may be more widespread in rural areas. Countries with sky-high toxoplasmosis rates, like Ethiopia, France, and Brazil, don't have elevated schizophrenia rates. Likewise, despite all of the new cats trotting around, the rate of toxoplasmosis infection has fallen recently in some parts of the developed world, including the United States, perhaps because of meat freezing and improved farming practices—yet schizophrenia diagnoses haven't dropped.

The evidence is tough to tease apart in part because toxoplasmosis is so universal. Some of the maddening inconsistencies in data, Yolken and Torrey say, could be resolved by better diagnostic tools, which identify the parasite's strain (some are far more virulent than others) or its precise whereabouts in the body (a liver cyst is likely less relevant than a brain cyst, in terms of neurological consequences).

Perhaps most important, toxoplasmosis tests don't reveal when the infection occurred. Schizophrenia typically surfaces in young adulthood, and Yolken and Torrey think that the parasite could be particularly damaging to developing brains—not only in fetuses, but also babies and little children. (Mice infected at four weeks of age have very different outcomes from those infected at nine weeks, for instance.) They are increasingly focused on early childhood acquisition.

Of course, it's also possible that the toxoplasmosis researchers' thinking is as compromised as their lab rats'—because Torrey, Dubey, Flegr, and other stars of the field are themselves infected with *Toxoplasma*, and they know it. Even if parasitic manipulation doesn't steer their research, observer bias might. At a certain point, viewing human life through the lens of a cat-poop parasite risks becoming pathological.

For me, it took not one but two negative blood tests before I bid adieu to the idea that a microorganism had suckered me into reclining with lions.

Even now, truth be told, I'm not totally convinced. As Yolken and Torrey say, the blood tests can be inaccurate.

Some neurologists worry that hyped-up toxoplasmosis research misinforms not only carried-away cat owners, but the seriously ill as well. "The toxoplasmosis-schizophrenia link is very tenuous," says Anita Koshy, a University of Arizona *Toxoplasma* researcher who also treats patients. "And it really is heartbreaking. Schizophrenia is such a terrible disease and I feel like you are throwing out false hope."

᷿

Meanwhile, new toxo theories keep hatching. A recent op-ed suggested that particular countries, like Brazil, owe their distinct machismo culture and World Cup prowess to high rates of male infection. (In soccer, heightened risk taking and aggression are good.)

Or maybe the parasite shaped all human cultures, period, via the first great civilization.

As everyone knows, the ancient Egyptians kept lots of house cats, and in fact bred them on an industrial scale. Not surprisingly, *Toxoplasma* is a major problem in modern Egypt—in fact, Torrey and Fuller recently participated in a study there, and are particularly interested in the threat of toxo-contaminated Nile River water.

Now, a young Stanford University researcher named Patrick House is hunting for the parasite in Egyptian mummies—specifically, bargain-basement Egyptian mummies in which lazy embalmers left the brains. "I have collected a list of every mummy in every museum that I know of," he says. "I have an Excel spreadsheet."

Assuming he can find the parasite, he wants to learn whether it was widespread in ancient populations, which strains people carried, and how those strains evolved. Whether a toxoplasmosis epidemic might have influenced the behavior of ancient Egyptians is fascinating to ponder. "To me, it could sort of rewrite the history of humanity," House says.

At first, the whole project strikes me as rather farfetched—crazy, even.

But then I learn that another scientific team, probing millennia-old mummy flesh, has already identified *Toxoplasma*.

Chapter 7

PANDORA'S LITTER BOX

P RINCE PERCY DOVETONSILS was an operatic Siamese, yowling arias while his breakfast was served as if to show appreciation for the food. During his seventeen years as a family pet—a period that spanned nearly my entire childhood—Percy eagerly followed our gazes with his slightly crossed, sky-blue eyes, hogged our laps whenever possible, and hovered near the door if we left the house.

Everybody knows a cat like that, who seems to love his home life and his humans. Such cats are often said to "act like dogs." But then there are the many cats that act like cats: elusive and beguiling—or neurotic and bizarre.

Take my sister's Fiona, who spends the daylight hours hidden among shoeboxes beneath the bed, in a tiny hollow formally known as "Fiona's office."

Or the still half-wild Annie, who vomits at the slightest change in daily routine, causing my mother to follow her around with a special barf spatula.

Or my own beloved Cheetoh, who is apt to sink his fangs into the flesh of honored houseguests, particularly if they try to pet him.

We've seen that house cats can thrive in the cruelest wildernesses. But how do these exquisite predators fare as pets amid the comforts of our homes? What do we know about the inner lives of these interior animals, their relationships with us, and their experience of our shared environment? Do they like to be cleansed with tearless kitten shampoo? Do they enjoy their dinners of free-range chicken with cheese, papaya, and kelp? And is cohabitation good for either of our species?

The truth is that cats' pampered persistence within our flat, painted walls is an evolutionary feat just as radical as their survival on wind-raked subantarctic isles and volcano cones. And if house cats do indeed drive some humans crazy, perhaps the problem is mutual.

It's the soul of this cloistered modern creature that I go searching for at the Global Pet Expo, held in a vast windowless Orlando convention center that is about as deep indoors as it gets. Wandering the endless cat product aisles of the $58 billion pet industry's biggest trade show, I examine cat nail tips in gothic black, cat dental picks, and cat strollers with quick-release tires. I learn that pumpkin is a natural hairball remedy, that silver vine is the new catnip, and that there's a "novelty protein" craze in cat food that should perhaps worry the world's buffalo and kangaroos. Every now and then, I politely decline samples of human-grade cat food. I pause to watch a grown man test the strength of a sequoia-like cat tree by climbing to the top of it, raising his arms in victory as the crowd roars.

Not long ago, cats didn't really have any "products," let alone forests of fake trees and handcrafted teepees and oatmeal sunscreen. They mostly made do with medications developed for dogs, and even basic items like cat carriers were scarce—a feline in need of restraint might be stuffed into an old boot. Commercial dog food was invented in the 1860s, but commercial cat food remained a tough sell until after World War II: it was assumed, with excellent reason, that cats could feed themselves.

As late as the 1960s, cat food and cat toys and cat everything else accounted for an astoundingly low 8 percent of the pet product market, lagging far behind not just dogs (40 percent) but also their ancient antagonists, the birds (16.5 percent) and even lesser prey species like reptiles and small mammals.

Today, though, cats have staked a huge market share and are gaining ground on the front-running canines. Americans now spend $6.6 billion on cat food alone every year, and even kitty litter is a $2 billion category.

What changed? Cat diapers and cat energy drinks with green tea extract and soothing purr pillows are all quite impressive innovations. But none of them would exist without the invention of the indoor cat.

Keeping cats indoors exclusively is a very recent arrangement. In his classic 1920 treatise on house cats, *The Tiger in the House*, Carl Van Vechten describes a fluid and often al fresco feline lifestyle that, not quite a century ago, was customary even in downtown Manhattan. "Persian pussies have been known to leave the silks and satins of the drawing-room for the free life of the rooftop," he writes. "A common tom cat, living on the domestic hearth, on the best of footing with the family, visits the rooftops and the fences, [becoming] a leading figure at prize-fights."

But today, over 60 percent of the American-owned cat population spends every waking moment inside, and millions of additional pet cats are indoors for the majority of their time, or at least at night. The change to a life lived beneath, as opposed to on top of, our rooftops transpired over just the last fifty years or so, driven at first by urbanization and enabled by neutering (intact tomcats and caterwauling females aren't very considerate roommates). As our own species retreated from the conquered natural world into cities, and then into the skies on ever-higher floors, many cats tagged along.

From the point of view of the individual indoor cat, the move indoors was a challenge, because it usually deprived them of the chance to do what they do best: have sex and hunt. But from the perspective of species-wide world conquest, coming inside was a brilliant stratagem. Though they account for a small proportion of cats worldwide, inside cats are vital ambassadors for their kind. Without indoor diplomacy, alley cats would probably not have so many human Allies, and, politically speaking, it would be a lot easier to purge fragile ecosystems of felines. Certainly, the modern cat craze would not be in full swing.

In nature and on its margins, felines are unseen animals. Only when trapped inside is the house cat transformed from a capricious presence into a true pet, with its elegant lethargy and splendid insolence and many de-lightful hidden habits suddenly on display around the clock. In the confines of the home, humanity's long-standing admiration for these creatures soon becomes something more obsessive. We go gaga. And the latest studies suggest that owners likely keep cats indoors neither to safeguard the neigh-borhood wildlife nor to protect their households from toxoplasmosis, but to shield their darling cats, which could otherwise fall prey to raccoons or Cadillacs.

This obsessive love, of course, costs cats not only their gonads and (sometimes) their claws, but often their dignity as well. As the door shuts or the elevator ascends, these apex predators become the purest depen-dents, needing us for everything: somewhere to poop, and something to do, and many, many things to eat.

At the Global Pet Expo, house cats are often billed not as archkillers but as cute, incompetent slackers whacked out on catnip bananas and whitefish-and-mint Meowjitos. The cat flap section is downright sad. In-stead of being portals to the green glory of the backyard, these tiny doors increasingly lead only to the basement litter box.

Yet maybe here, at last, in the intense bond that owners forge with their pets, it's finally humanity's turn to get something significant out of our millennia-old alliance with cats. Maybe the pleasure these cats afford us finally justifies our mysterious feline fixation.

The American Pet Products Association might like us to think so. The trade group has recently begun funding the research field known as human-animal interaction, the formal study of how people and their crit-ters influence one another. The business leaders have even founded a non-profit research organization to quantify the rewards of owning companion animals, and to promote pets "as a beneficial factor in human and animal health." Science isn't really supposed to take sides, but the emphasis here is stoutly positive: "Pets Make Us Happy," the group's website declares. "Pets Are Good for Us."

The science nonprofit is, at the time of the Expo, in the process of awarding its inaugural research grants, but I am disappointed to later learn that four out of five of these go to the dogs. (Canine studies is a rather overcrowded field these days, in part because the US government and other groups continue to look for useful new ways to harness these exceedingly handy animals.) The fifth grant goes to horse therapy. And so would-be investigators of America's most popular pet are left empty-handed.

But, as it turns out, a few scholars have already scrutinized human-cat affairs in the close quarters of the home—and their findings aren't always warm and fuzzy.

The father of human–house cat research is an American biologist named Dennis Turner. He began his scientific career in the 1970s with a very different animal subject: the vampire bat, studying the bat's "blood source selection" and other habits in the jungles of Costa Rica. Several times Turner was selected as a blood source himself, and after a bite from a rabid vampire, was subjected to the infamous series of 21 vaccination shots to save his life.

Perhaps this dicey fieldwork informed Turner's decision to study a cuddlier creature. Once back in the safety of his own living room, he contemplated switching to a variety of animals and at one point even entertained an offer to lead the famous Serengeti Lion Project.

"Exactly in the moment when I was considering taking over the Lion Project," Turner recalls, "my house cat came out from under the table and meowed. I jokingly said to her, 'You'll be my lion.' And then it clicked."

A few scientists were already investigating cats' outdoor roaming and hunting habits. But Turner was more interested in our increasingly intimate, and indoor, interspecies relationship. There was much to ponder: Do thermoregulatory problems explain why certain cats flee our laps? Does owner gender shape the play dynamic? He published papers with intriguing if oblique titles like "Spouses and Cats and Their Effects on Human Mood."

Several other labs around the world followed in Turner's footsteps, and soon lucky graduate students were rigorously petting kittens for their research projects. Their collective efforts now make up a small yet lively body of literature: as part of one recent study, researchers placed "a plush owlet with large glass eyes" on the floor of a home and watched the resident cats' reactions, recording behaviors such as lick lips and tail undulations and "events," including cats running at a "gallop" and "cat's eyes stretched open more widely than normal ('bug-eyed')."

Happily, the cat scientists' exertions converged with the brand-new, but expanding, human-animal interaction research field. As agriculture and animal husbandry fade from daily life, it's only natural to try and fathom our deepening relationships with those new beasts of emotional burden, household pets. And being self-interested creatures, humans have become especially interested in the quantifiable impacts that pets have on our health.

The groundbreaking study in this area was published in 1980, when a researcher named Erika Friedmann tracked factors influencing heart attack survival, and found that 94 percent of pet-owning patients survived the following year, while just 72 percent of nonpet owners lived. The resulting mantra that "pets are good for us" has since become entrenched. In his book *The Healing Power of Pets*, celebrity veterinarian and frequent *Today* show guest Marty Becker sums up the view this way: "A pet can be a miracle drug that keeps you healthier; home instead of hospitalized; reduc[ing] your risk of heart attacks . . . with the lick of a tongue, wag of a tail or rhythmic purring . . . and not for a fortune, but at the price of a can of Fancy Feast or Friskies."

When I meet with Alan Beck, a Purdue University animal ecologist who is helping to oversee the pet industry's new scientific endeavors, I've just finished reading a research summary entitled "The Attachment to Goats: Implications for Human Well-Being." ("When my favorite goat died, it was more of a loss than when my mother died," one study subject reported.) I know Beck himself has studied guinea pigs and autism, aquariums and Alzheimer's, and something to do with Clydesdales. I order a large coffee and brace myself for an onslaught of giddy feline findings. So when I ask him how cats are good for us, I am surprised to hear instead a long pause.

"As soon as you start bad-mouthing any one species or any one breed," he says, "and believe me, I've had that experience with pit bulls, you start getting into trouble. But—"

And now my ears really prick up.

"But the truth of the matter is there is less evidence for the health benefits of cats."

This isn't because people don't like cats, he hastens to assure me. "I just don't think people are using cats in a way that would lend itself to therapeutic outcomes."

The formal practice of cat therapy does indeed exist; trained "comfort cats" have been dispatched for petting during final exams at Pacific Lutheran University and other colleges, for instance. But it has clear limits. Lots of people—almost 20 percent, according to one survey—just don't like cats, clinical-grade cat phobias are surprisingly common, and studies suggest that cats occasionally seek to canoodle with people who hate them. (Much formal cat therapy seems to take place in prisons, where presumably neither party can get out of it.) Thus, feline healers can very quickly prove counterproductive.

But even for enthralled pet owners, cats don't seem to yield the health benefits that the "pets are good for us" mantra would suggest. Quite the contrary. When Erika Friedmann repeated her heart attack study in 1995, paying more attention to the type of pet owned than to pet ownership in general, she confirmed that dog ownership did indeed boost patients' survival rates—but cat ownership slightly lowered them. A more recent follow-up by another group pegged cats as a considerable cardiac liability: compared to dog ownership, or even having no pets at all, cat ownership was "significantly associated with increased risk of death or readmission," the authors write.

Other researchers have published similarly morbid results. While an American study of Medicaid records showed that dog owners visited the doctor less frequently, suggesting they had better health, cat owners saw doctors just as often as everybody else. Then a Dutch study concluded that cat owners more commonly sought out certain types of health care— namely, mental health care. Another group of scientists found that cat owners had higher blood pressure. A particularly damning Norwegian study confirmed the higher blood pressure, and also indicated that cat owners were heavier and reported poorer overall health.

"The lower the frequency of exercising, the more likely the person is a cat owner," the Norwegian authors warn. Noting the rising rates of European cat ownership, they call for further scientific surveillance of cat owners, to determine if "the cat keeps them indoors, with poorer health as an outcome."

Do indoor cats really corral their enraptured humans, cuddling us up until our weight balloons and our blood pressure surges? Is cardiac arrest the true return on that "can of Fancy Feast or Friskies" that Marty Becker mentions? These findings chilled my own cat-loving heart a little, so I was pleased to learn of several less sinister explanations for what's going on. The ritual of dog-walking alone accounts for some of the health differences between cat and dog owners: one study suggests that dog owners are 64 percent more likely than nonpet owners to do at least some walking, while cat owners walk 9 percent less than even the petless. Cat owners may also be a self-selecting group, less inclined to walk or dealing with preexisting health problems, which is perhaps why they chose a cat instead of a dog in the first place.

There's still another possibility: the extra exercise aside, dog owners may reap healthy social benefits from the fellow humans they encounter in the dog park and on the sidewalk. Cat ownership, on the other hand, doesn't exactly lend itself to frequent forays into public life.

That said, some of the experiments controlled for at least some of these variables, and there may yet be a fundamental difference in how dogs and cats influence people. "It's called social support theory," Beck says. "We want to be with other people, we feel less lonely, we find comfort in touch, we use each other to stay in the moment, and we also do this with our pets. Unfortunately we do this more with dogs than cats." In an age of family breakdown, geographic isolation, and general ennui, dogs seem to be a better substitute for the human presence.

Many cat owners will of course bristle at this criticism, and understandably so. I can myself recall many instances of being comforted by cats: when moving away from home after college, for instance, I took along a plump family pet named Coby, whom I would clutch all night, like a living teddy bear. (Though the more I reflect on this memory, the less comforting it becomes: in the bleak environment of my first apartment, Coby soon became despondent and began losing weight until I was forced to surrender him to my mother.)

Perhaps part of the problem is that even with pet cats cornered in our homes, we still have far more contact with our dogs. One study indicated that just 7 percent of pet owners spend all day with their cats, while half hang out with their dogs around the clock. Another revealed that, in 210 minutes of observation, cats and humans came within a meter of each other for just 6 minutes, and mutual exchanges were likely to last less than one minute. In a Japanese study, scientists showed, via analysis of feline ear twitching, that cats do in fact recognize their owners' voices, but simply choose not to respond to our calls.

And when they do approach, cats don't tend to relate to us in a human-like fashion. Recently, the British veterinarian Daniel Mills attempted to replicate a classic series of 1970s-era experiments meant to test children's attachment to parents—only instead of children and parents, he used cats and their owners. He'd already done the test with dogs, which behaved very much like human children, looking for reassurance and avoiding strangers as they explored a new room. When we spoke, Mills had yet to publish his feline findings, but someone had found his experimental video footage shocking enough to "leak" it, which is how it became an Internet sensation. In one video, the cat not only appears not to give a fig when the owner leaves the room, but elaborately snubs her and romances a stranger. Mills concluded that cats in a strange environment don't look to their owners for safety as dogs do, and play happily with random people.

The study "generated a lot of hate mail for me," Mill says. But "I have no problem saying that when it comes to safety and security, cats aren't attached to us."

Like so many feline matters, cats' interaction style, or lack thereof, comes down to protein and its procurement. And again, the best way to understand this deficit is in contrast with dogs. Reformed wolves, dogs evolved as social hunters. Their survival depended on working together to bring down game. Communication and cooperation are as much part of the dogs' survival arsenal as their teeth. Humans come from more or less the same evolutionary school, shaped by group living. Over tens of thousands of years together we may even have coevolved with dogs: Japanese researchers recently suggested that, while wolves avoid direct eye contact, dogs adopted humanity's intense eye-contact style during their long-ago domestication phase. Gazing eventually became such a key part of our mutual language that when a dog locks eyes with its owner, it is rewarded with a jolt of oxytocin, and the owner likewise receives a shot of the pleasure hormone for returning the look. (Human parents bond with their children in a similar manner.) Dogs and humans thus became "social partners." And today, after millennia of artificial selection and constant human dependence, there's no question that dogs are more attuned to our presence and personal cues than ever before. At the Global Pet Expo, I saw a machine that could remotely emit a whiff from an absent dog owner's sock drawer, which dogs apparently appreciate just as much as a treat.

But cats, as we've seen, are consummate loners. Almost all wild cats live and hunt solo, plying a tract of land that is exclusively theirs, only rarely meeting members of their own species. Cooperation of any sort is more or less impossible—even group-living lions don't really work in concert when they hunt—and status hierarchies simply don't apply. As nature's recluses, cats never evolved expressive skills, because there were no other cats around to read them—thus the cat family's trademark deadpan look. Cats don't wag their tails, cock their ears, or make puppy eyes, nor can they interpret such signs. Cats' few clear visual cues are typically delivered only in life-or-death moments, when they arch their backs and puff up like blowfish. Nor do cats, as ambush predators reliant on stealth, make much use of vocal signals. The cat's main communicative medium is pheromones, pungent messages that can be dispatched or received without any kind of unwelcome face time.

In short, house cats' communication style makes them almost uniquely ill-equipped to furnish the social give-and-take that humans desire. Cats crave space, not company, and protein, not praise. Humans and cats are a biological odd couple.

"Cats seem to have little or no instinctive appreciation either of how humans behave or the best ways to interact with them," the cat behaviorist

John Bradshaw points out in his book, *Cat Sense*. "An affectionate relationship with people is not most cats' main reason for living."

None of this stops humans, compulsive communicators that we are, from doing our best to read into these inscrutable animals, which is perhaps why scientists wind up writing conference papers with titles like "Affective Attitudes of Children and Adults in Relation to the Pupil Diameter of a Cat: Preliminary Data." Even to distinguished cat behaviorists like Bradshaw, a feline activity like leg rubbing poses an enduring mystery. "Despite years of research," Bradshaw laments, "I am still uncertain whether there is any significance in which part of the body the cat uses to rub."

In fairness to cats, there is some evidence that they make a good-faith effort to reach us through their limited, scent-based expressive repertoire, by spraying urine or spelling out subtler messages on our legs, using glands on their faces and rear ends. But humans are often too obtuse to register these clues: in fact, our sense of smell is notably dull. (In one study, cat owners could not even pick their own cats out of a lineup based on their odor, let alone register a smell's deeper significance.)

The mutual failure to communicate puts indoor cats in a precarious position, since once sealed in our homes they have no way to survive without human patronage. To complicate matters, due to what Bradshaw describes as their "weakness in social skills," cats are almost impervious to punishment, fixated on food exclusively as a reward, and so are very tough to train. We can't teach them our ways.

Which is where cat-human interaction studies take a fascinating turn: as they so often have in their relationship with humanity, cats take the initiative and tame us. Trapped in a house and with no other recourse, every pet cat sets about the daunting task of bringing its thick-skulled human to heel. Since this chore is well beyond the scope of normal feline (anti-) social life, the cat must more or less start from scratch, performing what amounts to a set of tests on human subjects. Indeed, it turns out that what we think of as cats' affection or love for us is not only not unconditional, it is actively conditioning. Cats are the experimental architects; we are Pavlov's dogs.

Some of this is obvious and even delightful to cat lovers. "Honeybun is the biggest love-mush," says an owner quoted in one study. "She demands affection and will actually 'hit' people with her paw to get them to pet her or keep petting her." But we are oblivious to much of the taming process.

Many cats somehow figure out, for instance, that humans respond well to sound. Take the pleasing trill of a purr. Among cats, this tonal buzzing in the vocal folds has no fixed significance—it can mean anything from "I am happy" to "I am about to die." But to humans the sound is welcome and even rather flattering. So within our earshot, many cats apparently rejigger their purposeless purr to include a barely audible, very annoying, and insistent signal, a cry—usually for food—that resembles a baby's wail. "The embedding of a cry within a call that we normally associate with contentment is quite a subtle means of eliciting a response," purr researcher Karen Mc-Comb has said. She described this "solicitation purr," which people register subconsciously, as "less harmonic and thus more difficult to habituate to," and claimed that cats increase the behavior when they realize it gets results.

Meowing can be similarly manipulative. In nature, this seldom-used call is not terribly meaningful, yet many owners are correct to interpret their own cats' meows as specific commands. For not only do pet cats meow more often—and more sweetly—than feral and wild cats, but within a given household, a cat devises a unique language of meows to instruct its owner. These cues are unique and don't translate across homes—an owner can heed his cat's specific directives, but not necessarily the cat next door's. Rather than "learning a common rule," one study suggests, "classification of cat meows is dependent on learning an individual cat's vocalizations." As usual, the human, not the cat, is the one taking notes.

With our hypercommunicative hardwiring, humans are prime targets for such exploitation. One investigation even showed, via functional magnetic resonance imaging, that the blood-flow patterns of our brains change with the tenor of the feline voice.

If formal analyses of human life under the feline influence remain rare, we know even less about our pets' private experience. It appears that, as usual, these asocial hypercarnivores do their darnedest to navigate the new circumstances, deploying various ingenious survival strategies to get by. For instance, house cats can relinquish their nocturnal lifestyle to match their owners' circadian rhythms. They make do with a territory that's one ten-thousandth the size of some of their feral brethren's. They renounce mating. And, for the most part, they give up killing, the pastime that defines every fiber of the feline being.

But is it enough? As Bradshaw points out, members of the cat family make notoriously poor prisoners—in zoos, only bears, another solitary carnivore, are as miserable. While big cats pace, house cats engage in what is called "apathetic resting," a description that strikes a chord: I picture Cheetoh's orange hulk beached on the bed for hours. How else is a matchless killer supposed to amuse himself? Indoor cats have been shown to interact more with their owners, presumably because there are few alternatives, but there's also a rather haunting study entitled "Caregiver Perceptions of What Indoor Cats Do 'For Fun.'" Apparently more than 80 percent of our cats spend up to five hours a day staring out the window—at wind chimes, butterflies, or sometimes "nothing" at all.

It's not just that our comfortable homes may be dull. There are elements that, to these high-strung, half-domesticated hunters, may be stressful in ways that humans can only begin to imagine. Apparently our refrigerators, computers, and other gadgets emit awful high-frequency sounds that cats must somehow endure—at the Global Pet Expo I met a woman who had composed a cat "symphony," heavy on flutes and harps, to disguise the cacophony. Household dust and certain toxins, especially secondhand smoke, can make cats ill with asthma and worse. And our holidays are no cause for feline celebration—we introduce poisonous Easter lilies, detonate deafening fireworks, and light menorahs that may subsequently ignite curious furry onlookers.

For some cats, though, our homes' most distasteful aspect is doubtless the other tenants.

Most cat-owning households have more than one cat, while dogs, who would actually appreciate the company, are more likely to be single pets. Cats, by design, typically loathe members of their own kind and wouldn't willingly share even miles of territory, but confusing feline solitude with loneliness, we perversely insist on crowding in more armed-to-the-teeth apex predators to cuddle with the first. Many cats interpret direct eye contact as a threat and literally can't even stand to look at each other: according to one study, cats in a household stay fastidiously out of each other's sight 50 percent of the time, though often they are no more than a few feet apart.

Of course, cats are also remarkably adaptable creatures, and we've all experienced or seen videos of cats "making friends" with each other, and with dogs, and even with hamsters. But these scenarios are intriguing in large part because they are exceptional.

And while some cats also seem partial to people in a proprietary sort of way, others are literally allergic to us, wheezing and sneezing, and even those that can tolerate our dandruff may find our companionship abhorrent. Some house cats, in addition to avoiding their fellow felines' stares, don't like humans to lock eyes with them either. Others may despise being petted. Studying stress by measuring cortisol levels in cat feces, researchers found that—despite the indignity of sharing territory—some timid cats actually seemed to fare better in multicat households, perhaps because the other cats bore the brunt of the owner's caresses.

Not surprisingly, then, indoor cats can develop the kind of behavioral problems that keep shows like *My Cat From Hell* in business. One phenomenon, known as "redirected aggression," flares up when something—anything, really—annoys a cat and it takes out its frustration on nearby humans. "For example, if two family cats have a spat, the losing cat, still aroused, may walk up and attack the family child," one animal welfare website explains.

Perhaps the most famous feline assailant of recent years was an unhinged Himalayan named Luxe who bit a seven-month-old baby in Seattle and then chased his entire family into a bedroom, where they dialed 911. An audio clip from the call went viral online.

"Do you think the cat will try to attack the police?" the emergency dispatcher asks.

"Yes," Luxe's owner replies unequivocally, while his 22-pound pet caterwauls in the background.

In 2008, a *New York Times* article about pet antidepressants introduced a cat named Booboo, described by his owner as "a cougar psycho little miniature stalker." Largely through violence, Booboo had conditioned his owner, Doug—a wealthy businessman who wouldn't give his last name because of possible professional repercussions—to wash his hands, and sometimes cleanse his entire body, if he'd had physical contact with another human, particularly any woman wearing perfume.

It was not enough. As the scratching, biting assaults intensified, Doug resorted to wearing pants "that he had lined with heavy-gauge ballistic nylon."

Abusive Booboo and Luxe may be extreme cases, but feline deviance is by no means unusual. Other well-publicized, gone-postal pet cats have had to be fended off with vacuums or doused with cups of tea. According to one study, nearly half of cats have been known to turn claws and teeth on their owners (imagine if dogs did the same), with cat wrath "most commonly associated with situations involving petting and play." Besides "petting intolerance," other environmental triggers include neuter status, access to the outside, the presence of visitors in a home, the presence of another cat, environmental lead levels, high-pitched noises, unusual odors—the list goes on. A study entitled "Reported Cat Bites in Dallas: Characteristics of the Cats, the Victims, and the Attack Events" determined that the typical victim is a woman between the ages of 21 and 35 on a summer morning. Many of the documented bites were from strays, but household pets tended to do more damage: indoor cat bites were more likely to be "delivered to the face or to multiple locations," and more likely to send the victim to an emergency room.

Along with anger management problems, other new indoor pathologies include the so-called Tom and Jerry syndrome, a mysterious epilepsy-like condition that has lately surfaced in England. Characterized by furniture collisions and convulsions, the bizarre cat behavior is almost always triggered by ordinary domestic sounds, including the crinkling of "newspapers and crisps packets," according to one account, as well as "the clicking of a computer mouse," "the popping of pills from blister packs," "the hammering of nails," and "the sounds of owners slapping their foreheads."

In cities there's also high-rise syndrome, in which house cats plum-
met from the upper floors of skyscrapers (and, being cats, often survive
the plunge of a dozen stories or more). Pent up in the penthouse, some
of these cats become so stupefied with boredom that they just fall out the
window by mistake. (In other cases, they are trying to land a longingly contemplated pigeon.)

But the most serious disease of feline modernity is feline idiopathic
cystitis—or as it's sometimes called, Pandora syndrome.

Pandora syndrome's key symptom is bloody or painful urination, often
outside the litter box. It's an exceedingly common and expensive problem,
usually ranked as a top veterinary insurance claim. Sometimes outbreaks
occur across whole cities. According to Tony Buffington, an Ohio State
University veterinarian who has devoted his career to studying the ailment,
it was long a leading cause of feline death. The sickness itself was not fatal,
but millions of owners—tired of urine-stained carpets and despairing of a
cure—put their Pandora-ridden pets to sleep.

In addition to the telltale litter box problems, feline idiopathic cystitis
is linked with a whole suite of gastrointestinal, dermatologic, and neurological issues. Hence the "Pandora": once you crack open a case, infinite
maladies emerge. "Lung signs, skin signs, all these kind of vague things,"
Buffington says.

When Buffington set out to study Pandora syndrome, "I was thinking it was a lower urinary tract disease, just like everyone else," he recalls.
He began amassing afflicted cats, who were not at all hard to find. One of
his first recruits was a splotchy Persian named Tiger, bestowed on him by
his own barber. He ensconced Tiger and the others in a spartan research
colony—each cat got a meter-wide cage, basic meals fed by the same person at the same times each day, and regular access to a communal hallway
full of toys.

And then, as Buffington set about trying to figure out how on earth to
study this baffling disease, something remarkable happened.

"The cats all got better," he says.

After about six months in the colony, not only did the study cats' urinary problems resolve, but so did their entire laundry list of respiratory and other symptoms. The full-of-wonder way in which Buffington describes this turn of events reminded me of *Awakenings*, the Oliver Sacks memoir about catatonic patients restored to life by an experimental drug—only in this case there was no drug. The health and behavioral changes in Buffington's cats were permanent as long as they remained in the research colony, and the formerly incorrigible Tiger became such a lovely pet that Buffington could not bear to kill and dissect her as he had planned. She lived out the rest of her days in the colony.

Quite by accident, Buffington had stumbled upon a cure and, by extension, a cause. Our homes had been making the animals sick. "The treatment is to improve the environment," he says.

Looking through the literature, Buffington noticed that the disease had sometimes been linked to indoor living—way back in 1925, one veterinarian blamed certain urinary problems on "too close confinement to the house." Seen in this light, suddenly the epidemic nature of the sickness made sense. Hard-hit areas, like the United Kingdom in the 1970s and Buenos Aires in the 1990s (when a desperate Argentinian cat food company contacted Buffington after pet owners blamed the food for an outbreak), are often undergoing swift urbanization, with migrants becoming apartment dwellers and their cats transitioning to life as total shut-ins.

For cats, the allure of the lost outdoors is painfully obvious. But Buffington didn't cure his research subjects by letting them hunt songbirds or prowl gardens. Could his colony's no-frills research cages—though obviously more peaceful than, say, the cages at your average animal shelter—really be more appealing than our lavish living rooms?

Apparently so. "We found that the things that mattered most to cats were consistency and predictability," Buffington says. Indoor cats are apex predators without a pyramid, and territorial overlords without territory. But in his own cage, safe from rivals, unexpected noises, unwanted eye contact, and us, every cat is what he was born to be: a king.

To heal our house pets, Buffington argues, we must find ways to restore them to their rightful station. For starters, we must grasp that cats are not the pets of convenience that humans believe them to be. It may seem like they can ride out the long weekend alone with a scattering of Meow Mix, but cats prefer that we not come and go as we please, and that we instead adhere to a strict schedule like trained butlers. And, especially for confined cats, strict means strict: not a generic "evening" feeding, Buffington suggests, but a rigid deference to the dinner hour. "If you are going to feed cats at 8 p.m., then you don't feed them at 6 p.m. or 10 p.m." An owner's grace period is more like 15 minutes either way, or cats may get fractious.

Cats also need a sense of physical control. Ironically, the stricken cats that Buffington acquired tended to come from the most adoring owners, more inclined to rack up massive vet bills than discreetly dump a problem animal. But sometimes the most affectionate people are also the most meddlesome. "They want to pet the cat, so they drag it from under the bed, hug it, try to show their love, and the cat is likely to feel threatened," Buffington says. He believes that stressed cats end up conceiving of us as outlandish predators, presumably toying with them extensively before we settle down to eat.

"I don't think I have ever met an owner who has set out to consciously abuse a cat," Buffington says, "but there are lots of people who screw up a relationship with family members as well, without ever meaning to."

Luckily, as many better-adjusted indoor cats have figured out, humans can be taught how to behave. To this end, Buffington has launched an online project called the Indoor Cat Initiative to diagnose and remedy owners' many flaws. Determining what exactly is driving your cat crazy is no small task. "It's just like Tolstoy's unhappy families—cats are unhappy for a thousand reasons," he says. "We have to think about the issues that the cat is facing, and it could be anything."

One of the first steps toward atonement is the raw concession of territory. Buffington suggests that each cat in a household be given an entire room for its exclusive use. This core domain should be rich in resources like food, water, and soft, restful substrates, but free from people and other cats. Borrowing from the language of beleaguered big cats, Buffington calls this cat-only room "a refuge."

Some owners apparently arrive at this solution on their own, perhaps by necessity. Doug, he of the structurally reinforced khakis, eventually yielded his master bedroom to the ruthless Booboo. "The 400-square-foot room had a walk-in closet, a four-poster bed and a floor-to-ceiling view of Beverly Hills mansions dotting a scenic canyon," the *Times* reported. "The suite belonged entirely to Booboo, though Doug said he was now able to sleep over a few nights a week."

However, many even more enlightened owners go much further, revamping their whole houses—or, as some feline aficionados prefer to call them, "habitats." Buffington (whose most recent book is entitled *Your Home, Their Territory*) and other cat experts offer various (and sometimes contradictory) pointers on how best to pursue a policy of complete feline appeasement.

First, dim the household lights, because cats don't like brightness. Crank up the thermostat—most cats prefer the temperature to be above a toasty 85 degrees. Consult a decibel reader to be sure that your booming human voice does not rise above a quiet conversational level. Purge "potentially objectionable odors," which obviously emanate from dogs and other inferior life-forms, but also from "alcohol (from hand rubs), cigarettes, cleaning chemicals (including laundry detergent but not bleach, they seem to like this odor), some perfumes, and citrus scents." Instead, you can mist your house with Feliway, a feline pheromone.

If you've foolishly become fond of any of your furniture, reupholster it in tinfoil, double-sided tape or another scratch-proof material. (The controversial option of declawing a cat is, from a cat whisperer's perspective, obviously a nonstarter.) Then, try not to ever move said furniture: cats find redecorating to be stressful.

If you must have a human baby, be sure to rub your own body with baby oils, lotions, and other products well in advance so the cat can acclimate to new and potentially repulsive smells—one animal welfare website suggests borrowing somebody's actual infant for a test run. Temporary houseguests are entirely unwelcome: perhaps knowing that your dinner party is "confusing and frightening" for your cat will prevent you from throwing one.

Understand, too, that what soothes one cat can provoke another. John Bradshaw writes of a cat that was a complete nutcase until his owner blocked off household windows, so the cat was free from the prying gaze of a garden-dwelling rival. But other cats get so attached to particular window vistas that seasonal change may upset them—should bustling fall become boring winter, for instance, consider setting up a fish tank, or devoting your big screen to a loop of high-definition cat DVDs with names like *Cat Dreams*, which are essentially prey porn. Buffington also stresses the importance of identifying your cat's prey preference—bird, bug, or rodent—and populating your home with anatomically correct toys.

And remember, always, that scooping a single household kitty litter box is nowhere near good enough for these possessive little sticklers. Mathematical-sounding laws determine the appropriate litter box numbers: one for every floor of the house, according to some experts; one box for every individual cat, plus one, argue others.

What's most fascinating about this campaign for total domestic capitulation is that it's not just some fringe agenda or academic pipe dream. It is, in widening circles, considered cool.

The best evidence of this is the wild popularity of decorating sites like Kate Benjamin's Hauspanther, which merges cat worship with haute design, and which has made her the standard-bearer for the new trendy cat lady. Before visiting her site, I had the impression that Benjamin's objective was to hide cat hair, mask litter box odors, and otherwise mitigate the hassles of cat ownership in the small yet thoughtfully appointed apartments popular with millennials.

Then I learned that Benjamin actually has thirteen cats. Her blog isn't about mutual solutions, but rather abject surrender to Dazzler, Simba, Ratso, and the rest. Festoon your dining room with cat hammocks! Stack your walls with vertically mounted cat beds! Some of the featured furniture pieces attempt to strike an interspecies balance—for instance, there's a walnut dining table where humans might really and truly dine, but with a stripe of spiky cat grass sprouting up the middle for feline delectation. Or there's an actual couch where you could at least theoretically recline before noticing that it conceals a long cat tunnel. But if you think a piece of furniture is just for human enjoyment, you're sadly mistaken: that modernist French sculpture is, in fact, a scratching post.

Hauspanther's forte, perhaps by necessity, is camouflaged litter boxes, which can double as nightstands and coffee tables. (Benjamin, by my dizzied calculations, needs at least fourteen boxes, and potentially twenty-eight if she inhabits a two-story house.)

In her full-color manifesto for a feline-centric lifestyle philosophy, co-authored with celebrity animal behaviorist Jackson Galaxy, Benjamin calls on cat owners to embrace what she calls Catification.

"Not wanting a litter box in the living room," she and Galaxy write, is not a mere aesthetic choice. It suggests "lack of true empathy toward, and an investment in, *love for* cats"—even a form of "cat shame." Catification, on the other hand, represents "the maturation of us as humans." To learn "the language of cats," to sacrifice our living spaces for their sake, "is a symbol of our evolution." (As a bonus, Jackson—host of *My Cat From Hell*—believes that extreme feline renovations might even deliver nicer cats.)

Aspiring Catifiers should begin on an introspective note. "Every parent has dreams for their children; what are your hopes for your cat?" Benjamin and Galaxy ask. What troubles does she face, and "what would 'stepping into her greatness' look like?" Next, look at your den like it's a lion's den—not a series of love seats and easy chairs, but a network of ambush zones and dead ends, with opportunities for you to build a "cat traffic circle" here and a cat "revolving door" there. The authors are most insistent about the "cat superhighway," a series of elevated platforms and catwalks that allows cats to navigate a space without ever setting foot on the floor. Perhaps you might also flank your entertainment center with climbing walls, or install what look like floor-to-ceiling sisal stripper poles for scratching posts, or wrap your dining table's legs in rope so they, too, become scratchable. Tapping into the hipster love of DIY, there is an emphasis on clever cat hacks, which involve taking a piece of furniture doomed for human consumption—an Ikea shelving unit, say—and turning it into a fabulous cat roost.

Sometimes Benjamin and Galaxy tsk-tsk a little at errant owners, like when Benjamin notices that "Beth and George didn't have a lot of cat-specific things in their home, just a single cat tree in the living room," or when Galaxy criticizes a hand-hewn sculptural masterpiece of a spiral feline staircase because it doesn't connect to a cat superhighway across the top of a cupboard. Again and again, they remind us: "When you think about Catifying your house, the first thing you have to consider is *What is my cat asking for?* And then everything else falls into place."

Sometimes your cat may be asking for you to drill a dozen scratching posts into your ceiling so it can laze overhead, or that you convert your tiny sliver of urban outdoor space into a catio. Your cat may suggest that you remove family photographs and other useless clutter from elevated flat surfaces and install no-slip mats instead so it can leap around like a leopard.

"We wanted to keep the décor in the living room minimalist," explain a pair of owners who erected a Churchill Downs–like "cat racetrack" in their new home. "(We) decided . . . not to hang any art or have bookshelves or other display furniture against the walls. We figured the cats would be our kinetic art installation."

Liath, Arleigh, Arbolina, Stanley, Irmo, Dido, Zaria, Simone, Dark Matter, Lucy, and Yani couldn't agree more.

☙

Of course, given how capably cats can take over a piece of turf, it was only a matter of time before they usurped our homes entirely. And there are indeed places—previews of a brave new world, perhaps—where this domestic seizure is already a fait accompli.

One is the cat café, a novel type of eatery that—in a viral and highly catlike manner—has swept the world over the last fifteen years or so. Cat cafés first emerged in Taiwan, became an absolute sensation in Japan, then Europe, and are at long last invading North America, with the first outposts in California and more cropping up in major cities coast to coast. Designs vary, but interestingly, the original Asian cafés are not laid out to look like cafés, nor feline Shangri-las, but rather like regular old living rooms.

"Highly domestic spaces," the cafés "evoke the feeling and ambience of being in one's apartment, through a carefully staged use of furniture, lighting, reading materials, and background music," according to one ethnographic account. (Luckily, social scientists have undertaken the formal study of these mystifying environments.)

Except, of course, the humans are just passing through: the only legitimate residents are cats, and people line up to pay for a temporary stay. Customers must sometimes read a feline etiquette book upon entering and peruse cat head shots and personality profiles. Only then may they observe such marvelous phenomena as cats being groomed, and cats eating their dinner—apparently this is so soothing that patrons frequently fall asleep on the cats' couches, and the cafés are often full of resonant human snoring. (Waking up a cat is explicitly against etiquette, but protections for passed-out humans are less clear.)

Cat sages might point out that cat cafés aren't perfectly ideal for their residents, given the stinky strangers who think they can just drop in whenever they like expecting petting. But these faux living rooms do illustrate how we have been groomed to delight in the idea of bestowing extravagant resources on cats, kowtowing to and tiptoeing around them, taking pleasure in our own subservience. (In a strange twist on social support theory, café customers apparently relish the shared experience of being snubbed by disdainful cats, a mutual public rejection that—in scholarly terms—becomes "a node or intermediary through which solitary patrons can connect.")

The next step, of course, is clear—living-room-like realms where cats rule completely, and people are banished. At least one such haven already exists. A high-end, long-term boarding and "retirement" facility for cats, the Sunshine Home in rural Honeoye, New York, opened in 2004, has operated at full capacity since 2008, and today fields calls from around the country from copycats interested in the business model.

It's a pretty simple one: life, finances, and time itself revolve completely around cats.

Some of the "retired" cats are not actually that old—though they may have rather savage behavioral problems, or require "an unusually rigorous routine of care," such as one cat with obscure allergies who licked off all of her fur and had to wear a frilly Elizabethan collar. Owners of these animals have bowed out for a few years, or even forever. Some have undertaken research in Antarctica, or secured contract work in Afghanistan. Some have simply died.

"We still don't know what happened to a few of them—they just vanish off the face of the earth," says owner Paul Dewey, who gallantly refers to the ex-owners as "old mommies" and "old daddies."

At the remarkably human rate of $460 a month—or for a much, much larger lump sum if the owner is prepared to cut a check up front for lifetime care—a Sunshine Home resident can enjoy a private room, which rivals many Manhattan studios, with seven-foot ceilings and a huge picture window, through which prey species of all preferences are visible.

Dewey encourages owners to trick out the cat suites with ottomans and futons and other elements from home. "One of our very first boarders replicated her entire living room down to the magazine rack, the lamp, and the La-Z-Boy chair," he says.

Except that now, of course, the furniture is for the cat alone. Old mommies may visit if they like, and for an extra five dollars per month they can set up a special toll-free number to contact their former pets day or night. But to be perfectly honest, Dewey confides, the cats aren't waiting by the phone.

"Some people have trouble making the change," he says, "but the cats always adjust."

Chapter 8

LIONS AND TOYGERS
AND LYKOI

THIS VOLUMINOUS Persian calico is properly known as Grand Champion Belamy's Desiderata of Cinema, but admirers just call her Desi. Whenever she is hauled, blow-dried derriere first, from her cage at the World Cat Show, awed spectators whisper praise: "Her tree-trunk legs! Her cobby body! Her iddy-biddy nose!"

Desi is more or less a series of perfect circles: a spherical torso, a domed head, a pair of tiny round ears, and two O-shaped eyes with acres of space between them. Some other Persians look rather mutinous, but Desi's expression is sweet. There is no guile in her penny-like eyes. She never attacks her prize ribbons. She never feigns sleep in the show ring. In profile, her face is so flat that it appears almost concave, and she occasionally raises it toward the ceiling lights, like a satellite dish searching for a signal.

It takes me a little while to discover Desi among the thousand top cats attending the Cat Fanciers' Association show in Novi, Michigan. (Cat fanciers are the show cats' most ardent human fans, often devoting large portions of their lives to "campaign" favorite felines for national titles.)

Pedigreed kitties from across the globe attend this particular contest: it is the "Super Bowl for Cats," according to one giddy announcer. I want to figure out which cats are in the running to be crowned the Best of the Best, but the show schematic turns out to be more byzantine than anticipated. The competition hall is a maze of booths and rings. There are lilac ribbons and mint rosettes signifying such obscure honors as "14th-best kitten." And what, exactly, is the difference between a Chartreux and a Russian Blue?

"Absolute final call for Balinese 321!" a hoarse voice exclaims over the loudspeaker. "Ring One is still looking for Oriental Shorthair 474 for the Championship Premier Final!"

Rental scooters rush all kinds of breeds—Cornish Rex and bald, sweater-clad Sphynx—to a dozen show rings; billowing Maine coons are carried high overhead, out of sticky-fingered fans' reach.

Not knowing where else to begin my purebred education, I started with the Persians, long considered the stiffest—yet also the fluffiest—competition in the cat fancy universe.

Hanging out with 150 Persians is a bit like standing too close to the cotton candy machine at a county fair—you inhale floating tufts of confectionary fur. The kittens are particularly tempting: I long to pocket one of these little pom-poms with eyes, but alas, for the most part, even petting is forbidden. Many owners have been awake since 3 a.m., degreasing, clarifying, and conditioning cats, blasting high-horsepower blow-dryers, and spritzing bay rum for volume and Evian water for static. (Often, feline grooming comes at the conspicuous expense of the owner's own toilette, and utilitarian "flip-and-clip" accessories for limp human hair are sold at the show alongside deluxe cat shampoos.) Around their necks many of the women wear intricate gold charm necklaces, which advertise past years' wins.

On this momentous day, with one of the cat fancy's most prestigious titles on the line, the Persian people gossip about who has "fur out to here" and which judge doesn't like silvers, while tweezing stray whiskers from their cats' wide English muffin faces. One murderous-looking chocolate, whose coat stands in peaks like black meringue, appears particularly equipped for victory.

And yet, despite all the flying fur and scuttlebutt and alleged suspense, the very first person I ask who will win the top prize answers, without a moment's hesitation: "Oh, the bicolor," which is what the competition calls Desi.

She is absolutely right.

"What a fabulous cat," says a judge a few hours later as she awards Desi the top prize in her division. "I've had the pleasure, the honor, the *opportunity* to see her several times before. I'm in *love* with this cat."

"Look at the coat on this girl," says another. "Little biddy nose. Little biddy ears. Just looking at her makes you want to smile. This is my best cat!"

Even rivals confess that Desi "has the flash" and "lives the standard." The judge who finally crowns her Best of the Best attempts stoicism, but upon hoisting Desi up to eye level and looking at her full in the face, his lips pucker almost reflexively into a kiss.

Desi's private cage is hung with ropes of pearls, a tiny vial of Chanel No. 19 and a sign that says "Good Girls Always Win," but she appears indifferent to these baubles.

"Dumb as a box of rocks," says one of her owners, Connie Stewart, whose eyeglass frames glimmer with a subtle leopard print. Stewart is at pains to be modest, since it is obvious to anyone with eyes that Desi's cream-puff physique and daft expression are the apogee of 100 years of artificial feline selection.

At first glance, show cats appear genuinely estranged from their apex-predator biology, more cartoon than carnivore. Here and there are reminders of these animals' fundamental nature—a baggie of bloody meat beside a pink-canopied cat bed, an owner's forearms partially mummified in bandages—but specimens like Desi seem to offer tentative evidence that humans have at last begun to engineer house cats more to our liking. Perhaps this is how we will finally master these creatures: by breeding them to our will.

Yet research suggests that so-called purebreds, even those who obligingly swallow water through a syringe to protect their elaborate hairdos, are not so very different from street cats, nor are their pedigrees necessarily proof of anything much. The cat fancy is only about a hundred years old, and our tinkering has just begun to touch the genetic trajectories of these animals.

Give us another few centuries to fiddle, and maybe—maybe—the human imprint may deepen. But beautiful, born-to-please kitties aren't all the future offers. The next generations of felines may be defined less by Desi's hothouse lineage than by the mutants that are just now being birthed in alleyways and barns. Some of these newcomers will not look much like cats at all, but rather like elves and werewolves, creatures that have already inspired some of today's emerging varieties.

Other new breeds, though, may seem hauntingly familiar.

Not long before the World Cat Show, and just a short drive away in rough-and-tumble northeast Detroit, a large, rangy feline with jungle-cat spots had been reported on the prowl. A cross between a house cat and a big-eared wild African feline called a serval, it was an escaped Savannah, a recently invented breed with skyrocketing worldwide popularity. This one was rumored to weigh a very leopard-like 90 pounds. (Really, it weighed 22.)

"That thing tried to get at my baby, man," one neighbor told the *Detroit Free Press*.

Like the tiger-slayers of old, locals eventually shot the wandering pet and threw its body in the trash.

Part creation, part reincarnation, these fierce-looking new beasts borrow from the gene pools of disappearing relatives and sharpen the ancient feline standard that the cherubic Desi defies. One flashy new hybrid, I'm a little tickled to learn, is called the Cheetoh.

Which sort of breeding strategy will prevail? Will cats of the future follow orders—or take command?

$\backsim$

The Egyptians are called the first cat "breeders," but they apparently failed to produce any distinctive cat breeds in their institutional catteries: as we've seen, the cats they idolized were mostly a succession of brown tabbies.

Even as millennia passed, the domestication process deepened, and the global feline population grew exponentially, few people paid much attention to changing cat coat colors or other variations that slowly emerged, let alone made aristocratic claims for particular animals. In nineteenth-century America, Katherine Grier writes, "the very concept" of a purebred cat would have "stunned" most cat owners.

As with the animal rights movement, it took the Victorians to invent the idea. The nineteenth-century British sought to impose order on the whole world, and the new discipline of natural history embodied this ideal—men subduing the chaos of nature through science, even as they simultaneously hunted down the most disruptive beasts in the wild. The Victorians dearly loved to rank and classify domestic animals, from puppies to pigeons, just as they liked to rank and classify all living things.

Yet the large numbers of house cats already roaming London and the countryside beyond were excluded from the first Victorian purebred pet pageants. If they were shown at all, it was usually as "an addendum to an exhibit of rabbits or guinea pigs," writes Harriet Ritvo in *The Animal Estate*.

Cats, you see, are extremely hard to rank and classify. Their general rebelliousness dismayed their Victorian masters, perhaps reminding them of the larger cats still digesting Englishmen in the far corners of the realm. But it also had major reproductive consequences. Because of the cats' "nocturnal and rambling habits, indiscriminate free-crossing cannot without much trouble be prevented," warned Charles Darwin, who pooh-poohed the notion of purebred cats. Humans, he suggested, would have as much luck policing the sex lives of honeybees.

Nonetheless, in 1871, an artist named Harrison Weir daringly proposed the first big cat show, at the premier Victorian venue of the Crystal Palace. "Many were the gibes, jokes, and jeers that were thrown at me," he later recalled. As the day of the "experiment" approached, even he expressed misgivings: "I felt somewhat more than anxious . . . what would it be like? Would there be many cats? How many? How would the animals comport themselves in their cages? Would they sulk or cry for liberty, refuse all food? Or settle down and take the situation quietly and resignedly, or give way to terror? I could in no way picture . . . the scene."

To his relief, the cats behaved, the crowds amassed, and Weir was awarded a silver tankard for his troubles. Cat shows soon proliferated "throughout the length and breadth" of England, Weir bragged, and hog-tied cats were sometimes packed into margarine hampers and shipped to distant competitions.

Yet the pesky problem of muddled bloodlines remained. Weir's first champions were no doubt beautiful: some early fanciers dripped show cats with cream so they would lick their fur to a patent leather shine, and amplified coat colors with dye. Yet all of them were essentially alley cats. The show did feature a few now-recognizable brand names, including long-haired "Persians" and dark-pointed "Royal Cats of Siam," whose natural genetics may have been mildly distinct. But these rather pedestrian creatures little resembled the coiffed beasts that we see today and had probably never been purposefully bred. At best, they were alley cats from particularly far-off alleys. And even among these exotics, there was none of the physical variety that distinguishes a dachshund from a Great Dane: the cats all looked more or less the same.

Undeterred, Victorian cat fanciers simply invented categories: "Most feline breeds were verbal rather than biological constructions," Ritvo writes. There were divisions for "fat" and "foreign" cats, "tortoiseshell" and "spotted." "Black and white cats" and "white and black cats" were considered to be entirely distinct creatures. The first American cat show, at the Boston Music Hall in 1878, paraded "Short-Haired Cats of Any or No Sex and Any Color," "long-haired cats," and "curiosities of any variety."

Breed definitions that rely exclusively on superficial traits like fur length or pattern can get slippery fast. These difficulties were acknowledged at the highest levels of the cat fancy. One early-twentieth-century judge cautioned that with cats, the term "breed" is always "used advisedly, for whatever the outer covering or coat, colour or length of fur, the contour of each and all is practically the same." A pioneering Persian breeder confessed that even she could not tell the difference between Persians and so-called Angoras and suspected they might be identical animals.

Amid so many desperate attempts to draw distinctions among ordinary house cats, perhaps it's no surprise that one early cat show was won by a ring-tailed lemur, a small primate that was much closer kin to the cat show's human judges than to its meowing contestants.

A century later, cat husbandry remains a somewhat stunted enterprise. The British did their best to produce respectable feline dynasties, but apparently the chaos of World War II undid many of their achievements, which were not terribly impressive to begin with. As late as the 1960s, the Cat Fanciers' Association still recognized only a handful of breeds. The majority of today's fifty or so types have debuted since then, many in just the last few decades.

Meanwhile, modern genetics has helped knock some the most famous "natural" breeds off their nineteenth-century pedestals. "I tend not to pay too much attention to the lore until you can prove it," says the University of Missouri feline geneticist Leslie Lyons. Some show cats with folkloric ties to far-off lands appear to be pretenders. Today's Persians, for instance, are not really Persian, descending instead from a more generic Western lineage. The same goes for Egyptian maus. In general, exotic cat names are far adrift from geographic reality: Havana browns have nothing to do with Cuba, for instance.

A few natural breeds, notably the Siamese and its relatives, have legitimate foreign blood. Early trade routes may have deposited random-bred cats in Southeast Asia, well beyond the range of the other *Felis silvestris* subspecies with which they are most likely to interbreed. In a small, long-isolated population, harmless mutations would have more easily proliferated, says feline geneticist Carlos Driscoll. Within the Asian family, though, the breeds typically still differ from each other in just a few basic features, most of which involve coat color: Siamese have dark points on their faces and feet, Birmans are white, Korats blue, and Burmese sepia-toned.

Such skin-deep distinctions, based on the simplest genetic traits, are typical of the cat fancy. Most feline breeds still feel rather imaginary. Especially outside of show halls, many so-called purebred cats of different varieties look like clones wearing different-colored fur coats. Shaved down to her off-season "lion cut," which leaves only a mane-like ruff of fluff, Desi isn't fundamentally very different from the ancestral strays from which all of these creatures came—at least, not in the way that a teacup poodle differs from a bull mastiff.

Interestingly, many modern dog types are of Victorian vintage as well, and superficial traits like coat color and curly fur sometimes distinguish closely related breeds. But nineteenth-century dog breeders were building on a much richer history of artificial selection, which created a plethora of canine shapes and profiles and builds—not to mention dispositions—long before the Westminster Kennel Club Dog Show's 1877 debut.

The difference between dog breeds and cat breeds (or lack thereof) highlights our historical rapport with each companion animal. First off, dogs were domesticated thousands of years before cats, and we've been putting selective pressure on dogs for much of that period; archaeological sites suggest that dogs have come in different sizes since hunter-gatherer days.

In addition to getting a head start on cats, dogs were largely hostage to their masters' decisions in ways that cats were not. Since dogs (unlike cats) depend so heavily on us, people got to decide which dogs got the best food, and—to a degree, at least—who mated with whom. As a consequence, dogs ceded control over their own DNA long ago. This tight genetic leash helps explain why today so many dogs—a staggering 60 percent of the American pet population—are purebreds, and why almost all of what we call "mutts" are mixtures of various pedigrees. (It's thought that less than 2 percent of cats worldwide have any purebred ancestors.)

By not outsourcing their own survival, and handling hunting and kitten-rearing independently, cats flouted our rules and escaped our meddling. We couldn't have micromanaged ancient cat breeding even if we had wanted to.

And we probably didn't. Just as we never tried to domesticate cats in the first place, we never had a reason to coax out different feline types. We always had far more practical uses for dogs, and more incentive to mold them, so that some could race after antelope and others could haul fishing nets or guard prisons. Even breeding for basic dog obedience may have had physical consequences. The striking range of canine skull shapes—a hallmark of the domestication syndrome that's almost totally absent in cats—may be a by-product of millennia of selection for amenable juvenile disposition, says Bob Wayne, an evolutionary biologist at the University of California at Los Angeles. The skulls of various modern dog breeds, he argues, resemble infant and adolescent wolves, arrested at various stages of development. (By contrast, kitten and cat skulls are shaped very much alike, and are quite similar to that of *Felis silvestris lybica*.)

When the Victorians began their largely decorative canine tinkering, they merely refined a preexisting array of dog body types. And although modern Fidos have become increasingly detached from real-world duties, notional functionality still shapes official breeding practices, even if most "retrievers" or "terriers" are destined to be house pets.

With cats, though, form can't follow function, because there is no clear function, unless you count their prolific but unpredictable killer instincts, which are not something farmers or herdsmen would necessarily want to amplify—making a feline mastiff, for instance, would more or less mean conjuring a lion.

"There probably wasn't much enthusiasm for creating giant cats," Wayne points out. "You wouldn't want that on your scratching post."

In the absence of functional objectives, "everybody tends to take cats to extremes," Leslie Lyons says. "That's the easiest thing to do." Under our care, the weirdest-looking animals often score the most sexual partners. Many top-drawer Persians can trace their aesthetic to three ridiculously pie-faced, prolific sires in the 1980s, one of which was named Lullaby Abracadabra.

If cat fanciers focused on selecting for behavior instead of looks alone, predicts Razib Khan, a feline geneticist at the University of California at Davis, not only might cats become better pets, but they might undergo a more doglike physical diversification as well. And a few new breeds have toyed with this concept: the Persian-derived Ragdoll is known for its lackadaisical outlook, and the Australian Mist is allegedly bred for a sedate indoor lifestyle (a peace offering to Australia's wildlife, the marketing pitch goes). But to date there have been no revolutionary developments.

"So far," Lyons tells me, "cat breeders have been playing with the easy stuff."

↶

Perhaps because house cats have been so reluctant to transform under our influence, breeders are constantly on the prowl for exciting new material. They hunt for undiscovered cats in exotic locales—one breeder told me that he'd scoured Haiti for strange-looking strays, and another reportedly paid Indian children to procure unusual street cats with a luminous coat quality known as "glitter." One fresh pedigree is the Sokoke, a castaway from coastal Kenya, whose genetics bear evidence of ancient African trade routes. (Alas, it's quite ordinary-looking.)

More and more, though, breeders are scoping out talent right under their noses, like model scouts at the local mall. Many so-called new breeds are based on mutations that have lately surfaced close to home. Some of these freaks have probably been popping up for centuries but are only now—as our collective cat obsession grows—being celebrated and inter-bred, rather than being singled out for gunnysack drowning.

But it's also likely that, with the booming global house cat population, greater numbers of mutations are arising naturally today than in the past. And while there are still many more official dog breeds (the Westminster Kennel Club acknowledges roughly 200 breeds, and the Cat Fanciers' Association only 41), the number of cat breeds appears to be growing at a faster rate, as humans take notice and start naming them.

Notable single-mutation newcomers, many of them plucked from barn cat populations, are the hairless Sphynx—the progeny of two 1970s-era Minnesota cats named Dermis and Epidermis—and a host of curly-coat mutants, including the Cornish Rex (England, circa 1950), the Devon Rex (England, 1960), the LaPerm (Oregon, 1982), and the Selkirk Rex (Montana, 1987). Taylor Swift's Scottish Fold—whose unusual bent ears, while perhaps suggestive of the advancing domestication process, also reflect potentially crippling cartilage abnormalities—was discovered in 1961, and the bent-eared American Curl followed in the 1980s. The last decade alone has seen a flood of additions, many of which have not been officially recognized: the Brooklyn Wooley, the Helki, the Ojos Azules.

One of the most controversial novelties—heralded by one major Amer-

ican cat club, but shunned by the other—is the dwarf Munchkin, first discovered beneath a truck in Rayville, Louisiana. The offspring of this squat
matriarch have been much sought after, but also decried as "the mutant
sausages" of the cat world.

Though based on a single dominant gene, like so many other breed-
defining feline traits, the Munchkin's half-sized legs are one of the most
visible alterations of the house cat body plan to date, and its 1995 accep-
tance at the International Cat Fanciers' Association prompted a prominent judge to resign.

But at present the emerging breed with the most bizarre physique and
the biggest buzz is the Tennessee-based Lykoi—or as it's more widely
known, the werewolf cat.

The Gobble family of Sweetwater, Tennessee, has bred practically everything under the sun: French black truffles, Japanese fighting fish, timber
trees, nectarines, snails, zebra finches, Yorkshire terriers, quarter horses,
and button quail. The huge, foggy aquarium in their living room attests to
a recently concluded infatuation with poison dart frogs. ("They just kept
breeding," Johnny Gobble says darkly.) Raising pedigreed cats, however,
was until relatively recently beyond their ambition; in this rural dairy
farming community, the concept of a purebred feline remains somewhat
amazing.

"We don't buy cats around here," advises Gobble, a veterinarian. "We go
out to the neighbor's barn and get one."

But curiosity got the best of Gobble and his wife, Brittney, and the couple finally coughed up the cash for a hairless. Before long they were prominent breeders and Brittney even founded a hobby magazine called *Owned
by a Sphynx*.

In 2010, through the Sphynx breeders' grapevine, they learned about
the appearance of two "ugly Sphynx" cats at a Virginia shelter on the other
side of the Appalachians. (The Gobbles allow that even a prizewinning
Sphynx is not a conventionally attractive creature.) These scrawny stray
kittens were bald on their toes, nose, and ears, where even the Sphynx

typically have a little bit of down—yet these strange cats had hair everywhere else.

After seeing them for the first time, Gobble concluded that they weren't Sphynx at all. Perhaps they were just strays suffering from ringworm or red mange or even a congenital abnormality.

"Most vets, when they see something like this, their first reaction is: 'spay and neuter,'" Brittney recalls.

But Johnny didn't believe the mysterious denuded cats were sick either, and he liked their golden eyes and what remained of their unusual roan-colored fur. He suspected a new mutation. If the pair turned out to be healthy, he wanted to breed them.

"He's a little weird, my husband is, and that's the truth," Brittney says.

So they acquired the two ratty-looking cats, a male and a female, along with their mother, a normal black cat. But the Gobbles' luck was just beginning. A few months later, a Sphynx-breeding associate located a look-alike pair of partially hairless cats near Nashville. This additional set of unrelated kittens enabled the Gobbles to launch their breeding program without the obstacle of incest.

Then came the real breakthrough—a killer marketing strategy. "In the beginning, we were calling the cats Capossums, because they looked like a cross between a possum and a cat," Johnny Gobble recalls. (They named one of their founding kittens Opie, short for Opossum Roadkill.) Happily, a catchier theme presented itself. With their exposed pale skin showing through dark, sparse hair, and naked, humanlike faces wreathed in fur, the cats resembled old-fashioned werewolves in mid-morph. Hence, "Lykoi," from the Greek "Lykos," wolf.

After a battery of skin samples and heart scans, both sets of cats proved healthy. The Gobbles still didn't know, however, if the mutation was heritable. In 2011, they bred the male of one litter with the female of the other and were crestfallen to produce one black female kitten with a perfectly lush coat. But within a few weeks, she started to shed profusely—a process the Gobbles now refer to as "wolfing out." They named her Daciana, Romanian for "wolf."

The Gobbles are working with the feline geneticist Leslie Lyons to pin down the relevant genetics, but it looks like the Lykoi rely on yet another recessive trait, based on just one gene. Fortunately for their breeding efforts, this mutation has also occurred outside of Appalachia: in the few years since they began developing the breed, dozens of Lykoi litters have been recovered around the world, "almost all of them from shelters and Dumpsters," Johnny Gobble says. (He has to get the cats quickly, as concerned veterinarians are typically poised to spay.)

It's all a numbers game, since more cats on the planet mean more mutants to choose from. But the Lykoi bumper crop is also likely a reflection of our intensifying feline obsession: the mutation may have been around for a while, but it's taken a cat-crazed culture to mine it, and the cat-distracted Internet to connect owners of similarly strange-looking beasts who otherwise never would have met.

Using their home and Johnny's veterinary kennels, the Gobbles are now running a veritable werewolf farm and, like their (no doubt baffled) dairying neighbors, are even certified by the United States Department of Agriculture. They spend some $600 a month on kitty litter and employ several full-time workers whose most important job is to pet the partially hairless cats.

There are still just a few score of standard Lykoi in the world, and the breed only recently gained rights to enter some cat shows, but that's about to change. Johnny, who calls himself "a very ambitious man," is distributing his cat stock throughout the global landscape. There are satellite operations in Canada, England, Israel, and South Africa, and when I visited the Gobbles, one Lykoi was being quarantined for travel to Australia. (How that country's cat-embattled Department of the Environment will greet the werewolf cat's arrival is anyone's guess.)

The rare felines are now available for purchase at $2,500 a pop, and the wait list of would-be werewolf owners is hundreds of people long.

Natural showfolk, the Gobbles keep me waiting, too, before they at long last trot three Lykoi into their living room. The cats' bald muzzles and blank-looking, lemon-drop eyes really are arresting, and their brown noses have—beneath my tentative forefinger—the unexpected texture of a rubber band.

The Gobbles insist that the cats exhibit unusual, canine-like behaviors and go wild for deer scent or the rustle of a Twinkie wrapper. But the "pointless" visual is clearly the main point. I stare at the cats' paws, which resemble bare human hands with the first lupine bristles pushing through.

"We've gotten hate mail from people saying they want to come burn down our laboratory," Brittney says, perhaps noticing my gaze.

"Yeah," Johnny says, "they thought I was creating them—"

"—in a test tube!" Brittney giggles.

"We've had people who want me to put wings on them next."

The Lykoi still appear to be healthy. That does not mean, however, that they are fit enough to survive on their own. Like the Sphynxes, which are sometimes confined in padded rooms before cat shows to safeguard their delicate skin, the Lykoi are extremely sensitive to cold and would likely die of exposure even in this moderate Tennessee climate. The werewolf cats also exhibit a creepy sensitivity to direct sunlight—if they bask on a windowsill, their alabaster skin begins to freckle, then turns completely black within a matter of days, like a form of extreme tanning.

New breeds tend to get weirder via crossing: a Sphynx plus an American Curl equals a naked, shrivel-eared Elf Cat, for instance, and a Meerkat is a tailless, stumpy-legged admixture of several new arrivals. There is apparently a growing, highly controversial movement to "Munchkinize" all existing pedigrees.

Some recent breeds are clearly abominations, like the so-called Twisty Cat, aka squitten, whose grotesquely curved bones give it a squirrel-like appearance. But it can be hard to say which others go too far.

Leslie Lyons can think of one potential test: "If you turned all the cats loose and came back five years later," she muses, "who would still be alive? The Sphynx? I don't know. The Persian? I don't know." (On the other hand, Lyons suspects that the much-maligned Munchkins would do fine if left to their own devices.)

At the World Cat Show, I witnessed one Persian escape attempt: a gentle plop from grooming table to floor, followed by utter befuddlement. The cat's round, headlight-shaped eyes stayed dim.

Though often only a couple of genes removed from rough-and-ready street cats, some modern breeds may have forfeited the most fundamental feline trait of all: the ability to survive.

Not all of them, though. Even as humans nurse these frail feline mutants, we are also populating our homes with a different sort of breed—hybrid cats, the progeny of house cats mixed with various wild species just a few generations out of the jungle.

For the hybrid cat breeders, there's nothing haphazard about cat aesthetics. Their guiding star is big-cat biology, not whatever oddity pads out from behind the local Dumpster. If most breeders push house cats toward arbitrary extremes, hybrid breeders try to preserve the feline essence, and to disguise, but not undo, domestication's handiwork. The names of their breeds—Toygers, Pantherettes, Cheetohs—pay homage to vanquished kings. For practicality's sake, house cats are typically crossed with the smaller species of wild cats, but the hybrid breeders dream big.

"The end game is to create the most beautiful example of something that looks wild but is domestic," says Anthony Hutcherson, who breeds Bengals, a mix of house cat and Asian leopard cat lineage whose name nods to a type of endangered tiger. "It's great to win a cat show, but it is more rewarding to make something that looks like a little leopard or jaguar or ocelot that eats cat food and purrs on sight."

"I want to make a kitty that looks like it walked out of the forest and into a kid's arms," says Carol Drymon, progenitor of the Cheetoh, another Asian leopard cat cross that is renowned for its spotted-coat pattern, its jungle-stalk walk, and (I'm not totally surprised to learn) its tremendous size. Some Cheetoh males approach 30 pounds, and the cats come in all different colors, including a shade of orange. Drymon bulks them up with red meat and hardboiled eggs.

Hybrid breeders debate whether a 45-degree or a 60-degree angle between the ears is most appropriate, what defines an ideal nose, and how one can best mimic the snowy white markings on many big-cat faces. One major challenge has been adding white spots to the back of the Bengals' ears—many big-cat species sport these, possibly so that trailing cubs can more easily follow behind their mothers in the wild. House cats, though, don't have them.

But just as the domestic disposition is associated with certain physical signatures, wild looks might come with wilder tempers attached. Scientists wonder if a particular animal's physique predicts its behavior—that is to say, if a domesticated silver fox born with floppy ears (in keeping with the domestication syndrome) is destined to be more docile than its wild-looking littermate with straight ears.

What's certain is that creating a sedate lap leopard is even trickier than its sounds. (The cats I met in veterinarian Melody Roelke-Parker's basement months earlier were also Asian leopard cat crosses, for instance, and most had by no means shed their jungle manners.) Developed in the 1970s, pedigreed Bengals are multiple generations removed from their wild forefathers and have thus inherited just a fraction of their genes, typically less than 12.5 percent. But they are still behaviorally distinct from other house cats, according to research published by University of California at Davis animal behaviorists Lynnette and Ben Hart. Bengals are more apt to act aggressively toward owners and strangers and are notorious for ignoring litter boxes and hosing down houses with pee.

Yet Bengals are considered the tamest of the hybrids. Savannahs, the serval-cross type that terrified Detroiters, are now considered a "championship breed" by some cat clubs and are shown alongside patrician Persians and Siamese. Yet on one recent episode of *My Cat From Hell*, Savannahs could be found devouring metal rods, sabotaging their owners' skydiving parachutes, and pouncing on stove hoods in a way that caused host Jackson Galaxy to yelp in horror.

Even hybrid breeders have prejudices about which small wild cats make good crossbreeding candidates. Some species have "attitude problems," according to Drymon. The Geoffroy's cat is a pretty, spotted wild feline species that's the co-parent of the new Safari hybrid breed. It's also, in Drymon's view, "an evil little creature that should be left in the forest."

Perhaps these cats should be left in the forest for other reasons. Some are imperiled species. The International Union for Conservation of Nature lists Geoffroy's cat as vulnerable in certain habitats. Other small cats used in hybridization include sand cats, oncillas, and margays, none of which are exactly flourishing. A few breeding programs have drawn on the Asian fishing cat, an endangered species now on the IUCN red list.

Typically the wild parents are already in captivity and so breeding them doesn't directly hurt natural populations. But some conservationists think that the mighty house cat has no business diluting dying bloodlines. (If it's avoidable, that is: amorous house cats in the wild have already hybridized some of their relatives, like the Scottish wildcat, almost out of existence.)

Hybrid breeders, including Hutcherson, have argued that living alongside mini-leopards will sensitize us to the plight of endangered big cats. But the reverse might just as easily be true, since watering down wild cat lineages could make the endangered seem commonplace and create the illusion of compassion toward creatures that humans are, in fact, systematically destroying. The practice clearly encroaches on the wild cats' mystique, which is pretty much all they have going for them at this point.

Hybrids may also trespass on the big cats' refuges of last resort. Because of their behavioral quirks, these expensive pets are frequently surrendered by repentant owners, and not always to ordinary shelters. They may end up, instead, in cash-strapped wild cat sanctuaries meant to aid abused circus lions and the like.

Some of the sanctuaries are so swarmed with unwanted Bengals and Savannahs that they've begun turning them away, offering overwhelmed owners tips on how to convert their garages into "heated dens" for their half-wild house cats. Hybrid-specialty refuges have opened, like the 16-acre Avalo Farm in Wagener, South Carolina, which was recently raising funds to beef up its perimeter fence.

Since not all owners have the wherewithal to install a customized barricade with a 45-degree angle on top, these cats do sometimes get out. In addition to the unlucky Savannah padding around Detroit, other escaped hybrids have been reported slinking across Las Vegas rooftops, patrolling abandoned farmsteads on the outskirts of Chicago, and casing the University of Maryland's basketball arena. Some of these creatures would look much more at home in the deep Serengeti, lounging under the acacia trees.

One October, a particularly strapping, spotted hybrid specimen stalking a Delaware suburb led terrified parents to consider keeping kids inside for Halloween.

The cat's name, as it happened, was Boo.

⌁

Far more than any man-made fad, though, what matters to the future of house cats is how they will change themselves. Regardless of how many strays are neutered, how closely pets are confined, or how crafty human matchmaking becomes, the vast majority of cats will always be conceived beyond our selective control. Will they get any bigger? Bolder?

In some places, it seems they already have. The biologist Luke Dollar studies the elusive fossa, a rare, mongoose-like carnivore at the top of the Madagascar food chain. The only cats on the huge African island are imports, most of them rather puny pets that inhabit rural villages. "Scrawny, spindly, high parasite load," Dollar says. "They are really pitiful."

But in 1999, while he was canvassing a slashed-and-burned agricultural zone on the edge of the deep interior forest, Dollar's carnivore traps ensnared a very different-looking sort of feline.

"This thing turned around on us and practically roared," he recalls. "It was absolutely huge, and it would have torn us apart if it could have—it was in 'oh, hell no' mode."

"Then we caught another one. And another one. Dozens of them. It was a 'holy shit' moment."

As the head of National Geographic's Big Cats Initiative, Dollar knows something about the feline family. But the burly cats looked so little like the local pets that he took the unusual step of testing their DNA to confirm they were house cats (they were). Dollar also weighed and measured them, "and they were blatantly anatomically distinct," he says, large and strong and in superb physical condition, nearly free of parasites. The village cats came in all different colors—calico, black, orange—but the forest cats were exclusively gray-brown tabbies with some black tiger stripes thrown in. The

Madagascar natives, he learned, have different words for the two types and consider them to be separate kinds of animals.

But whether white explorers introduced these house cats several centuries ago, or if they are more recent runaways, there hasn't been time for major genetic changes to naturally transform the population, which takes thousands of years.

The forest cats' distinct looks were simply the result of a much more immediate lifestyle choice. Bigger cats with well-camouflaged coats may quickly proliferate in a setting where "nobody is provisioning them," Dollar says, "and the forces of nature are not constrained." (Likewise, orange cats are said to dominate the ruddy Australian desert, while gray and black cats populate the shaded jungles.) "There is no cat food, no laser toys, no kitty litter," Dollar continues. Freaks and weaklings die young out there. The strong survive to become the fittest possible versions of themselves: house cats in the raw.

Dollar hasn't catalogued what precisely the Madagascar cats are hunting, but he feels sure that it's "everything." To confirm that they were killing the islands' sifaka lemurs, his colleagues used the same technique anthropologists once used to show that ancient leopards ate early humans, fitting cat fangs to the mysterious holes sometimes found in the skulls of dead primates.

These house cats have seemingly forsaken our houses for a better life in the wild. Yet they still likely draw on their domestic heritage as well. While they look a little different on the surface, they have the same shrunken brains as their housebound compatriots; even if superficial domestic attributes like coat color disappear over a few generations, the cognitive changes endure. Because they live amid Madagascar's former rice farms, in limbo between civilization and nature, it helps to not be so scared of humans. Unlike truly wild animals, for instance, they weren't shy of Dollar's traps—especially once they realized that they would always be released. He snared a few cats so often that he named them. "We caught Sylvester every day for three weeks in a row," Dollar marvels. "He wasn't going to purr or rub up against our legs or anything, but he figured, 'I go in this box, I eat the bait, and these guys come get me out the next day.'"

Reports of mammoth house cats have surfaced in other places, notably Australia, where rumors date back to the nineteenth-century colonial records; more recently, photographs of mega-cat corpses have made the Internet rounds. (It's unclear, however, if these alleged giants were photographed alongside particularly petite Aborigines.) Certainly such creatures roam our imaginations, in paranoid episodes like "The Lion of Essex" and others.

Maybe in a few million years, a real evolutionary leap will happen. Saber-tooth Siamese are not entirely out of the question. Catlike animals have sprouted saber teeth many times over the past 40 million years and the last saber-tooth tigers disappeared from Los Angeles only 11,000 years ago. Scientists fully anticipate an encore of the iconic dentition.

The clear evolutionary front-runner is the clouded leopard, which shares cranial characteristics with extinct saber-tooths. But, of course, there are now only a few thousand clouded leopards left, and these seem unlikely to survive the seven million years that scientists estimate must pass before the next-generation sabers sprout.

For the saber-tooth's successor, "I might bet on the domestic cat," La Brea Tar Pit paleontologist Christopher Shaw tells me.

I think he's joking. And yet: a feline population six hundred million strong and growing leaves serious room for experimentation.

But perhaps the most fascinating aspect of the house cats' evolutionary future is not how much they may change, but how little.

After all, house cats are already a perfect fit for our time, and sitting pretty at the top of the food chain. Outside of disease outbreaks, "in the situation that you have in most of the world, there is negligible selection on domestic cats," feline geneticist Carlos Driscoll says. "There is nothing hunting them. They can be any color they want" because—whether living inside our settlements, or on the compromised landscapes beyond—they already rule.

Besides, there is some evidence to suggest that—in many modern environments, at least—it does not behoove house cats to get bigger and meaner and more monstrous. (After all, brute strength alone didn't work out so well for lions and tigers.) As populations of people and house cats become denser in our growing cities, large, aggressive animals are at a disadvantage, as a study of stray French cats revealed.

The research focused on coat color—and on orange cats, in particular. Orange coat color is a sex-linked trait (orange males are more common than females) as well as a behavioral marker, a sign of size and strength. Orange males tend to be heavier and more aggressive than males of other colors (an observation that, via Cheetoh, I can anecdotally confirm).

The French researchers found that in the countryside, where cat populations are sparser, these big, mean orange males can often beat back their rivals and monopolize females.

In cities, however, where cat populations are ten times denser, it's impossible to fight the tide of suitors, and the best strategy is to mate with as many females as you can and politely ignore interlopers. The orange males, though, apparently spend too much time battling and not enough time mating, so their genes are not passed on as often as the smaller, calmer blacks' and tabbies'.

Perhaps the meek shall inherit the earth after all—or at least, the alleyways.

As far as the house cats' aesthetic future goes, there is only one guarantee: cats are getting fatter. Though environmental rather than genetic, this effect is extremely profound. Close to 60 percent of American pet cats are overweight or obese, and scientists report extremely rotund strays as well. I read endless news accounts of 31-pound feline Buddhas, 36-pound Meatballs, 35-pound pet McLovins. (A healthy weight is about a quarter of one of these kitties.)

So far, all this extra lard is humanity's most significant contribution to the feline form. True, many of our animal affiliates are plumping up, and even the street rats of Baltimore are 40 percent heavier today, thanks in large part to our heartier garbage. But house cats represent an extreme case, for a variety of human-driven reasons in addition to the ever-richer delicacies they enjoy in their food dishes and our trash cans. Locking cats indoors prevents them from getting exercise, spaying and neutering lowers their metabolic rate, and cats' delicate hypercarnivorous biology makes dieting extremely difficult.

I tour the University of Tennessee College of Veterinary Medicine, where animal obesity experts recently developed, by necessity, a new Body Fat Index chart for the twenty-first-century feline. The old version topped out at 45 percent body fat—totally inadequate for today's clientele. The new version goes up to 70 percent and beyond. The researchers— naturally—use pictures of orange cats to illustrate the various stages of corpulence, ranging from merely Botticellian to truly blimpish, and ending with a completely spherical state in which there's "no distinction between head and shoulder" and the ribs become "impossible to palpate."

But even this expanded guide may not prove helpful, as studies have shown that cat owners resolutely misclassify even the biggest whoppers as slender. As usual, we can't see our cats for what they are.

Perhaps we persist in fattening cats because—as research suggests, and all cat owners deep down know—cats pay the most attention to us when we feed them, and we want them to like us. Or perhaps we just don't want them to dislike us, since hungry cats can be more "persistent" in pressing their claims than dogs, feline obesity expert Angela Witzel tells me, and a bullying 30-pounder is no joke.

Feline fatness is also a potentially depressing twist on cats' ongoing environmental toll. One rather staggering estimate suggests that America's 100-odd million pet cats consume the equivalent of 3 million chickens every day. But that's assuming they need only two ounces of meat each. Tremendously fat cats may have bloated caloric requirements, whether these are met by felled neighborhood songbirds or canned fish caught in far-off oceans.

And yet even a finely calibrated scale can't tell the whole story here, and especially not how it ends. That's because the final frontier for all life-forms is the Internet, where creatures consist of pixels, not pounds. To conquer this vast new virtual territory, house cats—those die-hard hypercarnivores—have entirely transcended the flesh.

Chapter 9

NINE LIKES

THE CAT, alas, is not quite ready to receive me, and so the concierge leaves me to fidget in an elegant glass-walled lounge. The décor of this Manhattan hotel—the ritzy habitat of Lil Bub, a feline Internet celebrity—features faux bison skins tossed over sleek couches and a shelf full of natural history books, perhaps selected for their handsome spines.

I pick up one called *Life on Earth*. In photographs, a lone cheetah storms a wildebeest herd, and the big cat's chosen victim seems to bow its head in anticipation. "Of all the hunters, the cats are the most specialized for meat-eating," the text reads. Their teeth are "tools of butchery."

But Lil Bub has no teeth—they never grew in, and her physical idiosyncrasies don't end there. Her lower jaw is undeveloped, her femurs are twisted, she suffers from a disease called osteopetrosis and a form of dwarfism. Her bladder sometimes malfunctions; the cat's owner, Mike Bridavsky, has learned to "pee her" by scratching her belly in a particular way, and her urine, mingling with the perfume of her favorite coconut cat shampoo, smells spookily like Thai food.

And yet Lil Bub is part of a pantheon of elite online cats. These A-list felines have licensing agents and corporate ties; they may roll through Hollywood in chauffeured Escalades, negotiating movie deals. A few of the cats are said to bank a million dollars a year, and others are prominent philanthropists: Lil Bub, a four-pound mutant who would be doomed at any other moment in history, has campaigned to save the last of the tigers.

Finally summoned, I find Lil Bub pacing the floor of the meeting room, her shortened legs making for a somewhat serpentine gait. Her face is familiar to me from countless tank tops, tote bags, teacups, knee socks, and cell phone covers. Her green eyes appear especially huge, and her pink tongue protrudes so she looks permanently pleased. Bridavsky scripts Lil Bub's cheerful online persona around this famous "smile."

She emits a trilling purr when I enter. "Here, Bub," says Bridavsky, who is in his mid-thirties, scooping her up. He spends almost every minute of the day with the cat, and much of his body's surface area is tattooed with her image. His 2011 decision to adopt her was an act of kindness, and he had no inkling of the fame she would bring him. He was an in-arrears music producer who already owned four cats; she was the runt of a feral litter found in an Indiana tool shed. "She was the size of a Hacky Sack," he says. "It wasn't really an option not to take her home."

Yet even Bridavsky—Lil Bub's first fan—is a little mystified by the public response to his pet. One of her Tumblr photos, posted in April of 2012, went viral immediately. Soon she had Twitter and Instagram accounts, her own YouTube channel, and a Facebook page with more than two million likes. Along came book contracts and Animal Planet specials and alliances with Urban Outfitters, not to mention *Today* cameos and cuddle sessions with the likes of Robert De Niro and Ke$ha. (Though Lil Bub's real-world reproductive options are moot, she may have expanded Bridavsky's—he has dated beautiful women, and just a few hours before we met, a famous television actress had pressed her breast into his arm "like, aggressively.") Tonight Lil Bub is to be the guest of honor at a sold-out Internet Cat Video Festival in Brooklyn.

"It's all surreal," Bridavsky says. "At the meet and greets, people cry around her. They get really, really emotional." A pet psychic once divined "that Bub's a walk-in—a spirit that walks into another body. It's a soul that has been around for millions of years, or whatever, that stays around for a reason."

He's not sure if he believes this, but no one can deny that Lil Bub has managed to slip her earthly bonds.

"Oh my God, what time is it?" Bridavsky says suddenly. He has to go upload cat photos to one account or another—maybe he and Lil Bub will see me later at the festival. I'll certainly see them.

Internet stars like Lil Bub and Maru (a Scottish Fold from Japan) are just the tip of the virtual iceberg. There are so many felines loose online that when Google's X lab let an "unsupervised" gaggle of 1,600 computer processors analyze YouTube videos, the machines became so used to scanning kitty data that they learned to recognize cat faces almost as well as human faces, with 74.8 percent accuracy. Cute cat pictures are so irresistible that corporate IT departments use them as bait to catch employees misusing their company PCs. A recent study revealed that British Internet users alone upload 3.8 million cat pictures per day, compared to just 1.4 million selfies, and that several hundred thousand individual Britons maintain social media accounts for their cats.

Some tiny fraction of all of this cat content is useful. There are websites devoted to litter box crises, online forums featuring thoughtful pet care questions ("if I smoke in the same room as my kitten, will she get high?"), and, from Australia of course, an educational feral-cat-slaughtering app designed to teach seven-year-olds about invasive species. ("Move your crosshair and fire . . . all the while being conscious of your ammo count and accuracy.") Online cats deliver weather reports, teach Spanish, and battle writer's block. (The website Written? Kitten! sends writers cat pictures every hundred words, and it's too bad that I waited until I was writing the last chapter of this book to discover it.)

Yet, much like house cats themselves, most digital house cats are almost self-consciously useless, pure purposeless amusement. There have been virtual crazes for cats with their heads stuck through slices of bread, cats confronting cucumbers, cats yodeling and striking yoga poses and riding Roombas and hopping into boxes and bleating like goats and knocking things over, cats posed to resemble sushi and decadent, gun-toting gangsters, and cats that really do look like Hitler. People film themselves half-buried in cat food, and share images of three-legged cats wearing fascinators, and remake *The Hunger Games* with a cats-only cast. Current events are rife with random Internet cats. When Belgian leaders called for social media silence in the wake of a 2015 terror scare, Twitter was inexplicably swamped with cat pictures. During the 2016 presidential primaries, Vermont senator Bernie Sanders was endlessly photoshopped alongside cute cats.

Why does an animal called Grumpy Cat—arguably the most famous online feline—have a Honey Nut Cheerios endorsement deal? Why has the Bible been translated into LOLSpeak, the pidgin tongue of Internet cats? Nobody quite knows. When Sir Tim Berners-Lee, often called "the father of the Internet," was asked recently what aspect of modern web usage most surprised him, he replied, "Kittens." Scholars at the Harvard Kennedy School and the London School of Economics ponder these "cat objects," as one academic calls them; they have been examined from the perspective of "feminist media studies" and "corporate surveillance," while linguists parse the "orthography and phonetics" of LOLSpeak.

Internet cats have, at the same time, become a watchword for the most mindless online content, and for idiot culture in general; the media scholar Clay Shirky calls captioning cat pictures "the stupidest possible creative act."

Perhaps Internet cats are worse than dumb—they might be accidental. The seemingly inexplicable popularity of Internet cats "could just be random," says Katherine Milkman, a big data expert at the Wharton School of Business. If the web were to begin anew, maybe a different creature would prevail.

But it seems more likely that the house cats' Internet invasion relates to their unique flesh-and-blood capacities and their particular history. Their online takeover fits with a much larger pattern of ecological and cultural conquests. After all, cats have been going viral since the Ptolemies ruled the Nile.

⌒⤳

Certainly cat content seems to have a mysterious, almost magical, quality that makes it more likely to be shared among users at the highest rate. According to recent BuzzFeed data, the average BuzzFeed cat post gets nearly twice as many viral views—coming from outside sources like Facebook and Twitter—as the average BuzzFeed dog post. Over a span of two years, the top five BuzzFeed cat posts received about four times as many viral views as the top dogs.

And cat content isn't just viral—it's often also what's called "memetic." Memes are bits of (usually funny) viral content that change a little—or adapt, if you will—as they are passed along. (The media scholar Kate Miltner calls them " 'inside jokes or pieces of hip underground knowledge' that inhabit social networks.") Successive users might tweak a cat caption, doctor the original cat picture, or swap in a new one. For instance, the most famous cat meme is a picture of an open-mouthed gray cat with a caption that says "I Can Has Cheezburger?" Memetic permutations include a picture of a Hitler lookalike cat saying "I Can Has Poland." Whenever a misconjugated "has" or "haz" appears online, the gray cat—known as Happy Cat—rears its head.

A play on the word "genes," memes behave a lot like living things, mutating at high rates and competing fiercely with each other in a sort of virtual habitat where human attention is the only vital resource. And they are studied like organisms as well. Borrowing Darwinian ideas and models from real-world fields like epidemiology, computer scientists and others try to understand what survives online and why.

"If I knew what was making these cats popular I would be a billionaire," says Christian Bauckhage, a University of Bonn computer scientist who tracks memes. "I am not aware of another genre in which individual memes live for such a long time. They are pretty much immortal."

Animal memes in general tend to prosper—BuzzFeed employs a whole class of editors called Beastmasters just to handle all of the bio-content— and considering the global online audience, this makes obvious sense. The particulars of human politics and cultures don't always translate across borders and continents, while animal imagery reliably does. (The rash of post-terror Belgian cat pictures, for instance, overnight became "an internationally recognized symbol of solidarity," according to the *New York Times*.)

Yet cat content stands out even among creature memes. Graphed over time, cat memes tend to have an unusual shape. Some memes—the "O Rly" snowy owl, for instance, or the Montauk Monster (a decayed animal carcass that washed up on a Long Island beach)—are what's known as "long-tailed": they tend to spike once in popularity and then taper off into a long, rather sad appendage. Cat memes, on the other hand, may enjoy peaks that last for months or years. Internet cats are thus, ironically, "short-tailed."

Cats have withstood some formidable challengers. Sloths and slow lorises, for instance, had their day in the sun. "The Socially Awkward Penguin was everywhere for a while," says Michele Coscia, a digital humanities researcher at the Harvard Kennedy School. But it's "very rare to see the penguin going viral now. It's clearly in decline. The memes that are used so constantly over time, eventually people grow tired of them. After a couple of years, they just die out. But cats apparently don't.

"I really understand little about why they are so successful," he adds. "It doesn't fit anything I know about memes."

For instance, Coscia's analyses suggest that the one trait that highly successful memes tend to share is novelty—we haven't seen too many pictures of snowy owls or slow lorises, which gives them a temporary edge. Yet house cats are preposterously common. And cats, especially when compared to the huge range of dogs, look more or less the same, purebreds and mutants included. As the media scholar Radha O'Meara points out in a journal article on cat videos, it's "as if there is a single cat performing in millions of videos."

Sameness is also a defining feature of the videos' settings, no matter where in the world they were filmed. Almost always, it's a domestic tableau, typically a living room (though bathrooms are also big). The action is simple to the point of absurdity.

A cat attacks a home office printer, or a pet parrot hiding beneath the coffee table, or its owner, or a watermelon. A cat rockets out from under the couch, or skulks atop the kitchen cabinets, or hops into a cardboard box.

Sometimes the cat even hops back out.

Cats infiltrated the Internet very early—a spoof website called Bonsai Kittens (featuring kittens and jars), The Infinite Cat Project (cats and mirrors), My Cat Hates You, and even a popular "litter box cam" date back to the early years of the World Wide Web. "From the late 1990s, we would talk about cute cat pages," says Ethan Zuckerman, director of the MIT Center for Civic Media and an early Internet entrepreneur. "It was certainly one of the first species of user-generated culture."

Perhaps timing was everything. In nature, the first creatures to fill a void can thrive, and the foothold they gain may make it very difficult for higher organisms to dislodge them later on. (For instance, after overfishing and pollution emptied the Black Sea, invasive jellyfish moved in and have ruled there ever since.)

But the cats' Internet takeover is a more specifically feline scenario, and one that should sound extremely familiar to residents of Australia. Internet cats were introduced for a specific purpose, and then, simply put, they went wild.

The definitive online felines, clearing a path for all the cats to come, were the LOLCats, short for Laughing Out Loud Cats. They first emerged in the mid-2000s on 4chan, a clubby online community of technological elites, many of them young men, known for their transgressive humor. (Another 4chan-generated animal is Pedobear, a pedophilic bear.) In the mid-2000s, 4chan declared a weekly holiday called Caturday, which people celebrated by posting cat pictures, some of which had superimposed captions.

It's unclear whether the 4chan crowd was particularly fond of cats. Cat lovers may well be heavier Internet users, since we don't get outdoors as much as dog owners. The web is also the rare realm where cat people can connect over their shared feline passion. (The Internet has sometimes been termed a "cat park.") Certainly a cat-techie synergy seems to exist today, since a notorious hacker was recently foiled after using his cat's name as his computer password, and an unmasked Reddit troll named Violentacrez turned out to be a middle-aged man with seven cats.

Yet whether or not the first Caturday celebrants were bona fide cat fanciers is, from a sociological perspective, largely irrelevant. Media scholars think meme genesis and sharing is primarily a way for anonymous Internet users to display allegiance to a particular digital clan and to disqualify outsiders. Miltner calls this "in-group boundary establishment and policing." For a small community of privileged users, the "LOLCats' value rested in their subcultural capital" rather than their cuteness. The first captioned cat images were deliberately obscure, a classic inside joke.

But then something peculiar, yet also familiar, happened: the cats escaped. In Miltner's words, they "migrated."

In January of 2007, a Hawaiian software developer named Eric Nakagawa posted a picture of Happy Cat on his blog. The image of the gray cat had been doing the rounds since 2003, but Nakagawa imposed a LOLCat-style caption. The single post got (a then-astounding) 375,000 hits in March alone. Nakagawa featured more LOLCats, and readers flooded his site with their own cat creations. The traffic numbers for the blog—ultimately entitled I Can Has Cheezburger—doubled the next month, then doubled again. By May, he quit his day job, and within the year sold the site to media entrepreneur Ben Huh, who believed that LOLCats would capture an even larger audience.

"The original meme of cats belongs to 4chan," Huh told *The International Business Times* in 2014. "But 4chan was mostly for anonymous friends, it was not where everyone could go. They used crude language." I Can Has Cheezburger, on the other hand, was warm and cuddly and accessible even to outsiders.

"It was where cats entered the pop consciousness."

The LOLCats quickly carved out a particular niche with middle-aged women, who became regulars on Huh's site and began referring to themselves as Cheezfrenz or Cheezpeepz—much to the horror of the darkly ironic 4chan crowd, which soon abandoned its pet meme. From the web-savvy perspective, once LOLCats breached "the mainstream culture, they lost their punch," according to Miltner. "They became symbolic of an earnest, technologically inept audience." Soon the even lamer "Bored at Work" demographic tuned in.

But that demographic was the very one the cats needed to multiply like gangbusters. Freed from their original owners' plan to keep them as an "inside" joke, cats soon got out, overrunning online platforms from Twitter to GIFs to YouTube videos and adapting themselves to every new ecosystem.

Instead of mice, they survive on mouse clicks.

The story of feral LOLCats helps explain how cats gained online dominion but not why. Another early web icon was a picture of a walrus with a bucket; the term "lolrus," however, somehow lacked staying power. Why not LOLferrets, or viral foxes?

The answer starts with cats' real-world fecundity and cosmopolitanism. With more than half a billion house cats on the planet today, creating new cat content is cheap and easy. Pandas can be cute, too, but there are only about 2,000 of them left alive, mostly in the remote bamboo forests of China, so panda pictures are costlier and rarer, and achieving hilarity (and virality) is far harder. (True to form, one I Can Has Cheezburger panda–themed spinoff flopped.) Cats also provide a built-in audience: as the most popular pets, they have a paw in the door with many different types of people who use the Internet in myriad ways—an automatic leg up over, say, the walrus or the ferret. Some computer scientists think that a meme's quality is almost incidental to its success and that what matters most is how many social networks it crosses. Cats cross them all.

But there's more to this than raw numbers. The very recent trend toward complete feline confinement is also key, because cats' invasion of our computers is a logical extension of their invasion of the indoors. When cats lived most of their lives outside, their secretive, slinking habits made them not only very tough to observe, but also extraordinarily difficult to photograph, film, and otherwise record. In *The Photographed Cat*, Northeastern University sociologist Arnold Arluke and coauthor Lauren Rolfe recount valiant yet largely doomed attempts to photograph early-twentieth-century cats, many of them roaming neighborhoods—it seems that "pet horses, deer, goats" and also "baby coyotes" made for better pictures. The few completed cat portraits were technically abysmal, "even when compared to pictures of wild animals." But today, for the first time, we have the constant option of recording our cornered pet cats. It's telling that cat videos are almost always filmed in the living room, because imprisonment there is a prerequisite for their digital odysseys.

And yet, though modern pet-keeping practices make Internet cats logistically possible, it's cats' wildest instincts—and indeed, their very predatory style—that ultimately gives them the edge over their cutest online competition: namely, dogs and human babies.

For even once cornered and filmed or photographed, preferably amid cunning American Girl Doll accessories, house cats remain solitary, meat-eating ambush hunters. (The very phrase "I Can Has Cheezburger" is, at heart, a carnivorous battle cry.) And these lonely stalkers thrive in the solitude of cyberspace in ways that Labrador retrievers do not.

Indeed, dogs are so in tune with humans, and their behavior is such a perfect mirror of our own emotions, that without people in close proximity they are unfinished beings. Dogs are existentially rooted in their dealings with us: they take our cues and meet our gazes and engage in a sort of mutual communion. They come alive through personal interaction and cannot be fully enjoyed from afar. Cats, though, are self-contained. They don't need people to complete them. They are the most at home in perfect isolation, whether in nature or the virtual world. You can get similar satisfaction watching a cat from a nearby couch or from a computer continents away.

Interestingly, the behavioral biology that propels cats online has largely shut them out of traditional storytelling formats. The writer Daniel Engber points out that dogs far outnumber cats in most literary forms, from novels to short stories. Perhaps this is because dogs evolved in a kind of dialogue with us and can practically deliver their own lines. Dogs are born characters, and we understand each other to the extent that our tales are the same, with beginnings and endings, long distances traveled in between, and death waiting obediently at the end.

Literary cats, by contrast, hardly ever die, when they live at all. Cats are not characters but cryptic presences. Communication is not their forte, and they don't really have complications or denouements. They are agents of utter stillness or acute violence.

Engber points out that the one traditional genre where cats do seem to dominate is poetry, which is nonlinear, intuitive, and spontaneous: a literary ambush. And sure enough, cats weave in and out of everything from nursery rhymes to T. S. Eliot. In fact, the few memorable cats from long-form literature seem to be poetry's strays—the Cheshire Cat, for instance, is an unpredictable presence even in crazy Wonderland, his erratic appearances a kind of narrative attack.

The Internet is much more like poetry than a novel. It is fragmented, explosive, and outside of time, and full of stalking and pouncing instead of organized sagas told from start to finish. The cat's essential suddenness is a perfect fit for a six-second Vine or surprising tweet.

"A typical cat video establishes a state of calm, then suddenly disrupts it," O'Meara writes in her media journal analysis. "The most popular cat videos seem to have the most sudden and striking disruptions as well as the most abrupt endings." A cat bops a baby on the head without warning, or explodes from underneath the bed.

She is describing an ambush.

The web is also a uniquely visual platform, which of course means that cats get extra mileage out of the happy accident of their infant-like features, which we love to ogle.

But if babies are so great, why don't we just look at babies online? Why have we instead developed a social media tool called Unbaby.me that automatically substitutes cat pictures for photographs of our friends' kids? Why does LOLspeak dominate instead of the "goos" and "gaas" of baby talk?

Huh, the LOLCat mogul, has claimed that cats rule the Internet because "unlike dogs, who have a handful of emotional expressions, there are nuances in a cat's face and body language. They are expressive."

But in fact the opposite is true. (Here perhaps it's worth mentioning that Huh doesn't have a cat; he is allergic to them.) Cats are not expressive: they are largely impassive, having never needed a strong communicative capacity in their lives as solitary hunters. They have baby-like faces, but none of a baby's rubbery expressions. They play their cards close to the vest, something no human infant has ever been accused of doing.

As we've seen, this deadpan quality is problematic in close domestic quarters, where all too often cat owners can't really fathom their own pets or even tell if their beloved cat is sick.

But online, feline inscrutability is a major asset. Cat faces are blanks that human beings, as hypersocial beings, feel compelled to fill in. In effect, they cry out for captioning.

Internet users attribute human characteristics to all kinds of creatures; the lonely act of web browsing accentuates our ever-present anthropomorphizing tendencies. Yet with their unusual mix of humanlike features and expressive emptiness, "reading" cats is particularly irresistible. Even the first photographers understood this, which perhaps explains why they went to such heroic lengths to feature recalcitrant felines. "Rabbits are the easiest to photograph in costume, but incapable of taking many 'human' parts," one early-twentieth-century animal photographer complained. "The kitten is the most versatile animal actor, and possesses the greatest variety of appeal."

Captioning cat photos is such a widespread online pastime that scientists at the University of Lincoln invented a research tool called Tagpuss to study it. Participants could pick from a list of forty emotions to describe the various cat pictures, and "we found that users consistently applied overly complex human emotions and motivations to cats," the authors wrote. Indeed, the lengthy list of suggested descriptors (which included uniquely human feelings like "courage," "anxiety," and "anger") was woefully insufficient to capture the huge range of emotions that Tagpuss users perceived in felines who were feeling nothing of the sort. Dissatisfied participants also submitted dozens of their own tags, including "giggly," "nosy," "unamused," "cheeky," and "agoraphobic."

It's been suggested that simple emoticons like smiley faces :) were the original meme. If so, cats are a natural successor: with their illusory humanness, combined with their perfect blankness, feline faces have a highly adaptable, emoticon-like potential to have human feelings projected on and through them.

Yet the real feline luminaries like Lil Bub push the phenomenon still further. They fascinate us by stimulating our need to read faces and then also satisfying it. Many of these rare beasts are famous precisely because their "expressions" do *not* appear blank. Unlike ordinary felines, they are born with their captions built in.

The elite online cats, it's worth noting, are not the most beautiful animals. In fact, many of the famous cats have serious health problems, and are described as "special needs." Often something is wrong with their faces, typically their mouths, which gives rise to a sort of expressive mirage. Lil Bub's crippled jaw gives her a constant, quizzical smile; her rival, fellow feline dwarf Grumpy Cat, has a frown so deep that it was initially thought to be photoshopped.

Colonel Meow, a scowling Himalayan, is the angry cat. Princess Monster Truck's hideous underbite—a classic Persian deformity—looks like a crooked grin; Sir Stuffington has a piratical sneer; Hamilton the Hipster Cat's unusual white mouth markings resemble an ironic mustache.

Grimacing cats with cleft palates have hit it big, though the so-called OMG cat seems to have faded from popularity after she healed from her broken jaw, the source of her formerly shocked expression. She was no longer an emoticat.

These "expressions," of course, have nothing to do with the animals' interior states—Grumpy Cat is apparently an affable creature, and smiling Lil Bub is often in pain due to her health problems.

But online all that matters is whether we want to look.

Meme researchers, I was rather startled to learn, aren't even ultimately all that interested in the Internet. Memes are, to them, a means to track how all kinds of catchy ideas spread through human cultures, and to quantify how concepts pass from mind to mind offline as well.

In that case, perhaps they should quit studying computers and switch to cats. Cats were intellectually contagious long before I Can Has Cheezburger. In addition to invading ecosystems, bedrooms, and brain tissue, they've hijacked whole cultures.

Take Japan, home to Hello Kitty maternity hospitals and Hello Kitty tombstones and everything in between; the cartoon cat is so nationally important that the Japanese government has blasted a Hello Kitty doll into space orbit.

This bizarre modern cat cult began 40 years ago, when a Japanese silk manufacturing company crafted the feline face that launched a thousand lunch boxes, becoming a transnational totem of corporate dominance that's revered by marketing executives across the globe. Hello Kitty has an estimated 50,000 trademarked products, with approximately 500 new ones introduced *per month*, not counting all the copycats. (She is one of the most counterfeited brands on the planet, proof of her extreme memetic power.) Her goods range from toasters to themed Airbus jets. About 90 percent of the cat's revenue now comes from outside of Japan, and the first-ever Hello Kitty Con, complete with a permanent tattoo parlor, was recently convened in Los Angeles, not far from the La Brea Tar Pits. Even the cat's slogan is self-consciously viral: "You can never have too many friends."

Like the house cat itself, Hello Kitty is a flexible predator. She is an example of pure design—a mascot without a brand, and an image that exists for its own sake, which means she can inhabit almost any object, a very feline versatility that allows her to constantly invade new markets. Her smallness, too, is crucial: she appears most commonly on miniature goods, like pencil cases, and when sufficiently enlarged—lurching down 42nd Street in the Macy's Thanksgiving Day parade, for instance—she seems almost leonine.

But her signature feature is one that's entirely missing. Voracious as she is, Hello Kitty has no mouth. This handicap helps explain why—despite the fortunes to be made, and her remarkable adaptive capacity—she seldom appears on television or in films. It's worth forgoing that revenue, because her designers believe that the missing orifice is also the source of her charm and near-universal allure.

"Kitty has no mouth so that she may better reflect the feelings of those who look upon her," her official website explains.

The comic author Scott McCloud calls Hello Kitty "hard to read" and "delightfully inexplicable." The University of Hawaii anthropologist Christine Yano, who studies Hello Kitty fans, declares her a modern "sphinx."

But really she's a primitive LOLCat, with a fill-in-the-blank expression that demands captioning.

This cat has other secrets. The figurehead of Japan's indigenous *kawaii* or cute culture, she is technically of British origin. Yuko Shimizu, Hello Kitty's original cartoonist, says that her creation's peculiar name derives from the 1871 Lewis Carroll classic *Through the Looking Glass*. Before stepping through the magic mirror, Alice plays with a cat called Kitty.

In the grim postwar era, Japanese schoolgirls apparently found an escape in the children's literature of the British victors, and Carroll's work in particular "became part of the fantasy world of Japanese women," Yano says.

Of course, Carroll, author of *Alice's Adventures in Wonderland*, is the force behind another archetypal feline: the Cheshire Cat, who is also a perfectly ambiguous being in his way. From a memetic perspective, it's rather thrilling that the iconic cat with no mouth and the iconic cat that often appears only as a smile share the same pedigree.

But perhaps we should reach further back than either postwar Japan or Victorian England, and end where this madness began.

"The cat is a time-traveler from ancient Egypt," writes the literary scholar Camille Paglia. "It returns whenever sorcery or style is in vogue."

Felis sylvestris lybica first entered our lives in the neolithic Near East, but the cultural fascination with the house cat began thousands of years later in the Nile valley. It's no stretch to call what happened in Egypt the world's first real cat "craze."

As luck would have it, while Lil Bub is busy conquering Brooklyn, a show called *Divine Felines: Cats of Ancient Egypt* is on view at the Brooklyn Museum, and I decide to stop by.

I am prepared for the curated rows of dainty house cats cast in bronze and carved and gilded and even outfitted with dangly gold earrings.

The lions, though, are a surprise. Hewn from limestone and syenite, these statues look as large as life. The jewels have fallen out of one lion's eyes, and its drilled gaze is as vacant and endless as the desert.

Egypt, like much of the planet, was big-cat country once, and the Egyptians' primary feline muse—for most of the three millennia that their civilized endured—was not the house cat but the lion. Lions lived on the edge of the desert, where the early kings built their tombs. It was lions that the pharaohs chose to merge with in the form of the sphinx, and there were multiple lion-headed gods. Lions feature prominently in older tomb frescoes, as royal pets, alleged hunting companions, and—perhaps most often—glorious quarry.

In fact, the major Egyptian house cat goddess, Bastet, began her divinity as a lion. House cats, on the other hand, did not become an Egyptian obsession until the empire's last days.

The first domestic depictions of Egyptian house cats date from the Middle Kingdom, around 1950 BC. As befits a great agrarian society, many tomb frescoes show cats confronting rats. In others, cats are also seen slaying wild birds and dining on sumptuous portions of human-provided meat. In fact, some of these cats are downright fat; Egyptian scholar Jaromir Malek describes one as "an ungainly creature" and another, pictured wearing a beaded necklace, as "plump and rather cross-looking . . . one suspects that much of its diet was due to its owners' kindness rather than its own hunting efforts."

Though clearly already part of the Egyptian household, these cats were spoiled pets, not sacred creatures. House cats wouldn't become holy animals for many more centuries, by which point ancient Egyptian civilization was in decline, riven by internal factions and pressured by bullying neighbors. Also, the empire's once-abundant natural resources were dwindling. When Herodotus visited Egypt in the fifth century BC, he described it as "not a country of many animals." After so many centuries of farming and hunting, most of the big game was gone, or corralled in royal preserves. Perhaps the shortage of charismatic wildlife helps explain why, around this time, the cat goddess Bastet rather abruptly transformed from a lion into a house cat. It's a change that hints at the taming of an entire landscape.

Starting around 332 BC, the Greek Ptolemies ruled Egypt for a few hundred years. The brief, fraught reign of these foreigners was a period of religious ferment and hysteria, when Egypt's animal cults suddenly became far more prominent. Bastet and her house cats—her flesh-and-blood familiars—quickly outcompeted crocodiles and ibises and the rest of the cult animals to become perhaps the most popular devotion. Interestingly, the Greek rulers had no special fondness for cats, yet they supported—or, as Malek suggests, skillfully manipulated—this spike in animal-centric native religion. The sale of priestly offices was a handy source of government funds, and the cult of Bastet helped foster an entire pilgrimage industry of hoteliers, fortune-tellers, and artisans who crafted bedazzled cat statues that even Grumpy Cat might envy.

Bastet, whose cult was based in the Nile city of Bubastis, had especially raucous festivals, where revelers from across the country floated into town on party barges. At their peak, these celebrations—more or less cat raves, in which worshippers danced and tore off their clothes—were attended by an estimated 700,000 people, a huge chunk of Egypt's population. Bastet also had extravagant temples, including one smack in the middle of Bubastis, encircled by 100-foot-wide channels of flowing Nile water. Some of her temples had real catteries attached, where priests raised untold number of house cats. Ordinary pet felines throughout the kingdom basked in Bastet's elevated status, and Egypt allegedly even made efforts to ransom and repatriate cats from other countries.

In addition to the economic boost, the Egyptian government probably liked how cat cults and similar institutions smoothed over cracks in an increasingly fractured society. Rallying around these familiar creatures and their associated gods was a kind of national retrenchment, Malek points out, and a way for the conquered Egyptians to claim identity.

Maybe then as now, cats were something everybody could get behind, a happy distraction, a universal pleasure, and even a taming force. The chaotic, hostile, and faction-ridden atmosphere of Egypt's late antiquity, in fact, reminds me a little of the Internet.

Just as Internet cats exemplify low culture today, Egypt's feline ardor was attacked as an intellectual and spiritual shortcoming; classical writers often "commented scathingly on the oddity of the Egyptians' obsession with animals," writes Egyptian archaeologist Salima Ikram. These critics had a point, since some ancient Egyptians at times seemed to care more for felines than for their fellow humans. When a cat died of natural causes, people shaved their eyebrows in mourning, and cat killing became a major crime. According to the historian Diodorus, after a Roman visitor to Egypt accidentally killed a cat, a mob of cat lovers murdered him. Meanwhile, the Egyptians carefully mummified their cats; one very early cat embalmer hoped his pet would become "an imperishable star."

In our own age, this is a familiar wish—though today we digitally embed rather than embalm. Facebook, in particular, is the new funerary fresco, the idealized, two-dimensional legacy of our mortal lives. Online, we'd like to think that none of us have to die, and perhaps we use animals as proof of concept. I was a little shocked to learn that several prominent Internet celebrity cats—who, I had naively assumed, were purring away in some far-off living room—really are "imperishable stars." Keyboard Cat, whose video popularity peaked in the 2000s, has been dead since 1987. The Happy Cat died nearly a decade ago, shortly after I Can Has Cheezburger made him immortal. Colonel Meow succumbed to heart failure in early 2014 and has since nearly doubled his fan base, racking up "friends" and "likes" every day.

"He's kind of like the Tupac of cats," his owner, Anne Marie Avey, told me. "A lot of his fans don't even realize that he's passed." They still drink Scotch on his birthday and chuckle over old pictures with new captions.

But there's one even more striking similarity between the first cat lovers and ourselves. More than the animals' privileged treatment after death, it has to do with how many of Egypt's house cats died.

When archaeologists X-rayed the ancient cat mummies, they found that many of them contained not cats but kittens, and that these kittens had been violently killed. Their necks were snapped and their skulls were smashed in. They may have been animals bred only for slaughter, perhaps dispatched en masse to furnish corpses for votive mummy offerings around the time of Bastet's spring festivals, when pilgrims flocked to the cat god's temples. This wide-scale extermination may also have been a primitive (and, it goes without saying, doomed) attempt at population control.

It's unclear how much Bastet's pilgrims knew about the institutional killing, or if they approved. I am a sometime cat worshipper myself, and the pictures of strangled Egyptian kittens from thousands of years ago reminded me of a photograph that I'd quite recently averted my gaze from, of that fluffy pile of dead cats and kittens representing just one morning's euthanasia rounds at a single California animal shelter.

We are far more prolific killers than the Egyptians, dispatching millions of cats per year in America alone, and cremating the bodies. I'd never thought of them as sacrificial animals, but perhaps in a sense they are— the secret price of the almost spiritual pleasure that we get from our feline companions.

Human reverence and disregard have a dangerous way of coexisting, especially where animals are concerned. No matter how much we "love" something, it's never beyond us to destroy it. And this has serious implications for how we treat animals that are not as cuddly or convenient to live with or as good at surviving as house cats. Pets are, after all, increasingly the crucible in which we form our thoughts about the fading natural world.

Throughout this book, I've argued that it's important to appreciate an animal like the cat for what it really is, not our plaything but a powerful organism with a strategy and a story. Seeing cats in this light also means recognizing ourselves and acknowledging the full range of what we're capable of—our special mix of tenderness and cruelty, and our unlimited, often careless influence. If we don't, many life-forms on this planet may not stand a chance.

House cats, though, are going to be fine regardless, just as they weathered the fall of their cult to Christianity in the fourth century AD, when Bastet's temples were shuttered and the priests were killed. The house cats' nine lives are, after all, an Egyptian idea.

Even the mummified cats survived their sacrifice: Victorian archaeologists dug them up from mass graves two thousand years later, and they were shipped by the ton back to England to be used as agricultural fertilizer just as the formal cat fancy was getting started, and the great lion slayers returned from safari to take their tea.

So house cats will continue to succeed as long as we do, and maybe longer. At the same time, though, they never would have existed without us, and while not exactly our creations, they are our creatures. Perhaps "familiars" really is the right word.

Unlike us, though, they are always innocent.

The men played on pipes of lotus: the women on cymbals and tambourines, and [those that] had no instruments accompanied the music with clapping of hands and dances, and other joyous gestures. . . . when they reached Bubastis, then held they a wondrously solemn feast: and more wine of the grape was drank in those days than in all the rest of the year. Such was the manner of this festival . . . (HERODOTUS, ca. 450 BC)

Is this Brooklyn or Bubastis? It's disorientingly dark in the nightclub. Human silhouettes with cat ears and long tails sidle past. Some people are wearing their dead cats' collars as ankle bracelets, and lockets full of feline ashes dangle from their necks. Everyone seems to be guzzling something potent, perhaps wine of the grape, and feasting on artisanal pierogies and smuggled-in kale cookies as they wait for the festival to start. A girl band called Supercute! screeches through a set, cymbals clashing. Fans stand on tiptoes looking for Lil Bub, that modern-day Cheshire Cat, who must be here somewhere, her smile moving in and out of sight.

The Internet Cat Video Festival is simply a montage of online cat clips. Its logo is a roaring kitten, Metro-Goldwyn-Mayer's lion in miniature. Like Bastet's floating Nile festival, it is an itinerant affair—the tour's schedule has included stops in London, Sydney, and Memphis (Tennessee, that is).

I see only one real cat on the festival premises, a pale, elegant presence named Parsnip hovering on someone's shoulders like a ghost. Parsnip watches with dispassionate eyes, but no one seems to notice her.

"Unlike man who forgets his previous forms," Carl Van Vechten writes, the cat alone "really remembers, many generations back."

"Where are the cats! Where are the cats!" the boozy crowd begins to chant.

The human girls finish singing and, conspicuously, receive no encore. The real show is about to begin.

Acknowledgments

T HE TALE of the little house cat brushes up against some surprisingly big questions, and I am grateful to the dozens of scientists, activists, and enthusiasts—those mentioned by name in these pages and many more—who patiently shared their work and perspectives with me.

Thank you to my wonderful editor, Karyn Marcus, for taming the manuscript, and to Megan Hogan for fine grooming thereafter. Thank you to Scott Waxman, my literary agent, for his confidence and support.

Elizabeth Quill, E. A. Brunner, Stephen Kiehl, Michael Ollove, Patricia Snow, Maureen Tucker, Steven Dong, Judith Tucker, and Charles Douthat all delivered instrumental suggestions, and Lyn Garrity contributed her keen research skills. Mark Strauss, your words of wisdom and canny cat quotes arrived at just the right moment. Terence Monmaney, thank you for your comments and encouragement here, and for your guidance and many editorial insights over the years.

I am indebted to Michael Caruso and all the editors at *Smithsonian* for allowing me so many opportunities, and to other great editors and teachers, including Carey Winfrey, Laura Helmuth, Jean Marbella, the late Mary Corey, Will Doolittle, Andrew Botsford, Marjorie Guerin, Robert Cox, and Kathleen Wassall.

Most of all, I am grateful to my family, especially to my sweet and extraordinary husband, Ross, and to our three children, Gwendolyn, Eleanor and—now—Nicholas. Who can say what his first word will be?

Notes

Introduction

1   *In the summer of 2012:* David Wilkes, Inderdeep Bains, Tom Kelly, and Abul Taher, "On the prowl again! Teddy the 'mystery lion of Essex' is out and about, but this time the ginger tom cat doesn't need a police escort," *Daily Mail*, Aug. 27, 2012; John Stevens, Hannah Roberts, and Larisa Brown, "Here kitty, kitty: Image of 'Essex Lion' that sparked massive police hunt is finally revealed as officers call off the search and admit sightings were probably of a 'large domestic cat,'" *Daily Mail*, Aug. 26, 2012.

2   *The Essex Lion is what is known as a Phantom Cat:* For more on this phenomenon, see britishbigcats.org or Michael Williams and Rebecca Lang, *Australian Big Cats: An Unnatural History of Panthers* (Hazelbrook, NSW, Australia: Strange Nation Publishing, 2010).

2   *A few of the phantoms have been revealed as calculated frauds:* Max Blake, Darren Naish, Greger Larson, et al., "Multidisciplinary investigation of a 'British big cat': a lynx killed in southern England c. 1903," *Historical Biology: An International Journal of Paleobiology* 26, no. 4 (2014): 442–48.

2   *Former lords of the jungle, lions are now relics:* Erica Goode, "Lion Population in Africa Likely to Fall by Half, Study Finds," *New York Times*, Oct. 26, 2015.

2   *The global house cat population:* Philip J. Baker, Carl D. Soulsbury, Graziella Iossa, and Stephen Harris, "Domestic Cat (*Felis catus*) and Domestic Dog (*Canis familiaris*)," in *Urban Carnivores: Ecology, Conflict, and Conservation*, ed. Stanley D. Gehrt, Seth P. D. Riley, and Brian L. Cypher (Baltimore: Johns Hopkins University Press, 2010), 157.

2   *More of them are born in the United States:* Including strays and pets, the total American house cat population is somewhere between 100 and 200 million. For the population to hold steady, assuming an average life expec-

tancy of 12 years, between 22,000 and 44,000 kittens would need to be born every day.

2 *New York City's annual spring kitten crop:* Corrine Ramey, " 'Tis the Season for ASPCA's Kitten Nursery," *Wall Street Journal,* July 24, 2015. More than 2,000 kittens pass through a single New York City shelter each year. Meanwhile, the World Wildlife Fund reports that as few as 3,200 tigers persist in the wild, www.worldwildlife.org/species/tiger.

2 *Worldwide, house cats already outnumber dogs:* John Bradshaw, *Cat Sense: How the New Feline Science Can Make You a Better Friend to Your Pet* (New York: Basic Books, 2013), xix. Baker et al. put the ratio at a more modest three cats to two dogs, while other sources favor even more staggering cat numbers.

3 *The tally of pet cats in America rose by 50 percent:* E. Fuller Torrey and Robert H. Yolken, "*Toxoplasma* oocysts as a public health problem," *Trends in Parasitology* 29, no. 8 (2013): 380–84.

3 *today approaches 100 million:* The APPA puts the number of pets at 95.6 million. National Pet Owners Survey, 2013–2014, 169.

3 *Similar population jumps are happening across the planet:* From interviews with Paula Flores, Global Head of Pet Care Research at Euromonitor International.

3 *Australia's 18 million feral cats outnumber the pets:* Baker et al., "Domestic Cat (*Felis catus*) and Domestic Dog (*Canis familiaris*)," 160.

4 *It's especially confusing:* International Union for Conservation of Nature's 100 Worst Invasive Species list, www.issg.org/database/species/search .asp?st=100ss.

4 *Australian scientists recently described stray cats:* "Historic Analysis Confirms Ongoing Mammal Extinction Crisis," *Wildlife Matters* (Winter 2014): 4–9.

4 *in a landscape teeming with great white sharks:* Jared Owens, "Greg Hunt calls for eradication of feral cats that kill 75m animals a night," *Australian,* June 2, 2014.

4 *in some states, "pet trusts" enable:* David Grimm, *Citizen Canine: Our Evolving Relationship with Cats and Dogs* (New York: Public Affairs, 2014), 153, 266–67.

4 *New York City recently shut down:* Matt Flegenheimer, "9 Lives? M.T.A. Takes No Chances with Cats on Tracks," *New York Times,* Aug. 29, 2013.

4   *even as our country routinely euthanizes:* Hal Herzog, *Some We Love, Some We Hate, Some We Eat: Why It's So Hard to Think Straight About Animals* (New York: Harper Perennial, 2010), 6.

4   *said to compromise our thinking:* Carl Zimmer, "Parasites Practicing Mind Control," *New York Times,* Aug. 28, 2014.

5   *the world's largest fancy cat emporium:* Henry S. F. Cooper, "The Cattery," in *The Big New Yorker Book of Cats* (New York: Random House, 2013), 187.

7   *they eat practically anything that moves:* Christopher A. Lepczyk, Cheryl A. Lohr, and David C. Duffy, "A review of cat behavior in relation to disease risk and management options," *Applied Animal Behaviour Science* 173 (Dec. 2015): 29–39. This study points out that cats have been found to eat more than 1,000 species.

7   *Some of their imperiled feline relatives:* "Andean Cat," International Society for Endangered Cats Canada, www.wildcatconservation.org/wild-cats /south-america/andean-cat/.

7   *"the advantageous amino acid substitutions":* Michael J. Montague, Gang Li, Barbara Gandolfi, et al., "Comparative analysis of the domestic cat genome reveals genetic signatures underlying feline biology and domestication," *Proceedings of the National Academy of Sciences* 111 (Dec. 2014): 17230–35.

7   *"opportunistic, cryptic, solitary hunters":* Diane K. Brockman, Laurie R. Godfrey, Luke J. Dollar, and Joelisoa Ratsirarson, "Evidence of Invasive *Felis silvestris* Predation on *Propithecus verreauxi* at Beza Mahafaly Special Reserve, Madagascar," *International Journal of Primatology* 29 (Feb. 2008): 135–52.

7   *"subsidized predators":* Christopher A. Lepczyk, Angela G. Mertig, and Jianguo Liu, "Landowners and cat predation across rural-to-urban landscapes," *Biological Conservation* 115 (Feb. 2004): 191–201.

7   *"delightful and flourishing profiteers":* Carlos A. Driscoll, David W. Macdonald, and Stephen J. O'Brien, "From wild animals to domestic pets, an evolutionary view of domestication," *Proceedings of the National Academy of Sciences* 106, suppl. 1 (June 2009): 9971–78.

8   *More than half of the earth's human population:* Stanley D. Gehrt, "The Urban Ecosystem," in Gehrt et al., *Urban Carnivores,* 3.

8   *pet cats are statistically likely to:* About 35 percent of pet cats enter a household as wandering strays—the most common source for owners. By contrast, only 6 percent of dogs were found as wandering strays. *APPA Survey:* 64, 171.

Chapter 1 CATACOMBS

12 *Our competing needs for meat and space make us natural enemies:* Conversations with lion biologist Craig Packer of the University of Minnesota were indispensable throughout this chapter, as were interviews with Kris Helgen of the National Museum of Natural History.

13 *Most modern cat species:* Roughly two-thirds of cat species are listed in the top four categories of concern by the International Union for Conservation of Nature. The others are typically are found in areas far smaller than their natural range; David W. Macdonald, Andrew J. Loveridge, and Kristin Nowell, "*Dramatis personae*: an introduction to the wild felids," in *Biology and Conservation of Wild Felid*, ed. David Macdonald and Andrew Loveridge (Oxford: Oxford University Press, 2010), 15.

14 *the rare kittens often end up as highway roadkill:* Emily Sawicki, "Untagged Mountain Lion Kitten Killed," *Malibu Times*, Jan. 23, 2014.

14 *A mountain lion known as P-22:* Alexa Keefe, "A Cougar Ready for His Closeup," *National Geographic*, Nov. 14, 2013, http://proof.national geographic.com/2013/11/14/a-cougar-ready-for-his-closeup/.

14 *The cat family is part of the mammalian order Carnivora:* In addition to Macdonald et al., "*Dramatis personae*," the discussion of feline carnivory draws from these sources: Mel Sunquist and Fiona Sunquist, *Wild Cats of the World* (Chicago: University of Chicago Press, 2002); Elizabeth Marshall Thomas, *The Tribe of Tiger: Cats and Their Culture* (New York: Pocket Books, 1994); Alan Turner, *The Big Cats and Their Fossil Relatives: An Illustrated Guide to Their Evolution and Natural History* (New York: Columbia University Press, 1997); David Quammen, *Monster of God: The Man-Eating Predator in the Jungles of History and the Mind* (New York: W. W. Norton, 2003).

14 *cats require three times as much protein:* Sunquist and Sunquist, *Wild Cats of the World*, 5.

15 *"The important thing about big cats":* Thomas, *Tribe of Tiger*, 19.

15 *"the alpha and omega":* ibid., xi.

15 *"a key in a lock":* in Sunquist and Sunquist, *Wild Cats of the World*, 6.

15 *Cats can get the best of animals:* Thomas, *Tribe of Tiger*, 23–24.

15 *The modern Felidae have enjoyed:* Turner, *The Big Cats*, 30.

15 *Cats are partial to the tropical forests of Asia:* Macdonald et al., *"Dramatis personae,"* 4–5.

16 *most widely distributed wild land mammal ever:* Sunquist and Sunquist, *Wild Cats of the World,* 286, and Thomas, *Tribe of Tiger,* 47.

16 *typically less common:* Turner, *The Big Cats,* 15.

16 *very rough rule of thumb:* Todd K. Fuller, Stephen DeStefano, and Paige S. Warren, "Carnivore Behavior and Ecology, and Relationship to Urbanization," in *Urban Carnivores: Ecology, Conflict, and Conservation,* ed. Stanley D. Gehrt, Seth P. D. Riley, and Brian L. Cypher (Baltimore: Johns Hopkins University Press, 2010), 16.

16 *A host of creatures dined on us:* Rob Dunn, "What Are You So Scared of? Saber-Toothed Cats, Snakes, and Carnivorous Kangaroos," Slate.com, Oct. 15, 2012.

17 *we might not know nearly so much:* John Noble Wilford, "Skull Fossil Suggests Simpler Human Lineage," *New York Times,* Oct. 17, 2013.

17 *Scientists are just starting to formally study:* Donna Hart and Robert W. Sussman, *Man the Hunted: Primates, Predators, and Human Evolution* (New York: Westview Press, 2005), 170–80.

17 *Experiments have shown that even very young children:* Joseph Bennington-Castro, "Are Humans Hardwired to Detect Snakes?" io9.com, Oct. 29, 2013.

18 *Even less exalted primate relatives:* Joseph Bennington-Castro, "Monkeys Remember 'Words' Used by Their Ancestors Centuries Ago," io9.com, Oct. 30, 2013.

18 *small Amazonian cats called margays:* Wildlife Conservation Society, "Wild cat found mimicking monkey calls," *Science Daily,* July 9, 2010.

18 *Some scientists have even proposed that saber-tooth table scraps:* Alfonso Arribas and Paul Palmqvist, "On the Ecological Connection Between Sabretooths and Hominids: Faunal Dispersal Events in the Lower Pleistocene and a Review of the Evidence for the First Human Arrival in Europe," *Journal of Archaeological Science* 26, no. 5 (1999): 571–85.

19 *meat-eating may have literally expanded our minds:* Leslie C. Aiello and Peter Wheeler, "The Expensive-Tissue Hypothesis: The Brain and the Digestive System in Human and Primate Evolution," *Current Anthropology* 36, no. 2 (1995): 199–221.

19   *crown jewel of* Homo sapiens: Nikhil Swaminathan, "Why Does the Brain Need So Much Power?" *Scientific American,* Apr. 29, 2008.

20   *ancient stalemate:* The stalemate persists in some surviving hunter-gatherer cultures, as described in Thomas, *Tribe of Tiger,* 124.

20   *Victorians filled London's zoos:* Harriet Ritvo, *The Animal Estate: The English and Other Creatures in the Victorian Age* (Cambridge, MA: Harvard University Press, 1989), 208.

20   *Egypt, the first great agrarian culture:* Justin D. Yeakel, Mathias M. Pires, Lars Rudolf, et al., "Collapse of an Ecological Network in Ancient Egypt," *Proceedings of the National Academy of Sciences* 111, no. 40 (2014): 14472–77; Patrick F. Houlihan, *The Animal World of the Pharaohs* (London: Thames & Hudson, 1996), 45.

20   *Romans—who bagged big cats:* For a fabulous review of the lion's global decline, see Quammen, *Monster of God,* 24–29.

21   *Rufiji farming district:* Craig Packer, "Rational Fear: As human populations expand and lions' prey dwindles in eastern Africa, the poorest people—and the hungriest lions—pay the price," *Natural History,* May 2009, 43–47.

22   *Americans are no different:* The Beast in the Garden: A Modern Parable of Man and Nature* by David Baron (New York: W. W. Norton, 2004) offers an excellent snapshot of big-cat predation in a modern American suburb.

22   *Asian medicine market carves up:* For a list of tiger remedies, see "Tiger in Crisis: Promoting the Plight of Endangered Tigers and the Efforts to Save Them," www.tigersincrisis.com/traditional_medicine.htm.

22   *best when pan-seared:* For an account of a "Flintstone dinner" featuring lion meat, see PhilaFoodie, "Yabba-Dabba-Zoo!—Zot's Flintstone Dinner," July 7, 2008, philafoodie.blogspot.com/2008/07/yabba-dabba-zoo-zots -flintstone-dinner.html.

24   *Maybe it's telling that one of the few places in the world:* Euromonitor data; Jason Overdorf, "India: Leopards Stalk Bollywood," *GlobalPost,* March 20, 2013; Arvind Joshi, "Cats, Unloved in India," *India Times.* pets.indiatimes .com/articleshow.cms?msid=1736285885.

Chapter 2   CAT'S CRADLE

28   *The 11,600-year-old village of Hallan Çemi:* Brian L. Peasnall, "Intricacies of Hallan Çemi," *Expedition Magazine* 44 (Mar. 2002).

29   *archaeologist Melinda Zeder:* Conversations with the archaeologist Reuven Yeshurun, who studies the foxes of Hallan Çemi, were also extremely helpful.

29   *small yet graphic body of scientific literature:* Maria Joana Gabucio, Isabel Caceres, Antonio Hidalgo, et al., "A wildcat (*Felis silvestris*) butchered by Neanderthals in Level O of the Abric Romani site (Capellades, Barcelona, Spain)," *Quaternary International* 326 (2014): 307–18; Jacopo Crezzini, Francesco Boschin, Paolo Boscato, and Ursula Wierer, "Wild cats and cut marks: Exploitation of *Felis silvestris* in the Mesolithic of Galgenbühel/Dos de la Forca (South Tyrol, Italy)," *Quaternary International* 330 (Apr. 2014): 52–60.

30   *gluts of midsize hunters are actually a common feature:* Laura R. Prugh, Chantal J. Stoner, Clinton W. Epps, et al., "The Rise of the Mesopredator," *Bioscience* 59 (2009), 779–91.

30   *red foxes are a major nuisance:* Katrin Bennhold, "Forget the Hounds. As Foxes Creep In, Britons Call the Sniper," *New York Times*, Dec. 6, 2014.

31   *the process of animal domestication as a road or a pathway:* Melinda A. Zeder, "Pathways to Animal Domestication," in *Biodiversity in Agriculture: Domestication, Evolution and Sustainability*, ed. Paul Gepts, Thomas R. Famula, Robert L. Bettinger, et al. (New York: Cambridge University Press, 2012), 227–59.

31   *three times as many chickens:* "Counting Chickens," *Economist*, July 27, 2011, http://www.economist.com/blogs/dailychart/2011/07/global-live stock-counts.

32   *very tough for scientists to determine:* James Gorman, "15,000 Years Ago, Probably in Asia, the Dog Was Born," *New York Times*, Oct. 19, 2015; James Gorman, "Family Tree of Dogs and Wolves Is Found to Split Earlier Than Thought," *New York Times*, May 21, 2015.

32   *even today experts often can't tell house tabbies from wild cats:* Carlos A. Driscoll, Nobuyuki Yamaguchi, Stephen J. O'Brien, and David W. Macdonald, "A Suite of Genetic Markers Useful in Assessing Wildcat (*Felis silvestris*

ssp.)—Domestic Cat (*Felis silvestris catus*) Admixture," *Journal of Heredity* 102, suppl. 1 (2011): S87–S90.

32 *Darwin devotes just a few pages:* Charles Darwin, *The Variation of Animals and Plants Under Domestication*, vol. 1 (Teddington: Echo Library, 2007), 32–35.

32 *whether or not house cats really qualify as fully domesticated animals:* Carlos A. Driscoll, David W. Macdonald, and Stephen J. O'Brien, "From wild animals to domestic pets, an evolutionary view of domestication," *Proceedings of the National Academy of Sciences* 106, suppl. 1 (June 2009): 9971–78.

32 *ancestral sprinklings:* For some theories, see Juliet Clutton-Brock, *A Natural History of Domesticated Mammals* (Cambridge: Cambridge University Press, 1999), 136–37.

33 *project took nearly ten years:* Carlos A. Driscoll, Marilyn Menotti-Raymond, Alfred L. Roca, et al., "The Near Eastern Origin of Cat Domestication," *Science* 317 (July 2007): 519–23.

33 *Cats, by any reasonable standard, are terrible candidates:* ibid.

34 *average Australian household cat:* Chee Chee Leung, "Cats eating into world fish stocks," *Sydney Morning Herald*, Aug. 26, 2008.

34 *baseline comfort with humans:* Zeder, "Pathways to Animal Domestication," 232.

35 *"Beelzebina, Princess of Devils":* in John Bradshaw, *Cat Sense: How the New Feline Science Can Make You a Better Friend to Your Pet* (New York: Basic Books, 2013), 14.

35 *Studies of modern radio-collared wild* Felis silvestris lybica *suggest:* David Macdonald, Orin Courtenay, Scott Forbes, and Paul Honess, "African Wildcats in Saudi Arabia," in *The Wild CRU Review: The Tenth Anniversary Report of the Wildlife Conservation Research Unit at Oxford University*, ed. David Macdonald and Françoise Tattersall (Oxford: University of Oxford Department of Zoology, 1996).

37 *More than 50 years ago:* Evan Ratliff, "Taming the Wild," *National Geographic*, March 2011; Lyudmila N. Trut, "Early Canid Domestication: The Farm-Fox Experiment," *American Scientist*, Mar.–Apr. 1999.

38 *When researchers from Washington University:* Michael J. Montague, Gang Li, Barbara Gandolfi, et al., "Comparative analysis of the domestic cat genome

reveals genetic signatures underlying feline biology and domestication," *Proceedings of the National Academy of Sciences* 111 (Dec. 2014): 17230–35.

38   *Darwin, who first described it:* Adam S. Wilkins, Richard W. Wrangham, and W. Tecumseh Fitch, "The 'Domestication Syndrome' in Mammals: A Unified Explanation Based on Neural Crest Cell Behavior and Genetics," *Genetics* 197 (July 2014): 795–808.

39   *house cats' coats began to vary only:* Carlos A. Driscoll, Juliet Clutton-Brock, Andrew C. Kitchener, and Stephen J. O'Brien, "The Taming of the Cat," *Scientific American,* June 2009; James A. Serpell, "Domestication and History of the Cat," in *The Domestic Cat: The Biology of Its Behaviour,* 2nd ed., ed. Dennis C. Turner and Patrick Bateson (Cambridge: Cambridge University Press, 2000), 186.

39   *undergo more frequent reproductive cycles:* Perry T. Cupps, *Reproduction in Domestic Animals* (New York: Elsevier, 1991), 542–44.

39   *And they exhibit the single most vital:* Zeder, "Pathways to Animal Domestication," 232–36.

39   *because human beings weren't:* Helmut Hemmer, *Domestication: The Decline of Environmental Appreciation* (Cambridge: Cambridge University Press, 1990), 108.

40   *Scientists now suspect:* Wilkins et al., "The 'Domestication Syndrome' in Mammals."

40   *When the Washington University geneticists:* Montague et al., "Comparative analysis of the domestic cat genome."

40   *Our pets' legs:* Bradshaw, *Cat Sense,* 18.

40   *Their meow sounds a little sweeter:* Nicholas Nicastro, "Perceptual and Acoustic Evidence for Species-Level Differences in Meow Vocalizations by Domestic Cats (*Felis catus*) and African Wild Cats (*Felis silvestris lybica*)," *Journal of Comparative Psychology* 118 (2004): 287–96.

40   *recalibrated their social lives ever so slightly:* Mel Sunquist and Fiona Sunquist, *Wild Cats of the World* (Chicago: University of Chicago Press, 2002), 106.

40   *house cats have also lengthened their intestines:* Darwin, *The Variation of Animals and Plants Under Domestication,* vol. 1, 35.

Chapter 3 WHAT'S THE CATCH?

44   *include some 12 million more cats:* The 2012 US pet cat population was 95.6
     million, compared to 83.3 million dogs. *APPA Survey,* 7.

44   *they barked warnings:* David Grimm, *Citizen Canine: Our Evolving Relation-
     ship with Cats and Dogs* (New York: Public Affairs, 2014), 29–30.

44   *went whole hog:* Juliet Clutton-Brock, *A Natural History of Domesticated
     Mammals* (Cambridge: Cambridge University Press, 1999), 59.

45   *Hunting breeds similar to the greyhound:* "A Brief History of the Greyhound,"
     Grey2K USA, www.grey2kusaedu.org/pdf/history.pdf.

45   *Romans likely employed guide dogs:* Grimm, *Citizen Canine,* 220.

45   *sheep dogs:* Clutton-Brock, *Natural History,* 511–54.

45   *mastiff-like war dogs:* www.mastiffweb.com/history.htm.

45   *tiny lapdogs:* Bud Boccone, "The Maltese, Toy Dog of Myth and Legend,"
     American Kennel Club, akc.org/akc-dog-lovers/maltese-toy-dog-myth
     -legend/.

45   *A list of antique Tudor dog breed names:* Harriet Ritvo, *The Animal Estate: The
     English and Other Creatures in the Victorian Age* (Cambridge, MA: Harvard
     University Press, 1989), 93–94.

45   *we've fitted dogs with Kevlar vests:* Grimm, *Citizen Canine,* 209–12.

45   *Dogs comfort the victims of mass shootings:* Taylor Temby, "Therapy dogs
     brought to Aurora Theater Trial," 9news.com, June 14, 2015.

45   *help capture Osama bin Laden:* Grimm, *Citizen Canine,* 212.

45   *locate the scat of rare animals:* Sarah Yang, "Wildlife biologists put dogs'
     scat-sniffing talents to good use," *Berkeley News,* Jan. 11, 2011.

45   *discover the graves:* Cat Warren, *What the Dog Knows: The Science and Wonder
     of Working Dogs* (New York: Simon & Schuster, 2013), 235.

45   *"Dogs can detect incipient tumors":* Grimm, *Citizen Canine,* 224.

45   *"Cat purring . . . may boost bone density":* ibid.

45   *Indonesians paraded cats:* Mel Sunquist and Fiona Sunquist, *Wild Cats of the
     World* (Chicago: University of Chicago Press, 2002), 102.

45 *Seventeenth-century Japanese musicians:* Muriel Beadle, *The Cat: A Complete Authoritative Compendium of Information About Domestic Cats* (New York: Simon & Schuster, 1977), 89.

45 *The Chinese used the cats' dilating pupils:* James A. Serpell, "Domestication and History of the Cat," in *The Domestic Cat: The Biology of Its Behaviour,* 2nd ed., ed. Dennis C. Turner and Patrick Bateson (Cambridge: Cambridge University Press, 2000), 184.

45 *Cats were also an essential part:* Beadle, *The Cat,* 83.

46 *In the high-tech era, the cat hair:* Marilyn A. Menotti-Raymond, Victor A. Davids, and Stephen J. O'Brien, "Pet cat hair implicates murder suspect," *Nature* 386 (April 1997): 774.

46 *prisoners have employed cats as drug mules:* "Cat caught carrying marijuana into Moldovan prison," Associated Press, Oct. 18, 2013.

46 *cats have served as key indicators:* Beadle, *The Cat,* 90.

46 *Cat meat itself is still eaten:* Worldwide, some 4 million cats (compared to 13 to 16 million dogs) are eaten each year, according to Anthony L. Podberscek, "Good to Pet and Eat: The Keeping and Consuming of Dogs and Cats in South Korea," *Journal of Social Issues* 65 (2009): 615–32.

46 *cat skins are only seldom worn:* Steve Friess, "A Push to Stop Swiss Cats from Being Turned into Coats and Hats," *New York Times,* Apr. 1, 2008.

46 *hipster craze for harvesting shed cat fur:* Jun Hongo, "Cat Hair Is Festive for Japanese Craft Aficionados," *Wall Street Journal,* Apr. 18, 2014.

46 *a sixteenth-century German-language artillery manual:* Brad Scriber, "Why Do 16th-Century Manuscripts Show Cats with Flaming Backpacks?" *National Geographic,* Mar. 11, 2014, http://news.nationalgeographic.com/news /2014/03/140310-rocket-cats-animals-manuscript-artillery-history/.

46 *In the 1960s, the CIA did attempt:* Emily Anthes, *Frankenstein's Cat: Cuddling Up to Biotech's Brave New Beasts* (New York: Scientific American/Farrar, Straus and Giroux, 2013), 143–44.

46 *"In silence, in secret":* Donald W. Engels, *Classical Cats: The Rise and Fall of the Sacred Cat* (London: Routledge, 1999), 1.

47 *I first learned about:* Abigail Tucker, "Crawling Around with Baltimore Street Rats," Smithsonian.com, Nov. 18, 2009.

47   *He cracks it open to a section:* Some of these photos are published in James E. Childs, "Size-Dependent Predation on Rats (*Rattus norvegicus*) by House Cats (*Felis catus*) in an Urban Setting," *Journal of Mammalogy* 67 (Feb. 1986): 196–99. Some study results were replicated twenty years later: Gregory E. Glass, Lynne C. Gardner-Santana, Robert D. Holt, Jessica Chen et al., "Trophic Garnishes: Cat-Rat Interactions in an Urban Environment," *PLOS ONE* (June 2009).

48   *Foxes, their prehistoric doppelgängers:* Gilad Bino, Amit Dolev, Dotan Yosha, et al., "Abrupt spatial and numerical responses of overabundant foxes to a reduction in anthropogenic resources," *Journal of Applied Ecology* 47 (Dec. 2010): 1262–71.

48   *isotopic analysis of 4,000-year-old cat remains:* Yaowu Hu, Songmei Hu, Weilin Wang, et al., "Earliest evidence for commensal processes of cat domestication," *Proceedings of the National Academy of Sciences* 111 (Jan. 2014): 116–20.

48   *As late as the twentieth century, exterminators:* Katherine C. Grier, *Pets in America: A History* (2006; repr., Orlando: Harcourt, 2006), 45.

49   *only a few other studies:* Beadle, *The Cat*, 95–96.

49   *one recent California study:* Cole C. Hawkins, William E. Grant, and Michael T. Longnecker, "Effect of house cats, being fed in parks, on California birds and rodents," *Proceedings 4th International Urban Wildlife Symposium*, ed. W. W. Shaw, L. K. Harris, and L. VanDruff (2004): 164–70.

49   *One commensal adaptation to city living:* For more on the might of Norway rats, see Robert Sullivan, *Rats: Observations on the History & Habitat of the City's Most Unwanted Inhabitants* (New York: Bloomsbury, 2004).

50   *There's even a theory that the Catholic Church:* Engels, *Classical Cats*, 156–62.

50   *hurling cats from bell towers:* This tradition is still (symbolically) celebrated in Ypres, Belgium, Kattenstoet, http://www.kattenstoet.be/en/page/499/welcome.html.

50   *scientists now suspect that rat fleas:* In our interview, Kenneth Gage said that human fleas may be partially to blame. For another theory, see "Rats and fleas off the hook: humans actually passed Black Death to each other," *The Week*, March 30, 2014, http://www.theweek.co.uk/health-science/57918/rats-and-fleas-hook-humans-passed-black-death-each-other.

50   *house cats themselves can be major plague hosts:* Kenneth L. Gage, David T.

Dennis, Kathy A. Orioski, et al., "Cases of Cat-Associated Human Plague in the Western US, 1977–1998," *Clinical Infectious Diseases* 30 (2000): 893–900.

51   *cats were indeed the most commonly accused "imps"*: Serpell, "Domestication and History of the Cat," 188.

51   *Respiratory reactions to cat dander:* "Cat Allergy," from the American College of Allergies, Asthma and Immunology website, www.acaai.org.

51   *"Heckticks and consumptions"*: Serpell, "Domestication and History of the Cat," 188.

51   *"the impact of cats on commensal rodent populations"*: Philip J. Baker, Carl D. Soulsbury, Graziella Iossa, and Stephen Harris, "Domestic Cat (*Felis catus*) and Domestic Dog (*Canis familiaris*)," in *Urban Carnivores: Ecology, Conflict, and Conservation*, ed. Stanley D. Gehrt, Seth D. Riley, and Brian L. Cypher (Baltimore: Johns Hopkins University Press, 2010), 168.

52   *cats and humans last shared an ancestor:* Michael J. Montague, Gang Li, Barbara Gandolfi, et al., "Comparative analysis of the domestic cat genome reveals genetic signatures underlying feline biology and domestication," *Proceedings of the National Academy of Sciences* 111 (Dec. 2014).

53   *our own helpless neonates:* Hal Herzog, *Some We Love, Some We Hate, Some We Eat: Why It's So Hard to Think Straight About Animals* (New York: Harper Perennial, 2010), 39–41; John Archer, "Pet Keeping: A Case Study in Maladaptive Behavior," in *The Oxford Handbook of Evolutionary Family Psychology*, ed. Catherine A. Salmon and Todd K. Shackelford (Oxford: Oxford University Press, 2011), 287–88.

53   *enhanced fine-motor coordination:* John Bradshaw, *Cat Sense: How the New Feline Science Can Make You a Better Friend to Your Pet* (New York: Basic Books, 2013), 188–89.

53   *"misfiring of our parental instincts"*: Herzog, *Some We Love*, 92.

53   *"fooled by an evolved response"*: ibid., 40–41.

53   *Part of it is their size:* Elizabeth Marshall Thomas, *The Tribe of Tiger: Cats and Their Culture* (New York: Pocket Books, 1994), 104.

53   *Part of it is sound:* Karen McComb, Anna M. Taylor, Christian Wilson, and Benjamin D. Charlton, "The cry embedded within the purr," *Current Biology* 19, no. 13 (2009): R507–8.

53   *With their slitted pupils:* Alan Turner, *The Big Cats and Their Fossil Relatives: An Illustrated Guide to Their Evolution and Natural History* (New York: Columbia University Press, 1997), 96–98.

53   *an adult cat's eyes are almost as big:* Bradshaw, *Cat Sense*, 103.

53   *our own saucer-eyed offspring:* Abigail Tucker, "The Science Behind Why Pandas Are So Damn Cute," *Smithsonian*, Nov. 2013.

54   *so they evolved the best binocular vision:* Sunquist and Sunquist, *Wild Cats of the World*, 9.

54   *Primates are not ambush predators:* From interview with Adam Wilkins of Humboldt University in Berlin.

54   *got her start in infant gear:* Jennifer A. Kingson "Cool for Cats," *New York Times*, Dec. 18, 2013.

55   *Some scholars suggest that humans may reap benefits:* James A. Serpell and Elizabeth S. Paul, "Pets in the Family: An Evolutionary Perspective," in *The Oxford Handbook of Evolutionary Family Psychology*, 303–5.

55   *a cat is more akin to a "social parasite":* Archer, "Pet Keeping: A Case Study in Maladaptive Behavior," 293.

Chapter 4 THE CATS THAT ATE THE CANARIES

58   *Once common throughout Key Largo:* For a conservation summary, see U.S. Fish and Wildlife Service, Southeast Region, South Florida Ecological Services Office, "South Florida Multi-Species Recovery Plan, Recovery for the Key Largo Woodrat," Aug. 14, 2009.

60   *a number that has apparently tripled:* See chart in Christopher A. Lepczyk, Nico Dauphine, David M. Bird et al., "What Conservation Biologists Can Do to Counter Trap-Neuter-Return: Response to Longcore et al.," *Conservation Biology* 24, no. 2 (2010): 627–29.

60   *perhaps just as many strays:* One estimate of 60 to 100 million comes from David A. Jessup, "The welfare of feral cats and wildlife," *Journal of the American Veterinary Medical Association* 225 (Nov. 2004): 1377–83. The American Society for the Prevention of Cruelty to Animals estimates 70 million, www.aspca.org/animal-homelessness/shelter-intake-and-surrender /pet-statistics.

60 *House cats have populated every imaginable habitat:* For a sampling, see Table 1 in S. Pearre and R. Maass, "Trends in the prey size-based trophic niches of feral and House Cats *Felis catus L.*," *Mammal Review* 28, no. 3 (1998): 125–39.

60 *In all of these niches, they eat pretty much everything alive:* For a sampling, see Frank B. McMurry and Charles C. Sperry, "Food of Feral House Cats in Oklahoma, a Progress Report," *Journal of Mammalogy* 22, no. 2 (1941): 185–90.

60 *"Beefsteak and cockroaches":* in Carl Van Vechten, *The Tiger in the House: A Cultural History of the Cat* (1920; repr., New York: New York Review of Books, 2007), 11.

60 *house cats have even been known to prey on:* Diane K. Brockman, Laurie R. Godfrey, Luke J. Dollar, and Joelisoa Ratsirarson, "Evidence of Invasive *Felis silvestris* Predation on *Propithecus verreauxi* at Beza Mahafaly Special Reserve, Madagascar," *International Journal of Primatology* 29 (Feb. 2008), 135–52.

60 *Cats can drive extinctions, particularly on islands:* Félix M. Medina, Elsa Bonnaud, Eric Vidal, et al., "A global review of the impacts of invasive cats on island endangered vertebrates," *Global Change Biology* 17, no. 11 (2011): 3503–10.

61 *Domestic dogs, on the other hand:* Austin Ramzy, "Australia Deploys Sheepdogs to Save a Penguin Colony," *New York Times*, Nov. 3, 2015.

61 *"If we had to choose one wish":* "Historic Analysis Confirms Ongoing Mammal Extinction Crisis," *Wildlife Matters* (Winter 2014): 4–9.

61 *Australia's environmental minister:* "Australian official calls cats 'tsunamis of violence and death,'" *Atlanta Journal-Constitution*, Aug. 1, 2015.

61 *In 2013, federal scientists released a report:* Scott R. Loss, Tom Will, and Peter P. Marra, "The impact of free-ranging domestic cats on wildlife of the United States," *Nature Communications* (Dec. 2013), http://www.nature.com/ncomms/journal/v4/n1/full/ncomms2380.html.

61 *A Canadian governmental study:* Anna M. Calvert, Christine A. Bishop, Richard D. Elliot, et. al, "A Synthesis of Human-related Avian Mortality in Canada," *Avian Conservation & Ecology* 8, no. 2, article 11 (2013).

61 *one California facility reported cat injuries:* Jessup, "The welfare of feral cats and wildlife."

61   *"maimed, mauled, dismembered"*: ibid.

61   *"Kittycam" study:* Kerrie Anne T. Loyd, Sonia M. Hernandez, John P. Carroll, Kyler J. Abernathy, and Greg J. Marshall, "Quantifying free-roaming domestic cat predation using animal-borne video cameras," *Biological Conservation* 160 (Apr. 2013): 183–89.

62   *Australian scientists snagged:* www.youtube.com/watch?v=iwAmesMywFo.

62   *one Hawaiian researcher:* Seth Judge, Jill S. Lippert, Kathleen Misajon, Darcy Hu, and Steven C. Hess, "Videographic evidence of endangered species depredation by feral cat," *Pacific Conservation Biology* 18, no. 4 (2012): 293–96.

62   *In 2005, fearing the wood rat numbers:* For details on the program, see Association of Zoos & Aquariums, 2009 Edward H. Bean Award application, www.aza.org/uploadedFiles/Membership/Honors_and_Awards/bean09-disney.pdf.

64   *one eighteenth-century voyager lamented:* From Captain Cook's ship logs, www.captaincooksociety.com/home/detail/225-years-ago-april-june-1777.

64   *Some cats also enjoyed choice galley rations:* Val Lewis, *Ships' Cats in War and Peace* (Shepperton-on-Thames, UK: Nauticalia, 2001), 106.

65   *Hunting prowess aside:* John Bradshaw, *Cat Sense: How the New Feline Science Can Make You a Better Friend to Your Pet* (New York: Basic Books, 2013), 72.

65   *Sailors invented cat toys:* Lewis, *Ships' Cats,* 103.

65   *miniature hammocks:* Donald W. Engels, *Classical Cats: The Rise and Fall of the Sacred Cat* (London: Routledge, 1999), 13.

65   *Egyptians probably stalled:* Carlos A. Driscoll, Juliet Clutton-Brock, Andrew C. Kitchener, and Stephen J. O'Brien, "The Taming of the Cat," *Scientific American,* June 2009.

65   *ancient Greeks also furnished:* For an extensive summary of post-Egyptian cat dispersal, see Engels, 48–138.

65   *already holed up in Iron Age hill forts:* Bradshaw, *Cat Sense,* 51–52.

66   *many monks and nuns:* Kathleen Walker-Meikle, *Medieval Cats* (London: The British Library Publishing, 2011), 34–36.

66   *wealthy Cairo sultan:* Bradshaw, *Cat Sense,* 55.

66 *Cats were also beloved by the Vikings:* Neil B. Todd, "Cats and Commerce," *Scientific American*, Nov. 1977.

66 *The explorer Ernest Shackleton:* Engels, *Classical Cats*, 166.

66 *Starving Jamestown settlers ate theirs:* Joseph Stromberg, "Starving Settlers in Jamestown Colony Resorted to Cannibalism," Smithsonian.com, Apr. 30, 2013.

66 *Miners chauffeured them to California and Alaska:* Reginald Bretnar, "Bring Cats! A Feline History of the West," *The American West*, Nov.–Dec. 1978, 32–35, 60.

67 *"were perfect wrecks":* ibid.

67 *"it would be illogical to assume that the cats were supervised":* Ian Abbott, "Origin and spread of the cat, *Felis catus*, on mainland Australia, with a discussion of the magnitude of its early impact on native fauna," *Wildlife Research* 29, no. 1 (2002): 51–74.

67 *bronze statue of Trim:* Lewis, *Ships' Cats*, 111.

67 *"Many and curious":* in Lewis, *Ships' Cats*, 107.

67 *the British thoughtfully marooned cats:* David Cameron Duffy and Paula Capece, "Biology and Impacts of Pacific Island Invasive Species. 7. The Domestic Cat (*Felis catus*)," *Pacific Science* 66, no. 2 (2012): 173–212.

67 *cats paddled ashore:* Abbott, "Origin and spread of the cat."

67 *"Our cats . . . struck them with particular astonishment":* ibid.

67 *Among the Samoans, "a passion arose for cats":* Duffy and Capece, "Biology and Impacts of Pacific Island Invasive Species."

67 *On Ha'apai, natives stole:* Captain Cook's logs, http://www.captaincooksociety .com/home/detail/225-years-ago-april-june-1777.

67 *On Eromanga, natives exchanged cords of fragrant Polynesian sandalwood:* Duffy and Capece, "Biology and Impacts of Pacific Island Invasive Species."

68 *charming pets:* Abbott, "Origin and spread of the cat."

68 *By the 1840s, some Australian natives:* Ian Abbott, "The spread of the cat, *Felis catus*, in Australia: re-examination of the current conceptual model with additional information," *Conservation Science Western Australia* 7, no. 2 (2008): 1–17.

68   *in 2006, twelve wild dogs:* Megan Gannon, "Don't Just Blame Cats: Dogs Disrupt Wildlife, Too," LiveScience.com, Feb. 21, 2013.

68   *But it turns out that dogs:* Melinda A. Zeder, "Pathways to Animal Domestication," in *Biodiversity in Agriculture: Domestication, Evolution and Sustainability*, ed. Paul Gepts, Thomas R. Famula, Robert L. Bettinger, et al. (New York: Cambridge University Press, 2012), 238–39.

68   *unsurpassed breeders:* Perry T. Cupps, *Reproduction in Domestic Animals* (New York: Elsevier, 1991), 542–44.

68   *cats could produce 354,294 descendants:* Engels, *Classical Cats*, 8.

68   *In real life, five cats:* R. J. Van Aarde, "Distribution and density of the feral house cat *Felis catus* on Marion Island," *South African Journal of Antarctic Research* 9 (1979): 14–19.

69   *feline mothers teach:* Bradshaw, *Cat Sense*, 86–88.

69   *"The behavior of kittens at play":* Elizabeth Marshall Thomas, *The Tribe of Tiger: Cats and Their Culture* (New York: Pocket Books, 1994), 7.

69   *hunt more than 1,000 species:* Interview with Christopher Lepczyk about ongoing research.

69   *They can rule a thousand acres:* Jeff A. Horn, Nohra Mateus-Pinilla, Richard E. Warner, and Edward J. Heske, "Home range, habitat use, and activity patterns of free-roaming domestic cats," *Journal of Wildlife Management* 75, no. 5 (2011): 1177–85.

69   *tailor daytime hunting excursions:* "Stopping the slaughter: fighting back against feral cats," *Wildlife Matters* (Summer 2012–13): 4–8.

70   *In Bristol, England:* Philip J. Baker, Susie E. Molony, Emma Stone, Innes C. Cuthill, and Stephen Harris, "Cats about town: is predation by free-ranging pet cats *Felis catus* likely to affect urban bird populations?," *Ibis* 150, suppl. s1 (Aug. 2008): 86–99.

70   *In cities like Rome:* Olof Liberg, Mikael Sandell, Dominique Pontier, and Eugenia Natoli, "Density, spatial organization and reproductive tactics in the domestic cat and other felids," in *The Domestic Cat: The Biology of Its Behaviour*, 2nd ed., ed. Dennis C. Turner and Patrick Bateson (Cambridge: Cambridge University Press, 2000), 121–24.

70   *In some places, cats actually outnumber adult birds:* Victoria Sims, Karl Evans, Stuart E. Newson, Jamie A. Tratalos, and Kevin J. Gaston, "Avian assem-

blage structure and domestic cat densities in urban environments," *Diversity and Distributions* 14 (Mar. 2008): 387–99.

70 *This phenomenon is called hyperpredation:* Franck Courchamp, Michel Langlais, and George Sugihara, "Rabbits killing birds: modelling the hyperpredation process," *Journal of Animal Ecology* 69 (2000): 154–64.

71 *"secretive, flightless":* "Guam Rail," US Fish and Wildlife Service, Pacific Islands Fish and Wildlife Office, www.fws.gov/pacificislands/fauna /guamrail.html.

71 *The sub-Antarctic island of Kerguelen:* Leon van Eck, "The Kerguelen Cabbage," Genetic Jungle, May 25, 2009, www.geneticjungle.com/2009/05 /kerguelen-cabbage.html.

71 *"peculiar flavor":* ibid.

71 *The population exploded, and in 1951:* Dominique Pontier, Ludovic Say, François Debis, et al., "The diet of feral cats (*Felis catus* L.) at five sites on the Grande Terre, Kerguelen archipelago," *Polar Biology* 25 (2002): 833–37.

72 *In 1866, cat lover Mark Twain observed:* Mark Twain, *Mark Twain's Letters from Hawaii,* ed. A. Grove Day (Honolulu: University of Hawaii Press, 1975), 30–31.

72 *Cats even live 10,000 feet up:* Seth Judge, "Crouching Kittens, Hidden Petrels," pacificislandparks.com. Oct. 23, 2010, http://pacificislandparks .com/2010/10/23/crouching-kitten-hidden-petrels/.

72 *Wedge-tailed shearwaters, for instance, don't lay eggs:* Ted Williams, "Felines Fatales," *Audubon* magazine, Sept./Oct. 2009.

72 *last population of kakapo:* Elizabeth Kolbert, "The Big Kill," *New Yorker,* Dec. 22, 2014.

72 *"the ecological axis of evil":* Atticus Fleming, "Chief executive's letter," *Wildlife Matters* (Summer 2012–13): 2.

73 *In a rather heroic work of scholarship:* Abbott, "Origin and spread of the cat."

74 *In some places, tiny houses:* Elizabeth A. Denny and Christopher R. Dickman, *Review of cat ecology and management strategies in Australia: A report for the Invasive Animals Cooperative Research Centre* (Sydney: University of Sydney, 2010), http://www.pestsmart.org.au/wp-content/uploads/2010/03 /CatReport_web.pdf.

74   *"Rabbits have aided":* "The Feral Cat (*Felis catus*)," Australian Government, Department of Sustainability, Environment, Water, Population and Communities, www.environment.gov.au/system/files/resources/34ae02f7-9571 -4223-beb0-13547688b07b/files/cat.pdf.

74   *"scourge":* in Denny, *Review of cat ecology*.

74   *Turncoat cats are even said to conspire:* "Stopping the slaughter: fighting back against feral cats."

74   *The carnage is still being accounted for:* For a full account, see John C. Z. Woinarski, Andrew A. Burbidge, and Peter L. Harrison, *The Action Plan for Australian Mammals 2012* (Collingwood, Victoria, Australia: CSIRO Publishing, 2014).

74   *greater stick-nest rat:* From email interview with John Woinarski.

74   *"to tolerate electric shock":* Duffy and Capece, "Biology and Impacts of Pacific Island Invasive Species."

74   *In places like the Wongalara Wildlife Sanctuary:* "Restoring mammal populations in northern Australia: confronting the feral cat challenge." *Wildlife Matters* (Winter 2014): 10–11.

75   *to celebrate Easter with foil-wrapped bilbies:* "Easter Bilby," en.wikipedia.org /wiki/Easter_Bilby.

75   *shielded a few acres of bilby habitat:* Brian Williams, "Feral cats wreak havoc in raid on 'enclosed' refuge for endangered bilbies," *Courier-Mail*, July 19, 2012; John R. Platt, "3,000 Feral Cats Killed to Protect Rare Australian Bilbies," ScientificAmerican.com, Mar. 28, 2013.

75   *Several studies suggest:* For an example, see Colin Bonnington, Kevin J. Gaston, and Karl L. Evans, "Fearing the feline: domestic cats reduce avian fecundity through trait-mediated indirect effects that increase nest predation by other species," *Journal of Applied Ecology* 50 (Feb. 2013): 15–24.

75   *Bristle-thighed curlews in the Phoenix Islands:* Félix M. Medina, Elsa Bonnaud, Eric Fidal, and Manuel Nogales, "Underlying impacts of invasive cats on islands: not only a question of predation," *Biodiversity and Conservation* 23 (Feb. 2014): 327–42.

75   *In one Maryland study:* Nico Dauphiné and Robert J. Cooper, "Impacts of Free-ranging Domestic Cats (*Felis catus*) on Birds in the United States: A Review of Recent Research with Conservation and Management Recommen-

dations," *Proceedings of the Fourth International Partners in Flight Conference: Tundra to Tropics* (2009): 205–19.

75 *Cats likely spread:* R. Scott Nolen, "Feline leukemia virus threatens endangered panthers," *JAVMA News,* May 15, 2004.

76 *In the Balearic Islands:* Medina et al., "Underling impacts."

76 *In Hawaii, the droppings:* Williams, "Feral cats wreak havoc."

76 *"wide ranges and uncertainties":* Natalie Angier, "That Cuddly Kitty Is Deadlier Than You Think," *New York Times,* Jan. 29, 2013.

76 *lessons of island ecology:* From interview with Michael Hutchins.

77 *including the development of a toxic kangaroo sausage:* D. Algar, N. Hamilton, M. Onus, S. Hilmer et al., "Field trial to compare baiting efficacy of Eradicat and Curiosity baits," (2011), Australian Government, Department of the Environment, www.environment.gov.au/system/files/resources /d242c6f1-d2ab-43de-a552-61aaaf79c92c/files/cat-bait-wa.pdf.

77 *Australians have also tested the Cat Assassin:* Government of South Australia, Kangaroo Island Natural Resources Management Board, "Case Study: Feral cat spray tunnels trials on Kangaroo Island," www.pestsmart.org.au /wp-content/uploads/2013/11/FCCS2_cat-tunnel-trials.pdf.

77 *considered dispatching Tasmanian devils:* Ginny Stein, "Tasmanian farmers and environmentalists team up to eradicate feral cat threat," abc.net.au, Nov. 2, 2014.

77 *it can cost up to $100,000 per square mile:* Manuel Nogales, Eric Vidal, Félix M. Medina, Elsa Bonnaud, et al., "Feral Cats and Biodiversity Conservation: The Urgent Prioritization of Island Management," *BioScience* 63, no. 10 (2013): 804–10.

77 *Here's an idea of the process:* John P. Parkes, Penny Mary Fisher, Sue Robinson, and Alfonso Aguirre-Muñoz, "Eradication of feral cats from large islands: an assessment of the effort required for success," *New Zealand Journal of Ecology* 38, no. 2 (2014): 307–14.

77 *hard-won victory over the house cats of tiny San Nicolas Island:* Steve Chawkins, "Complex effort to rid San Nicolas Island of cats declared a success," *Los Angeles Times,* Feb. 26, 2012.

77 *"a monumental achievement":* ibid.

78   *Nearly 100 islands have been cleared so far:* Nogales et al., "Feral Cats and Bio-diversity Conservation."

78   *soaring bunny population gobbled 40 percent:* Dana M. Bergstrom, Arko Lu-cieer, Kate Kiefer, Jane Wasley, et al., "Indirect effects of invasive species re-moval devastate World Heritage Island," *Journal of Applied Ecology* 46, no. 1 (2009): 73–81.

78   *The devastation is visible from space:* Elizabeth Svoboda, "The unintended consequences of changing nature's balance," *New York Times*, Nov. 7, 2009.

78   *what scientists call "social acceptability":* Steffen Oppel, Brent M. Beaven, Mark Bolton, Juliet Vickery, and Thomas W. Bodey, "Eradication of Inva-sive Mammals on Islands Inhabited by Humans and Domestic Animals," *Conservation Biology* 25, no. 2 (2011): 232–40.

Chapter 5 THE CAT LOBBY

83   *Wandering dogs have been mostly eliminated:* See especially the comparison with India, in Brian Palmer, "Are No-Kill Shelters Good for Cats and Dogs?" Slate.com, May 19, 2014.

84   *nearly half of all house cats that enter shelters:* ASPCA, "Shelter Intake and Surrender: Pet Statistics," www.aspca.org/animal-homelessness/shelter -intake-and-surrender/pet-statistics.

84   *almost 100 percent:* "Cat Fatalities and Secrecy in U.S. Pounds and Shelters," Alley Cat Allies, http://www.alleycat.org/page.aspx?pid=396.

84   *"as part of the natural landscape":* "Save The Birds," Alley Cat Allies, http:// www.alleycat.org/page.aspx?pid=1595.

84   *The neuter-and-release method is sweeping the country:* Elizabeth Holtz, "Trap-Neuter-Return Ordinances and Policies in the United States: The Future of Animal Control," Law & Policy Brief (Bethesda, MD: Alley Cat Allies, 2004).

84   *and some 600 registered nonprofits:* "A Quarter Century of Cat Advocacy," *Alley Cat Action* 25, no. 2 (Winter 2015).

84   *Abroad, entire countries—like Italy:* From emails with Eugenia Natoli, an Ital-ian cat researcher.

85 *The modern animal welfare movement:* Katherine C. Grier, *Pets in America: A History* (2006; repr., Orlando: Harcourt, 2006), 160–233.

85 *"the Eden of home":* ibid., 197.

85 *"torture quiet, domestic animals":* ibid., 184.

86 *one eighteenth-century Philadelphia family:* ibid., 30.

86 *Cats were often excluded:* ibid., 45.

86 *They were underrepresented:* ibid., 335–36.

86 *People tended to use generic names for cats:* ibid., 87.

86 *most popular American pet:* By 1930, America was importing more than 800,000 birds per year (ibid., 318, 334). Also see NPR interview with Grier: Vikki Valentine, "From Canaries to Rocks: A Hardy Pet Is a Good Pet," NPR.org, May 16, 2007, http://www.npr.org/templates/story/story.php?storyId=10216089.

86 *many municipalities simply ignored the stray cat population:* Grier, *Pets in America,* 279.

86 *People called the stray cats "tramps":* ibid., 277.

86 *The cats were falsely accused:* ibid., 380.

86 *an example of "real brave humanity":* ibid., 133.

87 *In the 1930s, bands of well-meaning women:* ibid., 282.

87 *In 1948, Robert Kendell:* Katherine T. Kinkead, "A Cat in Every Home," in *The Big New Yorker Book of Cats* (New York: Random House, 2013), 91.

87 *some of London's first cat colonies:* Ellen Perry Berkeley, *Maverick Cats: Encounters with Feral Cats* (Shelburne, VT: New England Press, 2001), 16–17.

87 *in 1947, the invention of kitty litter:* Paul Ford, "The Birth of Kitty Litter," Bloomberg.com, Dec. 4, 2014.

87 *more sweeping social changes also drove the trend:* From interviews with Paula Flores, Global Head of Pet Care Research at Euromonitor International.

88 *something like 85 percent of owned cats are today spayed:* "Outdoor Cats: Frequently Asked Questions: Why Do People Consider Outdoor Cats a Problem?" Humane Society of the United States, http://www.humanesociety.org/issues/feral_cats/qa/feral_cat_FAQs.html.

88   *only about 2 percent of free-roaming cats are:* ibid.

88   *California alone kills about 250,000 cats annually:* Wayne Pacelle, "A Blueprint for Ending Euthanasia of Healthy Companion Animals," Humane Society of the United States, http://blog.humanesociety.org/wayne/2013/09/ending-euthanasia-healthy-pets-california.html.

88   *High-capacity shelters:* Grier, *Pets in America*, 277–79.

88   *"Allowing a cat or any living being":* Kate Hurley, "Making the Case for a Paradigm Shift in Community Cat Management, Part One," Maddie's Fund, www.maddiesfund.org/making-the-case-for-community-cats-part-one.htm.

88   *In Washington, DC, there are hundreds:* Lisa Grace Lednicer, "Is it more humane to kill stray cats, or let them fend alone?" *Washington Post* magazine, Feb. 6, 2014.

88   *in Oakland, California:* Nancy Barber, "Calif. Woman Fixes and Feeds 24 Cat Colonies," Pawnation.com, Jan. 22, 2014.

89   *Along with food:* For an example, see "Coyotes, Pets, and Community Cats: Protecting feral cat colonies," Humane Society of the United States, http://www.humanesociety.org/animals/coyotes/tips/coyotes_pets.html.

89   *how to shield their cats from a storm surge:* "Be Prepared for Disasters," Alley Cat Allies, http://www.alleycat.org/disastertips.

90   *have been at each other's throats since at least the 1870s:* Grier, *Pets in America*, 294–95.

90   *outdoor bird-watching is an increasingly popular pastime:* Melissa Milgrom, "The Birding Effect," *Nature Conservancy*, May/June 2013.

90   *"The world outside your front door can be a brutal place":* American Bird Conservancy, "Cats, Birds and You," https://abcbirds.org/program/cats-indoors/.

90   *The other pamphlet makes a less gentle case:* American Bird Conservancy, "Trap, Neuter, Release (TNR): Bad for Birds, Bad for Cats."

91   *researcher at the Smithsonian Migratory Bird Center:* Benjamin R. Freed, "Nico Dauphine Sentenced for Attempting to Kill Feral Cats," DCist.com, Dec. 15, 2011; Bruce Barcott, "Kill the Cat That Kills the Bird?" *New York Times Magazine*, Dec. 2, 2007.

91   *writer for* Audubon magazine: Christine Haughney, "Writer, and Bird Lover,

at Center of a Dispute About Cats Is Reinstated," *New York Times*, Mar. 26, 2013.

91 *"cat hoarding without walls":* Christopher A. Lepczyk, Nico Dauphine, David M. Bird et al., "What Conservation Biologists Can Do to Counter Trap-Neuter-Return: Response to Longcore et al.," *Conservation Biology* 24, no. 2 (2010): 627–29.

91 *it's estimated that 71 percent to 94 percent:* Travis Longcore, Catherine Rich, and Lauren M. Sullivan, "Critical Assessment of Claims Regarding Management of Feral Cats by Trap-Neuter-Return," *Conservation Biology* 23, no. 4 (2009): 887–94.

92 *Skeptics also contend:* Robert J. McCarthy, Stephen H. Levine, and J. Michael Reed, "Estimation of effectiveness of three methods of feral cat population control by use of a simulation model," *Journal of the American Veterinary Medical Association* 243, no. 4 (2013): 502–11.

94 *According to a 2011 Associated Press poll:* Sue Manning, "AP-Petside.com Poll: 7 in 10 pet owners: Shelters should kill only animals too sick or aggressive for adoption," Associated Press, Jan. 5, 2012.

94 *More than 40 million American households include cats:* National Pet Owners Survey 2013–2014, 6.

95 *the* Washington Post *was summoned:* Annie Gowen, "Wild Cats at Chantilly Trailer Park to Be Trapped, Probably Killed," *Breaking News* (blog), *Washington Post*, Mar. 12, 2008.

95 *and after three days of negative "local and national attention":* Annie Gowen, "Deal Reached to Keep Feral Cats," *Breaking News* (blog), *Washington Post*, Mar. 15, 2008.

96 *the website provides a political toolkit:* Alley Cat Allies, Advocacy Toolkit, http://www.alleycat.org/sslpage.aspx?pid=1552.

96 *"Mrs. Harper, raising awareness about cat welfare is a good look":* "Laureen Harper interrupted by Toronto activist at cat video festival," CBC News, Apr. 18, 2004, http://www.cbc.ca/news/canada/toronto /laureen-harper-interrupted-by-toronto-activist-at-cat-video-festival -1.2614936.

97 *A Twitter skirmish ensued:* Excerpts can be found at Christie Keith, "Michigan Mayor Taunts Cat Lovers on Twitter," previously available at Petconnection.com, Feb. 13, 2014.

99 *lingers in my mind:* Hurley, "Making the Case for a Paradigm Shift."

99 *biggest threat:* Philip H. Kass, "Cat Overpopulation in the United States," in *The Welfare of Cats,* ed. Irene Rochlitz (Dodrecht, the Netherlands: Springer, 2007), 119.

100 *One model showed that lethal control:* McCarthy et al., "Estimation of effectiveness of three methods of feral cat population control."

100 *newly proposed city Wildlife Action Plan:* Andrew Giambrone, "District May Target Feral Cats as Part of Wildlife Action Plan," *Washington City Paper,* Sept. 1, 2015.

100 *One proposed alternative:* McCarthy et al., "Estimation of effectiveness of three methods of feral cat population control."

Chapter 6 CAT SCAN

104 *one in three people:* Jaroslav Flegr, Joseph Prandota, Michaela Sovičková, and Zafar H. Isarili, "Toxoplasmosis—A Global Threat. Correlation of Latent Toxoplasmosis with Specific Disease Burden in a Set of 88 Countries," *PLOS ONE* (Mar. 2014).

104 *including some 60 million Americans:* Centers for Disease Control and Prevention, "Parasites—Toxoplasmosis (*Toxoplasma* infection)," www.cdc.gov/parasites/toxoplasmosis/.

105 *now perhaps the most successful parasite the world has ever seen:* Carl Zimmer, *Parasite Rex: Inside the Bizarre World of Nature's Most Dangerous Creatures* (New York: Atria, 2000), 195.

106 *Brain-burrowing parasites are almost always devastating:* Holly Yan, "Brain-eating amoeba kills 14-year-old star athlete," CNN.com, Aug. 31, 2015.

107 *The American infection rate is somewhere between:* Dolores E. Hill, J. P. Dubey, Rachel C. Abbott, Charles van Riper III, and Elizabeth A. Enright, *Toxoplasmosis,* Circular 1389 (Reston: US Geological Survey, 2014), 10.

107 *South Korea is perhaps the toxo-freest nation, at less than 7 percent:* João M. Furtado, Justine R. Smith, Rubens Belfort, Jr., and Kevin L. Winthrop, "Toxoplasmosis: A Global Threat," *Journal of Global Infectious Diseases* 3, no. 3 (2011): 281–84.

108 *In 1938, pathologists at Babies Hospital:* J. P. Dubey, "History of the discovery of the life cycle of *Toxoplasma gondii*," *International Journal for Parasitology* 39, no. 8 (2009): 877–82; J. P. Dubey, "Transmission of *Toxoplasma gondii*—From land to sea, a personal perspective," in *A Century of Parasitology: Discoveries, Ideas and Lessons Learned by Scientists Who Published in The Journal of Parasitology, 1914–2014,* ed. John Janovy, Jr., and Gerald W. Esch, eds. (Chichester, UK: Wiley-Blackwell 2016), 148.

109 *average cat owners don't even have unusually high rates of infection:* Marion Vittecoq, Kevin D. Lafferty, Eric Elguero, et al., "Cat ownership is neither a strong predictor of *Toxoplasma gondii* infection, nor a risk factor for brain cancer," *Biology Letters* 8, no. 6 (2012): 1042.

109 *It is outdoor cats:* Hill et al., *Toxoplasmosis,* 56.

109 *scientists estimate that 1 percent:* Dubey, "Transmission of *Toxoplasma gondii,*" 154.

109 *roughly 80 percent of Pennsylvania's black bears:* Nancy Briscoe, J. G. Humphreys, and J. P. Dubey, "Prevalence of *Toxoplasma gondii* Infections in Pennsylvania Black Bears, *Ursus americanus,*" *Journal of Wildlife Diseases* 29, no. 4 (1993): 599–601.

109 *nearly half of Ohio's deer:* S. C. Crist, R. L. Stewart, J. P. Rinehart, and G. R. Needham, "Surveillance for *Toxoplasma gondii* in the white-tailed deer (*Odocoileus virginianus*) in Ohio," *Ohio Journal of Science* 99, no. 3 (1999): 34–37.

110 *One Indian study showed:* Dubey, "History of the discovery."

110 *A well-known outbreak happened:* Judith Isaac-Renton, William R. Bowie, Arlene King, et al., "Detection of *Toxoplasma gondii* Oocysts in Drinking Water," *Applied and Environmental Microbiology* 64, no. 6 (1998): 2278–80.

110 *Another well-studied toxoplasmosis epidemic occurred:* J. P. Dubey and J. L. Jones, "*Toxoplasma gondii* infection in humans and animals in the United States," *International Journal for Parasitology* 38, no. 11 (2008): 1257–78.

110 *The parasite is now found even above the Arctic Circle:* Ian Sample, "Public health warning as cat parasite spreads to Arctic beluga whales," *Guardian,* Feb. 14, 2014.

110 *European colonists sailing to Brazil:* Tovi Lehmann, Paula L. Marcet, Doug H. Graham, Erica R. Dahl, and J. P. Dubey, "Globalization and the population structure of *Toxoplasma gondii,*" *Proceedings of the National Academy of Sciences* 103, no. 30 (2006): 11423–28.

112 *Like the house cat itself:* I am indebted to Vern Carruthers of the University of Michigan for explaining *Toxoplasma*'s activities in the human body, and to Mikhail Pletnikov of Johns Hopkins University and Wendy Ingram at the University of California, Berkeley.

112 *That was the gist of a sensational series:* M. Berdoy, J. P. Webster, and D. W. Macdonald, "Fatal Attraction in rats infected with *Toxoplasma gondii*," *Proceedings of the Royal Society B* 267, no. 1452 (2000): 1591–94; Zimmer, *Parasite Rex*, 92–94.

113 *toxo-infected chimpanzees are drawn*: Clémence Poirotte, Peter M. Kappeler, Barthelemy Ngoubangoye, Stéphanie Bourgeois, Maick Moussodji, and Marie J. E. Charpentier, "Morbid attraction to leopard urine in *Toxoplasma*-infected chimpanzees," *Current Biology* 26, no. 3 (2016), R98–R99.

114 *individuals with toxoplasmosis have an elevated risk of suicide:* Vinita J. Ling, David Lester, Preben Bo Mortensen, et al., "*Toxoplasma gondii* Seropositivity and Suicide Rates in Women," *The Journal of Nervous and Mental Disease* 199, no. 7 (2011): 440–44.

114 *higher suicide and homicide rates:* David Lester, "*Toxoplasma gondii* and Homicide," *Psychological Reports* 111, no. 1 (2012): 196–97.

114 *same spike shows up in car crash statistics:* Jaroslav Flegr, "Effects of *Toxoplasma* on Human Behavior," *Schizophrenia Bulletin* 33, no. 3 (2007): 757–60.

114 *"Maybe you take a toxo-infected human":* "Toxo: A Conversation with Robert Sapolsky," Edge, Dec. 2, 2009, edge.org/conversation/robert_sapolsky-toxo.

114 *toxo-positive sea otters:* C. Kreuder, M. A. Miller, D. A. Jessup, et al., "Patterns of Mortality in Southern Sea Otters (*Enhydra lutris nereis*) from 1998–2001," *Journal of Wildlife Diseases* 39, no. 3 (2003): 495–509.

115 *as many as 30 percent of AIDS patients:* Hill et al., *Toxoplasmosis*, 23.

115 *more eye-opening research:* Kathleen McAuliffe, "How Your Cat Is Making You Crazy," *Atlantic*, Mar. 2012.

115 *Perhaps inevitably:* Jaroslav Flegr, Pavlina Lenochová, Zdeněk Hodný, and Marta Vondrová, "Fatal Attraction Phenomenon in Humans—Cat Odour Attractiveness Increased for *Toxplasma*-Infected Men While Decreased for Infected Women," *PLOS Neglected Tropical Diseases* (Nov. 2011).

115 *may explain our fondness for sauvignon blanc:* Patrick House, "The Scent of a Cat Woman," Slate.com, July 3, 2012.

115 *New Zealand just happens to have the highest levels of cat ownership:* Karla Adam, "Cat wars break out in New Zealand," *Guardian*, May 21, 2013.

115 *toxoplasmosis rates hovering around 40 percent:* Matthew Theunissen, "Disease carried by cats not so 'trivial'—researchers," *New Zealand Herald*, Jan. 29, 2013.

116 *"There is no historical precedent for such numbers of cats":* E. Fuller Torrey and Robert H. Yolken, "*Toxoplasma* oocysts as a public health problem," *Trends in Parasitology* 29, no. 8 (2013): 380–84.

117 *"The rise of cats as pets":* E. Fuller Torrey and Judy Miller, *The Invisible Plague: The Rise of Mental Illness from 1750 to the Present* (New Brunswick, NJ: Rutgers University Press, 2007), 332–33.

117 *Yolken and Torrey introduced the notion:* E. Fuller Torrey and Robert H. Yolken, "Could Schizophrenia Be a Viral Zoonosis Transmitted from House Cats?" *Schizophrenia Bulletin* 21, no. 2 (1995): 167–71.

117 *Later, the scientists repeated the study:* R. H. Yolken, F. B. Dickerson, and E. Fuller Torrey, "Toxoplasma and schizophrenia," *Parasite Immunology* 31, no. 11 (2009): 706–15.

117 *that afflicts roughly 1 percent of the American population:* "Schizophrenia—Fact Sheet," Treatment Advocacy Center, "Eliminating Barriers to the Treatment of Mental Illness," www.treatmentadvocacycenter.org/problem /consequences-of-non-treatment/schizophrenia.

118 *But Yolken and Torrey believe:* For their excellent literature review, see "Toxoplasma-Schizophrenia Research," Stanley Medical Research Institute, www.stanleyresearch.org/patient-and-provider-resources/toxoplasmosis -schizophrenia-research/.

120 *particular countries, like Brazil:* Kevin D. Lafferty, "Look what the cat dragged in: do parasites contribute to human cultural diversity?" *Behavioural Processes* 68 (2005): 279–82; Patrick House, "Landon Donovan Needs a Cat," Slate.com, July 1, 2010.

120 Toxoplasma *is a major problem in modern Egypt:* Y. M. Al-Kappany, C. Rajendran, L. R. Ferreira, et al., "High Prevalence of Toxoplasmosis in Cats from Egypt: Isolation of Viable *Toxoplasma gondii*, Tissue Distribution, and Isolate Designation," *Journal of Parasitology* 96, no. 6 (2010): 1115–18.

120 *But then I learn that another scientific team:* Rabat Khairat, Markus Ball, Chun-Chi Hsieh Chang, et al., "First insights into the metagenome of Egyptian mummies using next-generation sequencing," *Journal of Applied Genetics* 54, no. 3 (2013): 309–25.

Chapter 7 PANDORA'S LITTER BOX

122 *$58 billion pet industry's biggest trade show:* "Pet Industry Market Size & Ownership Statistics," American Pet Products Association, www.american petproducts.org/press_industrytrends.asp.

122 *Not long ago, cats didn't really have any "products":* Katherine C. Grier, *Pets in America: A History* (2006; repr., Orlando: Harcourt, 2006), 22, 102, 122, 377.

122 *As late as the 1960s:* Kathleen Szasz, *Petishism? Pets and Their People in the Western World* (New York: Holt, Rinehart and Winston, 1968), 193.

123 *Americans now spend $6.6 billion:* 2012 Euromonitor data.

123 *"Persian pussies have been known to leave":* Carl Van Vechten, *The Tiger in the House: A Cultural History of the Cat* (1920; repr., New York: New York Review of Books, 2007), 14.

123 *But today, over 60 percent:* APPA Survey, 174.

124 *And the latest studies suggest:* Jennifer L. McDonald, Mairead Maclean, Matthew R. Evans, and Dave J. Hodgson, "Reconciling actual and perceived rates of predation by domestic cats," *Ecology and Evolution* 5, no. 14 (July 2015): 2745–53; Natalie Angier, "That Cuddly Kitty Is Deadlier Than You Think," *New York Times*, Jan. 29, 2013.

125 *as part of one recent study, researchers placed:* Manuela Wedl, Barbara Bauer, Dorothy Gracey, et al., "Factors influencing the temporal patterns of dyadic behaviours and interactions between domestic cats and their owners," *Behavioural Processes* 86, no. 1 (2011): 58–67.

126 *The groundbreaking study:* Erika Friedmann, Aaron Honori Katcher, James L. Lynch, and Sue Ann Thomas, "Animal Companions and One-Year Survival of Patients After Discharge from a Coronary Care Unit," *Public Health Reports* 95, no. 4 (1980): 307–12.

126 *"A pet can be a miracle drug":* Marty Becker, *The Healing Power of Pets: Har-*

nessing the Amazing Ability of Pets to Make and Keep People Happy and Healthy (New York: Hyperion, 2002), 64.

127 *Lots of people—almost 20 percent:* James A. Serpell, "Domestication and History of the Cat," in *The Domestic Cat: The Biology of Its Behaviour*, 2nd ed., ed. Dennis C. Turner and Patrick Bateson (Cambridge: Cambridge University Press, 2000). (By contrast, less than 3 percent of respondents disliked dogs.)

127 *studies suggest that cats occasionally seek:* John Bradshaw, *Cat Sense: How the New Feline Science Can Make You a Better Friend to Your Pet* (New York: Basic Books, 2013), 235.

127 *When Erika Friedmann repeated:* Erika Friedmann and Sue A. Thomas, "Pet Ownership, Social Support, and One-Year Survival After Acute Myocardial Infarction in the Cardiac Arrhythmia Suppression Trial (CAST)," *American Journal of Cardiology* 15 (Dec. 1995): 1213–17. (Hal Herzog and Alan Beck, in interviews, were kind enough to point me toward this fascinating body of scholarship.)

127 *A more recent follow-up:* G. B. Parker, Aimee Gayed, C. A. Owen, and Gabriella A. Heruc, "Survival following an acute coronary syndrome: A pet theory put to the test," *Acta Psychiatrica Scandinavica* 121, no. 1 (2010): 65–70.

127 *While an American study of Medicaid records:* Judith M. Siegel, "Stressful Life Events and Use of Physician Services among the Elderly: The Moderating Role of Pet Ownership," *Journal of Personality and Social Psychology* 58, no. 6 (1990): 1081–86.

127 *Dutch study concluded:* Mieke Rijken and Sandra van Beek, "About Cats and Dogs . . . Reconsidering the Relationship Between Pet Ownership and Health Related Outcomes in Community-Dwelling Elderly," *Social Indicators Research* 102 (July 2011): 373–88.

127 *Another group of scientists:* Erika Friedmann, Sue A. Thomas, Heesook Son, Deborah Chapa, and Sandra McCune, "Pet's Presence and Owner's Blood Pressures During the Daily Lives of Pet Owners with Pre- to Mild Hypertension," *Anthrozoös* 26 (Dec. 2013): 535–50.

127 *A particularly damning Norwegian study:* Ingela Enmarker, Ove Hellzén, Knut Ekker, and Ann-Grethe Berg, "Health in older cat and dog owners: The Nord-Trondelag Health Study (HUNT)-3 study," *Scandinavian Journal of Public Health* 40 (Dec. 2012): 718–24.

129 *one study indicated:* K. Robin Yabroff, Richard P. Troiano, and David Berri-

gan, "Walking the Dog: Is Pet Ownership Associated with Physical Activity in California?" *Journal of Physical Activity and Health* 5 (Mar. 2008): 216–28.

129 *Another revealed that, in 210 minutes of observation:* Penny L. Bernstein and Erika Friedmann, "Social behaviour of domestic cats in the human home," in *The Domestic Cat: The Biology of Its Behaviour,* 73.

129 *In a Japanese study:* Atsuko Saito and Kazutaka Shinozuka, "Vocal recognition of owners by domestic cats (*Felis catus*)," *Animal Cognition* 16, no. 4 (2013): 685–90.

130 *Japanese researchers recently suggested:* Jan Hoffman, "The Look of Love Is in the Dog's Eyes," *New York Times,* Apr. 16, 2015.

130 *"Cats seem to have little or no instinctive":* Bradshaw, *Cat Sense,* 132.

131 *"Despite years of research":* ibid., 199.

131 *In one study, cat owners could not even:* N. Courtney and Deborah Wells, "The discrimination of cat odours by humans," *Perception* 31 (2002): 511–12.

131 *"weakness in social skills":* Bradshaw, *Cat Sense,* xiv.

131 *"Honeybun is the biggest love-mush":* Janet Alger and Steven Alger, *Cat Culture: The Social World of a Cat Shelter* (Philadelphia: Temple University Press, 2002), 17.

132 *"The embedding of a cry":* "Cats Do Control Humans, Study Finds," Live Science.com, July 13, 2009.

132 *Rather than "learning a common rule":* Sarah Ellis, "Human classification of context-related vocalisations emitted by known and unknown domestic cats (*Felis catus*)" (from The Arts & Sciences of Human-Animal Interaction Conference 2012 literature).

132 *One investigation even showed:* Bernstein and Friedmann, "Social behaviour of domestic cats in the human home," 78.

133 *For instance, house cats can relinquish:* Giuseppe Piccione, Simona Marafioti, Claudia Giannetto, Michele Panzera, and Francesco Fazio, "Daily rhythm of total activity pattern in domestic cats (*Felis silvestris catus*) maintained in two different housing conditions," *Journal of Veterinary Behavior* 8, no. 4 (2013): 189–94.

133 *there's also a rather haunting study entitled:* Melissa R. Shyan-Norwalt, "Caregivers Perceptions of What Indoor Cats Do 'For Fun,' " *Journal of Applied Animal Welfare Science* 8, no. 3 (2005): 199–209.

133 *Most cat-owning households have more than one cat:* APPA survey, 169. (The average number of cats per household is 2.11.)

134 *according to one study, cats in a household:* J. L. Stella and C. A. T. Buffington, "Individual and environmental effects on health and welfare," in *The Domestic Cat: The Biology of Its Behaviour,* 196.

134 *others are literally allergic to us:* Maryann Mott, "Coughing Cats May Be Allergic to People, Vets Say," *National Geographic News,* Oct. 25, 2005.

134 *don't like humans to lock eyes:* Stella and Buffington, "Individual and environmental effects on health and welfare," 197.

134 *Studying stress by measuring cortisol levels:* "Stroking could stress out your cat," University of Lincoln, Oct. 7, 2013, www.lincoln.ac.uk /news/2013/10/772.asp.

134 "For example, if two family cats": "Understanding Cat Aggression Toward People," SPCA of Texas, http://www.spca.org/document.doc?id=38.

134 *An audio clip from the call:* Stuart Tomlinson, "Aggravated cat is subdued by Portland police after terrorizing family," *Oregonian,* Mar. 10, 2014.

135 *In 2008, a* New York Times *article:* James Vlahos, "Pill-Popping Pets," *New York Times Magazine,* July 13, 2008.

135 *According to one study, nearly half:* D. Ramos and D. S. Mills, "Human directed aggression in Brazilian domestic cats: owner reported prevalence, contexts and risk factors," *Journal of Feline Medicine and Surgery* 11, no. 10 (2009): 835–41.

135 *include the so-called Tom and Jerry syndrome:* Jasper Copping, "Cats suffering from 'Tom and Jerry' syndrome," *Telegraph,* Dec. 1, 2013.

137 *"too close confinement to the house":* in Stella and Buffington, "Individual and environmental effects on health and welfare," 188.

139 *"potentially objectionable odors":* ibid., 198.

139 *cats find redecorating to be stressful:* "New Furniture," Feliway, www.feliway .com/uk/What-causes-cat-stress-or-anxiety/New-Furniture-and-redeco rating.

139 *one animal website suggests borrowing somebody's actual infant:* "Preparing Your Pet for Baby's Arrival," www.oregonhumanesociety.org/resources -publications/resource-library/.

139 *"confusing and frightening"*: "The Indoor Cat Initiative," www.vet.ohio-state .edu/assets/pdf/education/courses/vm720/topic/indoorcatmanual.pdf.

141 *"Not wanting a litter box in the living room"*: Jackson Galaxy and Kate Benjamin, *Catification: Designing a Happy and Stylish Home for Your Cat (and You!)* (New York: Jeremy P. Tarcher/Penguin, 2014), 2–3.

141 *"Every parent has dreams"*: ibid., 42.

141 *"Beth and George"*: ibid., 175.

142 *"When you think about Catifying"*: ibid., 171.

142 *"We wanted to keep the décor"*: ibid., 208–9.

142 *Cat cafés first emerged in Taiwan:* Lorraine Plourde, "Cat Cafés, Affective Labor, and the Healing Boom in Japan," *Japanese Studies* 34, no. 2 (2014): 115–33.

142 *"Highly domestic spaces"*: ibid.

143 *"a node or intermediary"*: ibid.

143 *"unusually rigorous routine of care"*: "The Sunshine Home Frequently Asked Questions," www.thesunshinehome.com/faq.html#question08.

Chapter 8 LIONS AND TOYGERS AND LYKOI

148 *"That thing tried to get at my baby, man"*: Ryan Garza, "Big cat has northeast Detriot neighborhood on edge," Detroit Free Press video, www.youtube .com/watch?v=ciY29m9ZaWw.

149 *the "very concept"*: Katherine C. Grier, *Pets in America: A History* (2006; repr., Orlando: Harcourt, 2006), 33.

149 *If they were shown at all:* Harriet Ritvo, *The Animal Estate: The English and Other Creatures in the Victorian Age* (Cambridge, MA: Harvard University Press, 1989), 116.

149 *cats' "nocturnal and rambling habits"*: Charles Darwin, *The Variation of Animals and Plants Under Domestication*, vol. 1 (Teddington: Echo Library, 2007), 33–34.

149 *"Many were the gibes"*: Frances Simpson, *The Book of the Cat* (London: Cassell, 1903), viii, online at: archive.org/stream/bookofcatsimpson00sim prich/bookofcatsimpson00simprich_djvu.txt.

149 *"I felt somewhat more than anxious"*: Harrison Weir, *Our Cats and All About Them* (Turnbridge Wells: R. Clements, 1889), 3.

150 *"throughout the length and breadth"*: ibid., 5.

150 *margarine hampers*: Simpson, *The Book of the Cat*, 58.

150 *some early fanciers dripped*: Sarah Hartwell, "A History of Cat Shows in Britain," messybeast.com/showing.htm.

150 *"Most feline breeds were verbal rather than biological"*: Ritvo, *The Animal Estate*, 120.

150 *The first American cat show*: Grier, *Pets in America*, 49.

150 *always "used advisedly, for whatever the outer covering"*: John Jennings, *Domestic and Fancy Cats: A Practical Treatise on Their Varieties, Breeding, Management, and Disease* (London: L.U. Gill, 1901), 10.

150 *A pioneering Persian breeder confessed*: Simpson, *The Book of the Cat*, 98.

151 *ring-tailed lemur*: Hartwell, messybeast.com.

151 *A few natural breeds*: Carlos A. Driscoll, Juliet Clutton-Brock, Andrew C. Kitchener, and Stephen J. O'Brien, "The Taming of the Cat," *Scientific American*, June 2009.

152 *a staggering 60 percent*: APPA Survey, 62.

152 *less than 2 percent*: Philip J. Baker, Carl D. Soulsbury, Graziella Iossa, and Stephen Harris, "Domestic Cat (*Felis catus*) and Domestic Dog (*Canis familiaris*)," in *Urban Carnivores: Ecology, Conflict, and Conservation*, ed. Stanley D. Gehrt, Seth P. D. Riley, and Brian L. Cypher (Baltimore: Johns Hopkins University Press, 2010), 158; J. D. Kurushima, M. J. Lipinski, B. Gandolfi, et al., "Variation of cats under domestication: genetic assignment of domestic cats to breeds and worldwide random-bred populations," *Animal Genetics* 44, no. 3 (2013): 311–24.

154 *including the Cornish Rex*: Sarah Hartwell, "Breeds and Mutations Timeline," Messybeast.com/breed-dates.htm.

155 *"mutant sausages"*: "A Cat Fight Breaks Out Over a Breed," *New York Times*, July 23, 1995.

160 My Cat From Hell: "Thrill-seeking Savannahs Threaten Owner's Skydiving Gear," AnimalPlanet.com, www.animalplanet.com/tv-shows/my-cat-from -hell/videos/thrill-seeking-savannahs-threaten-owners-skydiving-gear/.

161 *Other small cats used in hybridization:* Sarah Hartwell, "Domestic X Wild Hybrids," Messybeast.com.

161 *They may end up:* Joan Miller "Wild Cat-Domestic Cat Hybrids—Legislative and Ethical Issues" (a white paper), Jan. 24, 2013, http://cfa.org/Portals /0/documents/minutes/20130628-transcript.pdf.

161 *"heated dens":* "What Is a Hybird Cat: Domestic Bengal Policy," Wildcat Sanctuary, http://www.wildcatsanctuary.org/education/species/hybrid -domestic/what-is-a-hybrid-domestic/.

161 *install a customized barricade with a 45-degree angle:* Ben Baugh, "Cat Sanctuary home to a variety of hybrids," *Aiken Standard,* Jan. 12, 2014.

162 *One October:* Kelly Bayliss, "Boo Is Back! Missing African Savannah Cat Found Safe," NBCPhiladelphia.com, Oct. 30, 2014.

163 *Likewise, orange cats are said to dominate:* John C. Z. Woinarski, Andrew A. Burbidge, and Peter L. Harrison, *The Action Plan for Australian Mammals 2012* (Collingwood, Victoria, Australia: CSIRO Publishing, 2014).

163 *To confirm that they were killing:* Diane K. Brockman, Laurie R. Godfrey, Luke J. Dollar, and Joelisoa Ratsirarson, "Evidence of Invasive *Felis silvestris* Predation on *Propithecus verreauxi* at Beza Mahafaly Special Reserve, Madagascar," *International Journal of Primatology* 29 (Feb. 2008): 135–52.

164 *where rumors date back:* Ian Abbott, "Origin and spread of the cat, *Felis catus,* on mainland Australia, with a discussion of the magnitude of its early impact on native fauna," *Wildlife Research* 29, no. 1 (2002): 51–74.

164 *Catlike animals have sprouted saber teeth:* Brian Switek, "How evolution could bring back the sabercat," io9, Oct. 4, 2013, http://io9.gizmodo.com /how-evolution-could-bring-back-the-sabercat-1441270558.

165 *a study of stray French cats revealed:* Michael Mendl and Robert Harcourt, "Individuality in the domestic cat: origins, development and stability," in *The Domestic Cat: The Biology of Its Behaviour,* 2nd ed., ed. Dennis C. Turner and Patrick Bateson (Cambridge: Cambridge University Press, 2000), 53.

165 *Close to 60 percent of American pet cats are overweight or obese:* "2013 Pet Obesity Statistics," Association for Pet Obesity Prevention, www.petobesity prevention.org/2013-pet-obesity-statistics/.

165 *even the street rats of Baltimore are 40 percent heavier:* Alla Katsnelson, "Lab animals and pets face obesity epidemic," Nature.com, Nov. 24, 2010.

166 *cat owners resolutely misclassify even the biggest whoppers:* Ellen Kienzle and Reinhold Bergler, "Human-Animal Relationship of Owners of Normal and Overweight Cats," *Journal of Nutrition* 136, no. 7 (2006): 1947S–50S.

166 *as research suggests, and all cat owners deep down know:* Dennis Turner, "The human-cat relationship," in *The Domestic Cat: The Biology of Its Behaviour,* 196–97.

166 *One rather staggering estimate suggests:* Hal Herzog, *Some We Love, Some We Hate, Some We Eat: Why It's So Hard to Think Straight About Animals* (New York: Harper Perennial, 2010), 6.

Chapter 9 NINE LIKES

168 *bank a million dollars:* Katie Van Syckle, "Grumpy Cat," *New York,* Sept. 29, 2013.

169 *with 74.8 percent accuracy:* Liat Clark, "Google's Artificial Brain Learns to Find Cat Videos," WiredUK, Wired.com, June 26, 2012.

169 *recent study revealed:* Rhiannon Williams, "Cat photos more popular than the selfie," *Telegraph,* Feb. 19, 2014.

169 *"Move your crosshair and fire":* "Feral cat phone app launch," abc.net.au, Dec. 1, 2013; "Feral Cat Hunter," Download.com, http://download.cnet.com /Feral-Cat-Hunter/3000-20416_4-76034817.html.

170 *he replied, "Kittens":* Nidhi Subbaraman, "Inventor of World Wide Wide Web Surprised to Find Kittens Took It Over," nbcnews.com, March 12, 2014.

170 *"cat objects"* and *"feminist media studies":* Leah Shafer, "I Can Haz an Internet Aesthetic?!? LOLCats and the Digital Marketplace," Northeast Popular Culture Association Conference (2012).

170 *"corporate surveillance":* Radha O'Meara, "Do Cats Know They Rule You Tube? Surveillance and the Pleasures of Cat Videos," *M/C Journal* 17, no. 2 (2014).

170 *"orthography and phonetics":* Lauren Gawne and Jill Vaughan, "I Can Haz Language Play: The Construction of Language and Identity in LOLspeak," in *Proceedings of the 42nd Australian Linguistic Society Conference* (2011).

170 *"the stupidest possible creative act":* Clay Shirky, "How cognitive surplus will

change the world," Ted Talk transcript, June 2010, www.ted.com/talks /clay_shirky_how_cognitive_surplus_will_change_the_world/transcript ?language=en.

171 *According to recent BuzzFeed data:* Suzanne Choney, "Why are cats better than dogs (according to the Internet)?" Today.com, Apr. 28, 2012.

171 *"'inside jokes or pieces of hip underground knowledge' that inhabit social networks":* in Kate M. Miltner, "Srsly Phenomenal: An Investigation into the Appeal of LOLCats," London School of Economic master's dissertation, 2011; https://dl.dropboxusercontent.com/u/37681185/MILTNER%20 DISSERTATION.pdf.

171 *And they are studied like organisms as well:* Josh Constine, "Facebook Data Scientists Prove Memes Mutate and Adapt Like DNA," techcrunch.com, Jan. 8, 2014.

171 *The particulars of human politics:* Tom Chatfield, "Cute cats, memes and understanding the internet," BBC.com, Feb. 23, 2012.

172 *"an internationally recognized symbol of solidarity":* Katie Rogers, "Twitter Cats to the Rescue in Brussels Lockdown," *New York Times,* Nov. 23, 2015.

172 *"as if there is a single cat":* O'Meara, "Do Cats Know They Rule YouTube?"

173 *They first emerged in the mid-2000s:* "LOLCats," KnowYourMeme.com, knowyourmeme.com/memes/lolcats.

174 *a notorious hacker was recently foiled:* Lily Hay Newman, "If You're a Wanted Cybercriminal, Maybe Don't Make Your Cat's Name Your Password," Slate .com, Nov. 13, 2014.

174 *an unmasked Reddit troll:* Adrian Chen, "Unmasking Reddit's Violentacrez, The Biggest Troll on the Web," Gawker.com, Oct. 12, 2012.

174 *"in-group boundary establishment and policing":* Kate M. Miltner, "'There's no place for lulz on LOLCats': The role of genre, gender, and group identity in the interpretation and enjoyment of an Internet meme," *First Monday* 19, no. 8 (2014).

174 *In January of 2007:* John Tozzi, "Bloggers Bring in the Big Bucks," Bloomberg .com, July 13, 2007.

174 *The image of the gray cat had been doing the rounds:* "Happy Cat," Know Your Meme, knowyourmeme.com/memes/happy-cat.

174 *"The original meme of cats belongs to 4chan"*: Barbara Herman, "Ben Huh Interview: Meet the Cat Philosopher Behind 'I Can Has Cheezburger?'" *International Business Times*, Nov. 3, 2014.

175 *one I Can Has Cheezburger panda-themed spinoff*: Jenna Wortham, "Once Just a Site with Funny Cat Pictures, and Now a Web Empire," *New York Times*, June 13, 2010.

175 *Some computer scientists think that a meme's quality is almost incidental*: Lilian Weng, Filippo Menczer, and Yong-Yeol Ahn, "Virality Prediction and Community Structure in Social Networks," *Nature Scientific Report* (Aug. 2013).

176 *"pet horses, deer, goats"*: Arnold Arluke and Lauren Rolfe, *The Photographed Cat: Picturing Human-Feline Ties, 1890–1940* (Syracuse: Syracuse University, 2013), 2.

176 *The writer Daniel Engber points out*: Daniel Engber, "The Curious Incidence of Dogs in Publishing," Slate.com, Apr. 5, 2013.

177 *"A typical cat video"*: O'Meara, "Do Cats Know They Rule YouTube?"

177 *Why have we instead developed*: Will Oremus, "Finally, a Browser Extension That Turns Your Friends' Babies into Cats," *Future Tense* blog, Slate.com, Aug. 3, 2012.

177 *"unlike dogs, who have a handful"*: Herman, "Ben Huh Interview."

178 *"Rabbits are the easiest to photograph"*: Cyriaque Lamar, "Even in the 1870s, humans were obsessed with ridiculous photos of cats," io9.com, Apr. 9, 2012.

178 *"we found that users consistently applied"*: Derek Foster, B. Kirman, C. Lineh, et al., "'I Can Haz Emoshuns?'—Understanding Anthropomorphosis of Cats Among Internet Users," *IEEE International Conference on Social Computing* (2011): 712–15.

178 *also submitted dozens of their own tags*: From email correspondence with Derek Foster.

180 *Hello Kitty has an estimated 50,00 trademarked products*: Sameer Hosany, Girish Prayag, Drew Martin, and Wai-Yee Lee, "Theory and strategies of anthropomorphic brand characters from Peter Rabbit, Mickey Mouse and Ronald McDonald, to Hello Kitty," *Journal of Marketing Management* 29, no. 1–2 (2013): 48–68.

180 *About 90 percent of the cat's*: Audrey Akcasu, "Hello Kitty now makes 90% of her money abroad," en.rocketnews24.com, Jan. 3, 2014.

180 *Like the house cat itself:* Hosany et al., "Theory and strategies of anthropomorphic brand characters."

181 *"Kitty has no mouth":* in Christine R. Yano, *Pink Globalization: Hello Kitty's Trek Across the Pacific* (Durham: Duke University Press, 2013), 79.

181 *"hard to read":* Jessica Goldstein, "Why We Care So Much If Hello Kitty Is or Is Not a Cat," Think Progress, Aug. 31, 2014, http://thinkprogress.org /culture/2014/08/31/3477683/hello-kitty-interview/.

181 *"sphinx":* Yano, *Pink Globalization,* 119.

181 *her creation's peculiar name derives:* Peter Larsen, "Hello Kitty, You're 30!" *St. Petersburg Times,* Nov. 15, 2004.

181 *"The cat is a time-traveler from ancient Egypt":* Camille Paglia, *Sexual Personae: Art and Decadence from Nefertiti to Emily Dickinson* (1990; repr. New York: Vintage Books, 1990), 66.

182 *Lions lived on the edge:* Jaromir Malek, *The Cat in Ancient Egypt* (Philadelphia: University of Pennsylvania Press, 1993), 22.

182 *It was lions that the pharaohs chose to merge with:* Patrick F. Houlihan, *The Animal World of the Pharaohs* (London: Thames & Hudson, 1996), 72–73 and 94.

182 *The first domestic depictions:* Malek, *The Cat in Ancient Egypt,* 49–50.

182 *"an ungainly creature":* ibid., 51.

182 *"plump and rather cross-looking":* ibid., 59.

182 *"not a country of many animals":* Houlihan, *The Animal World of the Pharaohs,* 44–45.

183 *the goddess Bastet rather abruptly:* Malek, *The Cat in Ancient Egypt,* 95–96.

183 *to become perhaps the most popular devotion:* ibid., 73.

183 *The sale of priestly offices was a handy source:* ibid., 98.

183 *an estimated 700,000 people:* ibid.

184 *"commented scathingly":* Salima Ikram, "Divine Creatures: Animal Mummies," in *Divine Creatures: Animal Mummies in Ancient Egypt,* ed. Salima Ikram (Cairo: American University in Cairo Press, 2005), 8.

184 *"an imperishable star":* Malek, *The Cat in Ancient Egypt,* 124.

184 *"When archaeologists X-rayed the cat mummies"*: Alain Zivie and Roger Lichtenberg, "The Cats of the Goddess Bastet," in *Divine Creatures*, 117–18.

185 *This wide-scale extermination may also have been:* Malek, *The Cat in Ancient Egypt*, 133.

186 *"The men played on pipes of lotus"*: William Smith, *Dictionary of Greek and Roman Geography*, Perseus Digital Library, http://www.perseus.tufts.edu /hopper/text?doc=Perseus:text:1999.04.0064:entry=bubastis-geo&high light=bubastis.

187 *"Unlike man who forgets his previous forms"*: Carl Van Vechten, *The Tiger in the House: A Cultural History of the Cat* (1920; repr., New York: New York Review of Books, 2007), 363.

Index

About the Author

Abigail Tucker is a correspondent for *Smithsonian* magazine, where she has covered a wide variety of subjects, from vampire anthropology to bioluminescent marine life to the archaeology of ancient beer. Her work has been featured in the Best American Science and Nature Writing series and recognized by the National Academy of Sciences. This is her first book.